Reprint Publishing

For People Who Go For Originals.

www.reprintpublishing.com

THE FEMALE EMIGRANT'S GUIDE,

AND

Hints on Canadian Housekeeping.

BY MRS. C. P. TRAILL,

AUTHORESS OF THE "BACKWOODS OF CANADA," "FOREST GLEANINGS," "THE CANADIAN CRUSOES," &C., &C.

SECOND THOUSAND.

TORONTO, C. W:
SOLD BY MACLEAR AND COMPANY,
AND ALL THE PRINCIPAL BOOKSELLERS THROUGHOUT CANADA, THE BRITISH AMERICAN PROVINCES, AND THE UNITED STATES.

1854.

Price Twenty-Five Cents, or One Shilling and Three-pence, each part, postpaid to any part of Canada, the British American Provinces, and the United States.

TO THE RIGHT HONOURABLE

THE EARL OF ELGIN AND KINCARDINE, K.T.

&c., &c., &c.

GOVERNOR-GENERAL OF BRITISH NORTH AMERICA,

THE FIRST PART OF THIS LITTLE HOUSEHOLD VOLUME

IS DEDICATED,

AS A RESPECTFUL TRIBUTE OF LOYAL ESTEEM,

BY HIS LORDSHIP'S

FAITHFUL FRIEND,

THE AUTHORESS.

TABLE OF CONTENTS.

Dedication iv
Preface ix
Introductory Remarks 14

Ague 197
Apples, Pears, Cherries 67, 79

Beer 136
Bees 201
Borrowing 38
Bread-making, &c., &c. 91
Buckwheat 109

Cakes, &c 101
Carpets, Home-made 177
Canada, Letters from 214
Candle-Making, ... 168
Cheese   do 185
Coffee and Tea, Substitutes for 133
Corn, Indian 112
Curing of Fish 159
    "   Meat 148

Dairy 180
Dysentery 199
Dying Wool, &c 172

Fish 159
Fire 194
Fruits, ... 79

Game 153

Gardening 60
Knitting, ... 178

Land, Value of 49
Letters From Canada 214

Miscellaneous Matter 221
Months, Summary of operations in .... 202 to 213

Oatmeal 110

Peaches 87
Poetry 22
Poultry 190
Potatoes 122
Pumpkins 127
Property, Security of 56
Productions, Natural, of Canada 202

Rice, Indian 107

Settlement, Description of New 51
Ship Stores 41
Soap-Making 163
Sugar, Making of Maple 141
Vegetables 62, 130
Venison 151
Wild Fruits 80
Wool 171

CONTENTS OF APPENDIX.

Table to calculate equivalent value of Currency and Cents	4
" " Sterling Money and Currency	5
" Land Measure	9
" Short Weight into Long Weight and Long Weight into Short	11
" To buy and sell by the Great Hundred	11
" Wages, to Calculate	12
" " Income and Expenses	30
" Length and Breadth of Imperial Acre, &c	9
" Interest Tables	12
" Useful Information to Farmers	7, 13
Emigrants, Information as to transmitting Moneys to Europe safely	36
Crown Lands, Conditions to be Observed	36
Deaths and Census of Deaths in the Canadas in 1853	12
Canada, Condition of, Collated from Census Returns	14 to 24
Deaths, Comparative Ratio of, in the Canadas and United States	27
Wheat, Average Produce of in ditto	29
Products Agricultural, Comparison of in ditto	40

Temperature and Climate :—

Comparative Meteorology in Toronto, U. C., and High-field House, Nottingham, England	37
Comparative Mean Temperature for the year and different seasons, and also the extremes of Temperature and climatic differences in various parts of Europe and America	10, 38

TARIFF :—

New, of Duties, to come into operation first of April, 1855	31

POSTAGE :—

New Book Regulations	40

VICTORIA COLLEGE, COBOURG, C.W.

PREFACE.

Among the many books that have been written for the instruction of the Canadian emigrant, there are none exclusively devoted for the use of the wives and daughters of the future settler, who for the most part, possess but a very vague idea of the particular duties which they are destined to undertake, and are often totally unprepared to meet the emergencies of their new mode of life.

As a general thing they are told that they must prepare their minds for some hardships and privations, and that they will have to exert themselves in a variety of ways to which they have hitherto been strangers ; but the exact nature of that work, and how it is to be performed, is left untold. The consequence of this is, that the females have everything to learn, with few opportunities of acquiring the requisite knowledge, which is often obtained under circumstances, and in situations the most discouraging ; while their hearts are yet filled with natural yearnings after the land of their birth, (dear even to the poorest emigrant), with grief for the friends of their early days, and while every object in this new country is strange to them. Disheartened by repeated failures, unused to the expedients which the older inhabitants adopt in any case of difficulty, repining and disgust take the place of cheerful activity ; troubles increase, and the power to overcome them decreases ; domestic happiness disappears. The woman toils on heart-sick and pining for the home she left behind her. The husband reproaches his broken-hearted partner, and both blame the Colony for the failure of the individual.

Having myself suffered from the disadvantage of acquiring all my knowledge of Canadian housekeeping by personal experience, and having heard other females similarly situated lament the want of some simple useful book to give them an insight into the customs and occupations incidental to a Canadian settler's life, I have taken upon me to endeavor to supply this want, and have with much labour collected such useful matter as I thought best calculated to afford the instruction required.

As even the materials differ, and the method of preparing food varies greatly between the colony and the Mother-country, I have given in this little book the most approved recipes for cooking certain dishes, the usual mode of manufacturing maple-sugar, soap, candles, bread and other articles of household expenditure; in short, whatever subject is in any way connected with the management of a Canadian settler's house, either as regards economy or profit, I have introduced into the work for the benefit of the future settler's wife and family.

As this little work has been written for all classes, and more particularly for the wives and daughters of the small farmers, and a part of it is also addressed to the wives of the labourer and mechanics, I aimed at no beauty of style. It was not written with the intention of amusing, but simply of instructing and advising.

PREFACE. xi

I might have offered my female friends a work of fiction or of amusing facts, into which it would have been an easy matter to have interwoven a mass of personal adventure, with useful information drawn from my own experience during twenty-two years sojourn in the Colony ; but I well knew that knowledge conveyed through such a medium is seldom attended with practical results ; it is indeed something like searching through a bushel of chaff to discover a few solitary grains of wheat. I therefore preferred collating my instruction into the more homely but satisfactory form of a Manual of Canadian housewifery, well contented to abandon the paths of literary fame, if I could render a solid benefit to those of my own sex who through duty or necessity are about to become sojourners in the Western Wilderness.

It is now twenty years ago since I wrote a work with the view of preparing females of my own class more paiticularly, for the changes that awaited them in the life of a Canadian emigrant's wife. This book was entitled " Letters from the Backwoods of Canada," and made one of the volumes in Knight's " Library of Useful and Entertaining Knowledge," and was, I believe, well received by the public ; but as I had then been but a short time resident in the country, it was necessarily deficient in many points of knowledge which I have since become aware were essential for the instruction of the emigrant's wife. These deficiencies I have endeavoured to supply in the present work, and must here acknowledge with thanks the assistance that I have received from several ladies of my acquaintance, who have kindly supplied me with hints from their own experience on various matters.

To Mr. W. McKyes, Mrs. McKyes and Miss McKyes I am

PREFACE.

largely indebted for much useful information ; also to Mrs. Stewart of Auburn, Douro, and her kind family; and to Misses A. and M. Ferguson ; with many others, by whose instruction I have been largely benefitted ; and take the present opportunity of publicly acknowledging my obligations.

Hoping that my little volume may prove a useful guide, I dedicate it with heartfelt good wishes to the Wives and Daughters of the

CANADIAN EMIGRANT.

INTRODUCTORY REMARKS,

ADDRESSED TO HUSBANDS AND FATHERS.

Before the master of the household fully decides upon taking so important a step as leaving his native land to become a settler in Canada, let him first commune with himself and ask the important question, Have I sufficient energy of character to enable me to conform to the changes that may await me in my new mode of life?—Let him next consider the capabilities of his partner; her health and general temper; for a sickly, peevish, discontented person will make but a poor settler's wife in a country where cheerfulness of mind and activity of body are very essential to the prosperity of the household.

In Canada persevering energy and industry, with sobriety, will overcome all obstacles, and in time will place the very poorest family in a position of substantial comfort that no personal exertions alone could have procured for them elsewhere.

To the indolent or to the intemperate man Canada offers no such promise; but where is the country in which such a person will thrive or grow wealthy? He has not the elements of success within him.—It is in vain for such a one to cross the Atlantic; for he will bear with him that fatal enemy which kept him poor at home. The active, hard-working inhabitants who are earning their bread honestly by the sweat of their brow, or by the exertion of mental power, have no sympathy with such men. Canada is not the land for the idle sensualist. He must forsake the error of his ways at once, or he will sink into ruin here as he would have done had he staid in the old country. But it is not for such persons that our book is intended.

TO WIVES AND DAUGHTERS.

As soon as the fitness of emigrating to Canada has been fully decided upon, let the females of the family ask God's blessing upon their undertaking; ever bearing in mind that "unless the Lord build the house, their labour is but lost that build it ; unless the Lord keep the city, the watchman waketh but in vain." In all their trials let them look to Him who can bring all things to pass in His good time, and who can guard them from every peril, if they will only believe in His promises, and commit their ways to Him.

As soon, then, as the resolution to emigrate has been fixed, let the females of the house make up their minds to take a cheerful and active part in the work of preparation. Let them at once cast aside all vain opposition and selfish regrets, and hopefully look to their future country as to a land of promise, soberly and quietly turning their attention to making the necessary arrangements for the important change that is before them.

Let them remember that all practical knowledge is highly valuable in the land to which they are going. An acquaintance with the homely art of baking and making bread, which most servants and small housekeepers know how to practice, but which many young females that live in large towns and cities where the baker supplies the bread to the family, do not, is necessary to be acquired.

Cooking, curing meat, making butter and cheese, knitting, dress-making and tailoring—for most of the country-people here make the everyday clothing of their husbands, brothers or sons—are good to be learned. By ripping to pieces any well-fitting old garment, a suitable pattern may be obtained of men's clothes ; and many a fair hand I have seen occupied in making garments of this description. For a quarter of a dollar, 1s. 3d., a tailor will cut out a pair of fine cloth trowsers ; for a coat they charge more ; but a good cloth is always better to have made up by a regular tailor : loose summer coats may be made at home, but may be bought cheap, ready-made, in the stores.

My female friends must bear in mind that it is one of the settler's great objects to make as little outlay of money as possible. I allude to such as come out to Canada with very little available capital excepting what arises from the actual labour of their own hands, by which they must realize the means of paying for their land or the rental of a farm. Everything that is done in the house by the hands of the family, is so much saved or so much earned towards the pay-

INTRODUCTORY REMARKS.

ing for the land or building houses and barns, buying stock or carrying on the necessary improvements on the place : the sooner this great object is accomplished, the sooner will the settler and his family realize the comfort of feeling themselves independent.

The necessity of becoming acquainted with the common branches of household work may not at first be quite agreeable to such as have been unaccustomed to take an active part in the duties of the house. Though their position in society may have been such as to exempt them from what they consider menial occupations, still they will be wise to lay aside their pride and refinement, and apply themselves practically to the acquirement of such useful matters as those I have named—if they are destined to a life in a colony—even though their friends may be so well off as to have it in their power to keep servants, and live in ease and comfort. But if they live in a country place, they may be left without the assistance of a female-servant in the house, a contingency which has often happened from sudden illness, a servant's parents sending for them home, which they will often do without consulting either your convenience or their daughter's wishes, or some act on the part of the servant may induce her to be discharged before her place can be filled ; in such an emergency the settler's wife may find herself greatly at a loss, without some knowledge of what her family requires at her hands. I have before now seen a ragged Irish boy called in from the clearing by his lady-mistress, to assist her in the mystery of making a loaf of bread, and teaching her how to bake it in the bake-kettle. She had all the requisite materials, but was ignorant of the simple practical art of making bread.

Another who knew quite well how to make a loaf and bake it too, yet knew nothing of the art of making yeast to raise it with, and so the family lived upon unleavened cakes, or dampers, as the Australians call them, till they were heartily tired of them : at last a settler's wife calling in to rest herself, and seeing the flat cakes baking, asked the servant why they did not make raised bread : " Because we have no yeast, and do not know how to make any here in these horrible backwoods," was the girl's reply. The neighbour, I dare say, was astonished at the ignorance of both mistress and maid ; but she gave them some hops and a little barm, and told the girl how to make the yeast called hop-rising ; and this valuable piece of knowledge stood them in good stead : from that time they were able to make light bread ; the girl shrewdly remarking to her mistress, that a little help was worth a deal of pity. A few simple directions for making barm as it is here practiced, would have obviated the difficulty at first. As this is one of the very first things that the housewife has to attend to in the cooking department, I have placed the raising and making of bread at the beginning of the work. The making and baking of REALLY GOOD HOUSEHOLD BREAD is a thing of the greatest consequence to the health and comfort of a family.

As the young learn more quickly than the old, I would advise the daughters of the intending emigrant to acquire whatever useful arts they think likely to prove serviceable to them in their new country. Instead of suffering a false pride to stand in their way of acquiring practical household knowledge, let it be their pride—their noble, honest pride—to fit themselves for the state which they will be called upon to fill—a part in the active drama of life ; to put in practice that which they learned to repeat with their lips in childhood as a portion of the catechism, "To do my duty in that state of life, unto which it may please God to call me." Let them earnestly believe that it is by the will of God that they are called to share the fortunes of their parents in the land they have chosen, and that as that is the state of life they are called to by his will, they are bound to strive to do their duty in it with cheerfulness.

There should therefore be no wavering on their part; no yielding to prejudices and pride. Old things are passed away. The greatest heroine in life is she who knowing her duty, resolves not only to do it, but to do it to the best of her abilities, with heart and mind bent upon the work.

I address this passage more especially to the daughters of the emigrant, for to them belongs the task of cheering and upholding their mother in the trials that may await her. It is often in consideration of the future welfare of their children, that the parents are, after many painful struggles, induced to quit the land of their birth and the home that was endeared to them alike by their cares and their joys ; and though the children may not know this to be the main-spring that urges them to make the sacrifice, in most cases it is so; and this consideration should have its full weight, and induce the children to do all in their power to repay their parents for the love that urges them to such a decision.

The young learn to conform more readily to change of country than the old. Novelty has for them a great charm : and then hope is more lively in the young heart than in the old. To them a field of healthy enterprise is open, which they have only to enter upon with a cheerful heart and plenty of determination, and they will hardly fail of reaching a respectable state of independence.

The wives and daughters of the small farmers and of the working class, should feel the difficulties of a settler's life far less keenly than any other, as their habits and general knowledge of rural affairs have fitted them for the active labours that may fall to their lot in Canada. Though much that they have to perform will be new to them, it will only be the manner of doing it, and the difference of some of the materials that they will have to make use of: enured from childhood to toil, they may soon learn to conform to their change of life. The position of servants is much improved in one respect : their services are more valuable in a country where there is less competition among the working class. They can soon save enough to be independent. They have the cheering prospect always before them: It depends upon ourselves to better our own condition. In this country honest industry always commands respect : by it we can in time raise ourselves, and no one can keep us down.

Yet I have observed with much surprize that there is no class of emigrants more discontented than the wives and daughters of those men who were accustomed to earn their bread by the severest toil, in which they too were by necessity obliged to share, often with patience and cheerfulness under privations the most heartbreaking, with no hope of amendment, no refuge but the grave from poverty and all its miseries. Surely to persons thus situated, the change of country should be regarded with hopeful feelings ; seeing that it opens a gate which leads from poverty to independence, from present misery to future comfort.

At first the strangeness of all things around them, the loss of familiar faces and familiar objects, and the want of all their little household conveniences, are sensibly felt ; and these things make them uncomfortable and peevish : but a little reasoning with themselves would show that such inconveniences belong to the nature of their new position, and that a little time will do away with the evil they complain of.

After a while new feelings, new attachments to persons and things, come to fill up the void : they begin to take an interest in the new duties that are before them, and by degrees conform to the change ; and an era in their lives commences, which is the beginning to them of a better and more prosperous state of things.

It frequently happens that before the poor emigrant can settle upon land of his own, he is obliged to send the older children out to service. Perhaps he gets employment for himself and his wife, on some farm, where they can manage to keep the younger members of the family with them, if there is a small house or shanty convenient, on or near the farm on which they are hired. Sometimes a farmer can get a small farm on shares ; but it is seldom a satisfactory mode of rental, and often ends in disagreement. As no man can serve two masters, neither can one farm support two, unless both parties are which rarely happens, quite disinterested and free from selfishness, each exacting no more than his due. It is seldom these partnerships turn out well.

There is an error which female servants are very apt to fall into in this country, which as a true friend, I would guard them against committing. This is adopting a free and easy manner, often bordering upon impertinence, towards their employers. They are apt to think that because they are entitled to a higher rate of wages, they are not bound to render their mistresses the same respect of manners as was usual in the old country. Now, as they receive more, they ought not to be less thankful to those who pay them well, and should be equally zealous in doing their duty. They should bear in mind that they are commanded to render " honor to whom honor is due." A female servant in Canada whose manners are respectful and well-behaved, will always be treated with consideration and even with affection. After all, good-breeding is as charming a trait in a servant as it is in a lady. Were there more of that kindly feeling existing between the upper and lower classes, both parties would be benefitted, and a bond of union established, which would extend beyond the duration of a few months or a few years, and be continued through life : how much more satisfactory than that unloving strife where the mistress is haughty and the servant insolent.

But while I would recommend respect and obedience on the part of the servant, to her employer I would say, treat your servants with consideration : if you respect her she will also respect you ; if she does her duty, she is inferior to no one living as a member of the great human family. The same Lord who says by the mouth of his apostle, " Servants obey your masters," has also added, " and ye masters do ye also the same, forbearing threatening ; knowing that your master also is in heaven, and that with him there is no respect of persons."

Your servants as long as they are with you, are of your household, and should be so treated that they should learn to look up to you in love as well as reverence.

If they are new comers to Canada, they have everything to learn ; and will of course feel strange and awkward to the ways of the colony, and require to be patiently dealt with. They may have their regrets and sorrows yet rankling in their hearts for those dear friends they have left behind them, and require kindness and sympathy.— Remember that you also are a stranger and sojourner in a strange land, and should feel for them and bear with them as becomes Christians.

Servants in Canada are seldom hired excepting by the month.— The female servant by the full calendar month ; the men and boys' month is four weeks only. From three to four dollars a month is the usual wages given to female servants ; and two, and two dollars and a half, to girls of fourteen and sixteen years of age, unless they are very small, and very ignorant of the work of the country ; then less is given. Indeed, if a young girl were to give her services for a month or two, with a good clever mistress, for her board alone, she would be the gainer by the bargain, in the useful knowledge which she would acquire, and which would enable her to take a better place, and command higher wages. It is a common error in girls coming direct from the old country, and who have all Canada's ways to learn, to ask the highest rate of wages, expecting the same as those who are twice as efficient. This is not reasonable ; and if the demand be yielded to from necessity, there is seldom much satisfaction or harmony, both parties being respectively discontented with the other. The one gives too much, the other does too little in return for high wages.

Very little if any alteration has taken place nominally in the rate of servants' wages during twenty-one years that I have lived in Canada, but a great increase in point of fact. * Twenty years ago the servant-girl gave from 1s. 6d. to 2s. 6d. a yard for cotton prints, 10s. and 12s. a pair for very coarse shoes and boots : common white calico was 1s. and 1s. 3d. per yard, and other articles of clothing in proportion. Now she can buy good fast prints at 9d. and 10d., and some as low as 7½d. and 8d. per yard, calicoes and factory cottons from 4½d. to 9d. or 10d. ; shoes, light American-made and very pretty, from 4s. 6d. to 7s. 6d., and those made to order 6s. 3d. to 7s. 6d. ; boots 10s. ; straw bonnets from 1s. 6d., coarse beehive plat, to such as are very tasteful and elegant in shape and quality, of the most delicate fancy chips and straws, proportionably cheap.

Thus while her wages remain the same, her outlay is decreased nearly one-half.

Ribbons and light fancy goods are still much higher in price than they are in the old country ; so are stuffs and merinos. A very poor, thin Coburg cloth, or Orleans, fetches 1s. or 1s. 3d. per yard ; mousselin de laines vary from 9d. to 1s. 6d. Probably the time will come when woollen goods will be manufactured in the colony ; but the time for that is not yet at hand. The country flannel, home-spun, home-dyed and sometimes home-woven, is the sort of material worn in the house by the farmer's family when at work. Nothing can be more suitable to the climate, and the labours of a Canadian settler's wife or daughter, than gowns made of this country flannel : it is very

---

* Since the above statement was written the wages both of men and women have borne a higher rate ; and some articles of clothing have been raised in price. See the tables of rates of wages and goods for 1854.

durable, lasting often two or three seasons. When worn out as a decent working dress, it makes good sleigh-quilts for travelling, or can be cut up into rag-carpets, for a description of which see the article—*Rag-Carpets:* and for instructions in dyeing the wool or yarn for the flannel see *Dyeing.* I have been thus minute in naming the prices of women's wearing apparel, that the careful wife may be enabled to calculate the expediency of purchasing a stock of clothes, before leaving home, or waiting till she arrives in Canada, to make her needful purchases. To such as can prudently spare a small sum for buying clothes, I may point out a few purchases that would be made more advantageously in England or Scotland than in Canada: 1st. A stock, say two pairs a piece for each person, of good shoes.— The leather here is not nearly so durable as what is prepared at home, and consequently the shoes wear out much sooner, where the roads are rough and the work hard. No one need encumber themselves with clogs or pattens: the rough roads render them worse than useless, even dangerous, in the spring and fall, the only wet seasons: in winter the snow clogs them up, and you could not walk ten yards in them; and in summer there is no need of them: buy shoes instead; or for winter wear, a good pair of duffle boots, the sole overlaid with india-rubber or gutta percha.

India-rubber boots and over-shoes can be bought from 4s. to 7s. 6d., if extra good, and lined with fur or fine flannel. Gentlemen's boots, long or short, can be had also, but I do not know at what cost. Old women's list shoes are good for the house in the snowy season, or good, strongly-made carpet shoes; but these last, with a little ingenuity, you can make for yourself.

Flannel I also recommend, as an advisable purchase: you must give from 1s. 9d. to 2s. 6d. for either white or red, and a still higher price for fine fabrics; which I know is much higher than they can be bought for at home. Good scarlet or blue flannel shirts are worn by all the emigrants that work on land or at trades in Canada; and even through the hottest summer weather the men still prefer them to cotton or linen.

A superior quality, twilled and of some delicate check, as pale blue, pink or green, are much the fashion among the gentlemen; this material however is more costly, and can hardly be bought under 3s. 6d. or 4s. a yard. A sort of overshirt made full and belted in at the waist, is frequently worn, made of homespun flannel, dyed brown or blue, and looks neat and comfortable ; others of coarse brown linen, or canvas, called logging-shirts, are adopted by the choppers in their rough work of clearing up the fallows : these are not very unlike the short loose slop frocks of the peasants of the Eastern Counties of England, reaching no lower than the hips.

Merino or cottage stuffs are also good to bring out, also Scotch plaids and tweeds, strong checks for aprons, and fine white cotton stockings : those who wear silk, had better bring a supply for holiday wear : satin shoes are very high, but are only needed by the wealthy, or those ladies who expect to live in some of the larger towns or cities ; but the farmer's wife in Canada has little need of such luxuries—they are out of place and keeping.

ON DRESS.

It is one of the blessings of this new country, that a young person's respectability does by no means depend upon these points of style in dress ; and many a pleasant little evening dance I have seen, where the young ladies wore merino frocks, cut high or low, and prunella shoes, and no disparaging remarks were made by any of the party. How much more sensible I thought these young people, than if they had made themselves slaves to the tyrant fashion. Nevertheless, in some of the large towns the young people do dress extravagantly, and even exceed those of Britain in their devotion to fine and costly apparel. The folly of this is apparent to every sensible person. When I hear women talk of nothing but dress, I cannot help thinking that it is because they have nothing more interesting to talk about ; that their minds are uninformed, and bare, while their bodies are clothed with purple and fine linen. To dress neatly and with taste and even elegance is an accomplishment which I should desire to see practised by all females ; but to make dress the one engrossing business and thought of life, is vain and foolish. One thing is certain, that a lady will be a lady, even in the plainest dress ; a vulgar minded woman will never be a lady, in the most costly garments. Good sense is as much marked by the style of a person's dress, as by their conversation. The servant-girl who expends half her wages on a costly shawl, or ma... a, and bonnet to wear over a fine shabby gown, or with coarse shoes and stockings, does not show as much sense as she who purchases at less cost a complete dress, each article suited to the other. They both attract attention, it is true ; but in a different degree. The man of sense will notice the one for her wisdom ; the other for her folly.— To plead fashion, is like following a multitude to do evil.

CANADA A FIELD FOR YOUNGER WORKING FEMALES.

Quitting the subject of dress, which perhaps I have dwelt too long upon, I will go to a subject of more importance : the field which Canada opens for the employment of the younger female emigrants of the working class. At this very minute I was assured by one of the best and most intelligent of our farmers, that the Township of Hamilton alone could give immediate employment to five hundred females ; and most other townships in the same degree. What an inducement to young girls to emigrate is this ! good wages, in a healthy and improving country ; and what is better, in one where idleness and immorality are not the characteristics of the inhabitants: where steady industry is sure to be rewarded by marriage with young men who are able to place their wives in a very different station from that of servitude. How many young women who were formerly servants in my house, are now farmers' wives, going to church or the market towns with their own sleighs or light waggons, and in point of dress, better clothed than myself.

Though Australia may offer the temptation of greater wages to female servants ; yet the discomforts they are exposed to, must be a great drawback ; and the immoral, disjointed state of domestic life, for decent, well-conducted young women, I should think, would more than counterbalance the nominal advantages from greater wages.— The industrious, sober-minded labourer, with a numerous family of daughters, one would imagine would rather bring them to Canada, where they can get immediate employment in respectable families ; where they will get good wages and have every chance of bettering their condition and rising in the world, by becoming the wives of thriving farmers' sons or industrious artizans ; than form connexions with such characters as swarm the streets of Melbourne and Geelong, though these may be able to fill their hands with gold, and clothe them with satin and velvet.

In the one country there is a steady progress to prosperity and lasting comfort, where they may see their children become landowners after them, while in the other, there is little real stability, and small prospect of a life of domestic happiness to look forward to. I might say, as the great lawgiver said to the Israelites, "Good and evil are before you, choose ye between them."

Those whose destination is intended to be in the Canadian towns will find little difference in regard to their personal comforts to what they were accustomed to enjoy at home. If they have capital they can employ it to advantage; if they are mechanics, or artizans they will have have little difficulty in obtaining employment as journeymen.— The stores in Canada are well furnished with every species of goods; groceries, hardware and food of all kinds can also be obtained. With health and industry, they will have little real cause of complaint. It is those who go into the woods and into distant settlements in the uncleared wilderness that need have any fear of encountering hardships and privations; and such persons should carefully consider their own qualifications and those of their wives and children before they decide upon embarking in the laborious occupation of backwoodsmen in a new country like Canada. Strong, patient, enduring, hopeful men and women, able to bear hardships and any amount of bodily toil, (and there are many such,) these may be pioneers to open out the forest-lands; while the old-country farmer will find it much better to purchase cleared farms or farms that are partially cleared, in improving townships, where there are villages and markets and good roads; by so doing they will escape much of the disappointment and loss, as well as the bodily hardships that are too often the lot of those who go back into the unreclaimed forest lands.

Whatever be the determination of the intended emigrant, let him not exclude from his entire confidence the wife of his bosom, the natural sharer of his fortunes, be the path which leads to them rough or smooth. She ought not to be dragged as an unwilling sacrifice at the shrine of duty from home, kindred and friends, without her full consent : the difficulties as well as the apparent advantages ought to be laid candidly before her, and her advice and opinion asked; or how can she be expected to enter heart and soul into her husband's hopes and plans ; nor should such of the children as are capable of forming opinions on the subject be shut out from the family council ; for let parents bear this fact in mind, that much of their own future prosperity will depend upon the exertion of their children in the land to which they are going ; and also let them consider that those children's lot in life is involved in the important decision they are about to make. Let perfect confidence be established in the family : it will avoid much future domestic misery and unavailing repining.— Family union is like the key-stone of an arch : it keeps all the rest of the building from falling asunder. A man's friends should be those of his own household.

Woman, whose nature is to love home and to cling to all home ties and associations, cannot be torn from that spot that is the little centre of joy and peace and comfort to her, without many painful regrets. No matter however poor she may be, how low her lot in life may be cast, home to her is dear, the thought of it and the love of it clings closely to her wherever she goes. The remembrance of it never leaves her ; it is graven on her heart. Her thoughts wander back to it across the broad waters of the ocean that are bearing her far from it. In the new land it is still present to her mental eye, and years after she has formed another home for herself she can still recal the bowery lane, the daisied meadow, the moss-grown well, the simple hawthorn hedge that bound the garden-plot, the woodbine porch, the thatched roof and narrow casement window of her early home. She hears the singing of the birds, the murmuring of the bees, the tinkling of the rill, and busy hum of cheerful labour from the village or the farm, when those beside her can hear only the deep cadence of the wind among the lofty forest-trees, the jangling of the cattle-bells, or strokes of the chopper's axe in the woods. As the seasons return she thinks of the flowers that she loved in childhood ; the pale primrose, the cowslip and the bluebell, with the humble daisy and heath-flowers ; and what would she not give for one, *just one* of those old familiar flowers! No wonder that the heart of the emigrant's wife is sometimes sad, and needs to be dealt gently with by her less sensitive partner ; who if she were less devoted to home, would hardly love her more, for in this attachment to home lies much of her charm as a wife and mother in his eyes.—But kindness and sympathy, which she has need of, in time reconciles her to her change of life ; new ties, new interests, new comforts arise; and she ceases to repine, if she does not cease to love, that which she has lost : in after life the recollection comes like some pleasant dream or a fair picture to her mind, but she has ceased to grieve or to regret ; and perhaps like a wise woman she says—" All things are for the best. It is good for us to be here."

ADORNMENT OF HOME.

What effect should this love of her old home produce in the emigrant-wife? Surely an earnest endeavour to render her new dwelling equally charming ; to adorn it within and without as much as circumstances will permit, not expending her husband's means in the purchase of costly furniture which would be out of keeping in a log-house, but adopting such things as are suitable, neat and simple ; studying comfort and convenience before show and finery. Many inconveniences must be expected at the outset; but the industrious female will endeavor to supply these wants by the exercise of a little ingenuity and taste. It is a great mistake to neglect those little household adornments which will give a look of cheerfulness to the very humblest home.

Nothing contributes so much to comfort and to the outward appearance of a Canadian house as the erection of the verandah or stoup, as the Dutch settlers call it, round the building. It affords a grateful shade from the summer heat, a shelter from the cold, and is a source of cleanliness to the interior. It gives a pretty, rural look to the poorest log-house, and as it can be put up with little expense, it should never be omitted. A few unbarked cedar posts, with a slab or shingled roof, costs very little. The floor should be of plank; but even with a hard dry earthen floor, swept every day with an Indian broom, it will still prove a great comfort. Those who build frame or stone or brick houses seldom neglect the addition of a verandah ; to the common log-house it is equally desirable ; nor need any one want for climbers with which to adorn the pillars.

SHADE PLANTS.

Among the wild plants of Canada there are many graceful climbers, which are to be found in almost every locality. Nature, as if to invite you to ornament your cottage-homes, has kindly provided so many varieties of shade-plants, that you may choose at will.

First, then, I will point out to your attention the wild grape, which is to be found luxuriating in every swamp, near the margin of lakes and rivers, wreathing the trees and tall bushes with its abundant foliage and purple clusters. The Fox-grape and the Frost-grape* are among the common wild varieties, and will produce a great quantity of fruit, which, though very acid, is far from being unpalatable when cooked with a sufficiency of sugar.

From the wild grape a fine jelly can be made by pressing the juice from the husks and seeds and boiling it with the proportion of sugar usual in making currant-jelly, i. e., one pound of sugar to one pint of juice. An excellent home-made wine can also be manufactured from these grapes. They are not ripe till the middle of October, and should not be gathered till the frost has softened them ; from this circumstance, no doubt, the name of Frost-grape has been given to one species. The wild vine planted at the foot of some dead and unsightly tree, will cover it with its luxuriant growth, and convert that which would otherwise have been an unseemly object into one of great ornament. I knew a gentleman who caused a small dead tree to be cut down and planted near a big oak stump in his garden, round which a young grape was twining : the vine soon ascended the dead tree, covering every branch and twig, and forming a bower above the stump, and affording an abundant crop of fruit.

The commonest climber for a log-house is the hop, which is, as you will find, an indispensable plant in a Canadian garden, it being the principal ingredient in making the yeast with which the household bread is raised. Planted near the pillars of your verandah, it forms a graceful drapery of leaves and flowers, which are pleasing to look upon, and valuable either for use or sale.

---

* There are many other varieties of wild grapes, some of which have, by careful garden cultivation, been greatly improved. Cuttings may be made early in April, or the young vines planted in September or October.

The Canadian Ivy, or Virginian Creeper, is another charming climber, which if planted near the walls of your house, will quickly cover the rough logs with its dark glossy leaves in summer, and in the fall delight the eye with its gorgeous crimson tints.

The Wild Clematis or Traveller's Joy may be found growing in the beaver meadows and other open thickets. This also is most ornamental as a shade-plant for a verandah. Then there is the climbing Fumatory, better known by the name by which its seeds are sold by the gardener, "Cypress vine." This elegant creeper is a native of Canada, and may be seen in old neglected clearings near the water, running up the stems of trees and flinging its graceful tendrils and leaves of tender green over the old grey mossy branches of cedar or pine, adorning the hoary boughs with garlands of the loveliest pink flowers. I have seen this climbing Fumatory in great quantities in the woods, but found it no easy matter to obtain the ripe seeds, unless purchased from a seedsman : it is much cultivated in towns as a shade plant near the verandahs.

Besides those already described I may here mention the scarlet-runner, a flower the humming-birds love to visit. The wild cucumber, a very graceful trailing plant. The Major Colvolvulus or Morning Glory. The wild honeysuckle, sweet pea and prairie-rose. These last-named are not natives, with the exception of the wild or bush honeysuckle, which is to be found in the forest. The flowers are pale red, but scentless ; nevertheless it is very well worth cultivating.

I am the more particular in pointing out to you how you may improve the outside of your dwellings, because the log-house is rough and unsightly; and I know well that your comfort and cheerfulness of mind will be increased by the care you are led to bestow upon your new home in endeavouring to ornament it and render it more agreeable to the eye. The cultivation of a few flowers, of vegetables and fruit, will be a source of continual pleasure and interest to yourself and children, and you will soon learn to love your home, and cease to regret that dear one you have left.

I write from my own experience. I too have felt all the painful regrets incidental to a long separation from my native land and my beloved early home. I have experienced all that you who read this book can ever feel, and perhaps far more than you will ever have cause for feeling.

CONTRAST NOW TO PERIOD OF EARLY SETTLEMENT.

The emigrants of the present day can hardly now meet with the trials and hardships that were the lot of those who came to the Province twenty years ago, and these last infinitely less than those who preceded them at a still earlier period.

When I listen, as I often do, to the experiences of the old settlers of forty or fifty years standing, at a time when the backwoodsman shared the almost unbroken wilderness with the unchristianized Indian, the wolf and the bear; when his seed-corn had to be carried a distance of thirty miles upon his shoulders, and his family were dependent upon the game and fish that he brought home till the time of the harvest; when there were no mills to grind his flour save the little handmill, which kept the children busy to obtain enough coarse four to make bread from day to day; when no sabbath-bell was ever heard to mark the holy day, and all was lonely, wild and savage around him. Then my own first trials seemed to sink into utter insignificance, and I was almost ashamed to think how severely they had been felt.

Many a tale of trial and of enterprize I have listened to with breathless interest, related by these patriarchs of the colony, while seated beside the blazing log-fire, surrounded by the comforts which they had won for their children by every species of toil and privation. Yet they too had overcome the hardships incidental to a first settlement, and were at rest, and could look back on their former struggles with that sort of pride which is felt by the war-worn soldier in fighting over again his battles by his own peaceful hearth.

These old settlers and their children have seen the whole face of the country changed. They have seen the forest disappear before the axe of the industrious emigrant; they have seen towns and villages spring up where the bear and the wolf had their lair. They have seen the white-sailed vessel and the steamer plough those lakes and rivers where the solitary Indian silently glided over their lonely waters in his frail canoe. They have seen highways opened out through impenetrable swamps where human foot however adventurous had never trod. The busy mill-wheels have dashed where only the foaming rocks broke the onward flow of the forest stream. They have seen God's holy temples rise, pointing upwards with their glittering spires above the lowlier habitations of men, and have heard the sabbath-bell calling the Christian worshippers to prayer. They have seen the savage Indian bending there in mute reverence, or lifting his voice in hymns of praise to that blessed Redeemer who had called him out of darkness into his marvellous light. And stranger things he may now behold in that mysterious wire, that now conveys a whispered message from one end of the Province to the other with lightning swiftness; and see the iron railway already traversing the Province, and bringing the far-off produce of the woods to the store of the merchant and to the city mart.

Such are the changes which the old settler has witnessed; and I have noted them for your encouragement and satisfaction, and that you may form some little notion of what is going on in this comparatively newly-settled country; and that you may form some idea of what it is likely to become in the course of a few more years, when its commerce and agriculture and its population shall have increased, and its internal resources shall have been more perfectly developed.

In the long-settled portions of the Province a traveller may almost imagine that he is in England; there are no stumps to disfigure the fields, and but very few of the old log-houses remaining: these have for the most part given place to neat painted frame, brick or stone cottages, surrounded with orchards, cornfields and pastures. Some peculiarities he will notice, which will strike him as unlike what he has been used to see in the old country; and there are old familiar objects which will be missed in the landscape, such as the venerable grey tower of the old church, the ancient ruins, the old castles and fine old manor-houses, with many other things which exist in the old country. Here all is new; time has not yet laid its mellowing touch upon the land. We are but in our infancy; but it is a vigorous and healthy one, full of promise for future greatness and strength.

FURNISHING LOG HOUSE.

In furnishing a Canadian log-house the main study should be to unite simplicity with cheapness and comfort. It would be strangely out of character to introduce gay, showy, or rich and costly articles of furniture into so rough and homely a dwelling. A log-house is better to be simply furnished. Those who begin with moderation are more likely to be able to increase their comforts in the course of a few years.

Let us see now what can be done towards making your log parlour comfortable at a small cost. A dozen of painted Canadian chairs, such as are in common use here, will cost you £2 10s. You can get plainer ones for 2s. 9d. or 3s. a chair: of course you may get very excellent articles if you give a higher price; but we are not going to buy drawing-room furniture. You can buy rocking chairs, small, at 7s. 6d.; large, with elbows, 15s.: you can cushion them yourself. A good drugget, which I would advise you to bring with you, or Scotch carpet, will cover your rough floor; when you lay it down, spread straw or hay over the boards; this will save your carpet from cutting. A stained pine table may be had for 12s. or 15s. Walnut or cherry wood costs more; but the pine with a nice cover will answer at first. For a flowered mohair you must give five or six dollars. A piece of chintz of suitable pattern will cost you 16s. the piece of twenty-eight yards. This will curtain your windows: and a common pine sofa stuffed with wool, though many use fine hay for the back and sides, can be bought cheap, if covered by your own hands. If your husband or elder sons are at all skilled in the use of tools, they can make out of common pine boards the frame-work or couches, or sofas, which look when covered and stuffed, as well as what the cabinet-maker will charge several pounds for. A common box or two stuffed so as to form a cushion on the top, and finished with a flounce of chintz, will fill the recess of the windows. A set of book-shelves stained with Spanish brown, to hold your library.— A set of corner shelves, fitted into the angles of the room, one above the other, diminishing in size, form an useful receptacle for any little ornamental matters, or for flowers in the summer, and gives a pleasant finish and an air of taste to the room. A few prints, or pictures, in frames of oak or black walnut, should not be omitted, if you can bring such ornaments with you. These things are sources of pleasure to yourselves, and of interest to others. They are intellectual luxuries, that even the very poorest man regards with delight, and possesses if he can, to adorn his cottage walls, however lowly that cottage may be.

I am going to add another comfort to your little parlour—a clock: very neat dials in cherry or oak frames, may be bought from 7s. 6d. to $5. The cheapest will keep *good time*, but do not strike. Very handsome clocks may be bought for ten dollars, in elegant frames; but we must not be too extravagant in our notions.

I would recommend a good cooking-stove in your kitchen : it is more convenient, and is not so destructive to clothes as the great log fires. A stove large enough to cook food for a family of ten or twelve persons, will cost from twenty to thirty dollars. This will include every necessary cooking utensil. Cheap stoves are often like other cheap articles, the dearest in the end : a good, weighty casting should be preferred to a thinner and lighter one ; though the latter will look just as good as the former : they are apt to crack, and the inner plates wear out soon.

There are now a great variety of patterns in cooking-stoves, many of which I know to be good. I will mention a few :—" The Lion," " Farmers' Friend," " Burr," "Canadian Hot-Air," "Clinton Hot-Air;" these two last require dry wood ; and the common " Premium" stove, which is a good useful stove, but seldom a good casting, and sold at a low price. If you buy a small-sized stove, you will not be able to bake a good joint of meat or good-sized loaves of bread in it.

If you have a chimney, and prefer relying on cooking with the bake-kettle, I would also recommend a roaster, or bachelor's oven : this will cost only a few shillings, and prove a great convenience, as you can bake rolls, cakes, pies and meat in it. An outside oven, built of stones, bricks, or clay, is put up at small cost, and is a great comfort. * The heating it once or twice a week, will save you much work, and you will enjoy bread much better and sweeter than any baked in a stove, oven or bake-kettle.

Many persons who have large houses of stone or brick, now adopt the plan of heating them with hot air, which is conveyed by means of pipes into the rooms. An ornamented, circular grating admits

---

* Two men, or a man and a boy will build a common-sized clay oven in a day or less, if they understand the work and prepare the materials beforehand.

the heated air, by opening or shutting the grates. The furnace is in the cellar, and is made large enough to allow of a considerable quantity of wood being put in at once.

A house thus heated is kept at summer heat in the coldest weather; and can be made cooler by shutting the grates in any room.

The temperature of houses heated thus is very pleasant, and certainly does not seem so unhealthy as those warmed by metal stoves, besides there being far less risk from fire.

Those who wish to enjoy the cheerful appearance of a fire in their sitting room, can have one; as little wood is required in such case.

The poorer settlers, to whom the outlay of a dollar is often an object, make very good washing tubs out of old barrels, by sawing one in half, leaving two of the staves a few inches higher than the rest, for handles. Painted washing-tubs made of pine, iron hooped, cost a dollar; painted water-pails only 1s. 6d. a piece; but they are not very durable. Owing to the dryness of the air, great care is requisite to keep your tubs, barrels and pails in proper order. Many a good vessel of this kind is lost for want of a little attention.

The washing tubs should be kept in the cellar, or with water in them. Those who keep servants must not forget to warn them of this fact.

In fitting up your house, do not sacrifice all comfort in the kitchen, for the sake of a best room for receiving company.

If you wish to enjoy a cheerful room, by all means have a fireplace in it. A blazing log-fire is an object that inspires cheerfulness. A stove in the hall or passage is a great comfort in winter; and the pipe conducted rightly will warm the upper rooms; but do not let the stove supersede the cheering fire in the sitting-room. Or if your house has been built only to be heated by stoves, choose one that, with a grate in front, can be opened to show the fire. A handsome parlour-stove can now be got for twelve dollars. Tanned and dyed sheep-skins make excellent door mats, and warm hearth-rugs. With small outlay of money your room will thus be comfortably furnished.

A delightful easy-chair can be made out of a very rough material —nothing better than a common flour barrel. I will, as well as I can, direct you how these barrel-chairs are made. The first four or five staves of a good, sound, clean flour barrel are to be sawn off, level, within two feet of the ground, or higher, if you think that will be too low for the seat : this is for the front : leave the two staves on either side a few inches higher for the elbows ; the staves that remain are left to form the hollow back : augur holes are next made all round, on a level with the seat, in all the staves ; through these holes ropes are passed and interlaced, so as to form a secure seat : a bit of thin board may then be nailed, flat, on the rough edge of the elbow staves, and a coarse covering, of linen or sacking, tacked on over the back and arms : this is stuffed with cotton-wool, soft hay, or sheep's wool, and then a chintz cover over the whole, and well-filled cushion for the seat, completes the chair. Two or three of such seats in a sitting-room, give it an air of great comfort at a small cost.

Those settlers who come out with sufficient means, and go at once on cleared farms, which is by far the best plan, will be able to purchase very handsome furniture of black walnut or cherry wood at moderate cost. Furniture, new and handsome, and even costly, is to be met with in any of the large towns ; and it would be impertinent in me to offer advice as to the style to be observed by such persons : it is to the small farmer, and poorer class, that my hints are addressed.

The shanty, or small log-house of the poorer emigrant, is often entirely furnished by his own hands. A rude bedstead, formed of cedar poles, a coarse linen bag filled with hay or dried moss, and bolster of the same, is the bed he lies on ; his seats are benches, nailed together ; a table of deal boards, a few stools, a few shelves for the crockery and tinware ; these are often all that the poor emigrant can call his own in the way of furniture. Little enough and rude enough. Yet let not the heart of the wife despond. It is only the first trial ; better things are in store for her.

Many an officer's wife, and the wives of Scotch and English gentlemen, in the early state of the colony have been no better off.— Many a wealthy landowner in Canada was born in circumstances as unfavourable. Men who now occupy the highest situations in the country, have been brought up in a rude log-shanty, little better than an Indian wigwam. Let these things serve to cheer the heart and

smooth the rough ways of the settler's first outset in Canadian life.—
And let me add that now there is more facility for the incoming emigrant's settling with comfort, than there was twenty or thirty years ago ; unless he goes very far back into the uncivilized portions of the country, he cannot now meet with the trials and privations that were the lot of the first settlers in the Province. And there is no necessity for him to place himself and family beyond the outskirts of civilization. Those who have the command of a little capital can generally buy land with some clearing and buildings ; and the working man can obtain good employment for his wife and elder girls or boys, so as to enable them by their united savings, to get a lot of land for themselves, to settle upon. This is more prudent than plunging at once into the bush, without possessing the experience which is necessary for their future welfare, almost for their very existence, in their new mode of life. When they have earned a little money and some knowledge of the ways of the country, they may then start fair, and by industry and sobriety, in a few years become independent.

To pay for his land by instalments, is the only way a poor man can manage to acquire property : to obtain his deed, is the height of his ambition : to compass this desirable end all the energies of the household are directed, For this the husband, the wife, the sons and the daughters all toil : each contributes his or her mite : for this they endure all sorts of privations, without murmuring. In a few years the battle is won. Poverty is no longer to be feared.

The land is their own : with what pride they now speak of it ; with what honest delight they contemplate every blade of wheat, every ear of corn, and the cattle that feed upon their pastures. No rent is now to be paid for it. God has blessed the labours of their hands. Let them not forget that to him is the glory and praise due.

When they have acquired land and cattle, let them not in the pride of their hearts say—"My hand and the power of my arm has gotten me all these ;" for it is God that giveth the increase in all these things.

ON TEMPERANCE.

With habits of industry long practiced, cheered by a reasonable hope, and with experience gained, no one need despair of obtaining all the essential comforts of life ; but strict sobriety is indispensably necessary to the attainment of his hopes. Let not the drunkard flatter himself that success will attend his exertions. A curse is in the cup ; it lingers in the dregs to embitter his own life and that of his hapless partner and children. As of the sluggard, so also may it be said of the intemperate—"The *drunkard* shall starve in harvest." It is in vain for the women of the household to work hard and to bear their part of the hardships incidental to a settler's life, if the husband gives himself up as a slave to this miserable vice.

I dwell more earnestly upon this painful subject, because unfortunately the poison sold to the public under the name of whiskey, is so cheap, that for a few pence a man may degrade himself below the beasts that perish, and barter away his soul for that which profiteth not ; bring shame and disgrace upon his name, and bitterness of heart into the bosom of his family. I have known sad instances of this abhorrent vice, even among the women ; and they have justified themselves with saying—"We do it in self-defence, and because our husbands set us the example : it is in vain for us to strive and strive; for everything is going to ruin." Alas that such a plea should ever be made by a wife. Let the man remember that God has set him for the support of the wife : he is the head, and should set an example of virtue, and strength, rather than of vice and weakness. Let both avoid this deadly sin, if they would prosper in life, and steadfastly resist the temptation that besets them on every side. And not to the poor man alone would I speak; for this evil habit pervades all classes; and many a young man of fair expectations is ruined by this indulgence, and many a flourishing home is made desolate by him who founded it. The last state of this man is worse than the first.

FEMALE ENERGY.

It is a matter of surprize to many persons to see the great amount of energy of mind and personal exertion that women will make under the most adverse circumstances in this country. I have marked with astonishment and admiration acts of female heroism, for such it may be termed in women whose former habits of life had exempted them from any kind of laborious work, urged by some unforeseen exigency, perform tasks from which many men would have shrunk. Sometimes aroused by the indolence and inactivity of their husbands or sons, they have resolutely set their own shoulders to the wheel, and borne the burden with unshrinking perseverence unaided ; forming a bright example to all around them, and showing what can be done when the mind is capable of overcoming the weakness of the body.

A poor settler was killed by the fall of a tree, in his fallow. The wife was left with six children, the youngest a babe, the eldest a boy of fourteen. This family belonged to the labouring class. The widow did not sit down and fold her hands in utter despair, in this sad situation; but when the first natural grief had subsided, she roused herself to do what she could for the sake of her infants. Some help no doubt she got from kind neighbours ; but she did not depend on them alone. She and her eldest son together, piled the brush on the new fallow ; and with their united exertions and the help of the oxen, they managed to log and burn off the Spring fallow. I dare say they got some help, or called a logging Bee, to aid in this work.— They managed, this poor widow and her children, to get two or three acres of wheat in, and potatoes, and a patch of corn ; and to raise a few vegetables. They made a brush fence and secured the fields from cattle breaking in, and then harvested the crops in due time, the lad working out sometimes for a week or so, to help earn a trifle to assist them.

That fall they underbrushed a few acres more land, the mother helping to chop the small trees herself, and young ones piling the brush. They had some ague, and lost one cow, during that year ; but still they fainted not, and put trust in Him who is the helper of the widow and fatherless. Many little sums of money were earned by the boys shaping axe-handles, which they sold at the stores, and beech brooms : these are much used about barns and in rough work. They are like the Indian brooms, peeled from a stick of iron-wood, blue-beech, or oak. Whip-handles of hickory, too, they made. They sold that winter maple sugar and molasses ; and the widow knitted socks for some of the neighbours, and made slippers of listing. The boys also made some money by carrying in loads of oak and hemlock bark, to the tanners, from whom they got orders on the stores for groceries, clothes and such things. By degrees their stock increased, and they managed by dint of care and incessant labour to pay up small instalments on their land. How this was all done by a weak woman and her children, seems almost a miracle, but they brought the strong will to help the weak arm.

I heard this story from good authority, from the physician who attended upon one of the children in sickness, and who had been called in at the inquest that was held on the body of her husband.

Dr. H. often named this woman as an example of female energy under the most trying circumstances; and I give it to show what even a poor, desolate widow may do, even in a situation of such dire distress.

BORROWING.

And now I would say a few words about borrowing—a subject on which so much has been said by different writers who have touched upon the domestic peculiarities of the Canadians and Yankees.

In a new settlement where people live scattered, and far from stores and villages, the most careful of housewives will sometimes run out of necessaries, and may be glad of the accommodation of a cupful of tea, or a little sugar; of barm to raise fresh rising, or flour to bake with. Perhaps the mill is far off, and the good man has been too much occupied to take in a grist. Or medicine may be needed in a case of sudden illness.

Well, all these are legitimate reasons for borrowing, and all kindly, well-disposed neighbours will lend with hearty good-will: it is one of the exigencies of a remote settlement, and happens over and over again.

But as there are many who are not over scrupulous in these matters, it is best to keep a true account in black and white, and let the borrowed things be weighed or measured, and returned by the same weight and measure. This method will save much heart-burning and some unpleasant wrangling with neighbours; and if the same measure is meted to you withal, there will be no cause of complaint on either side. On your part be honest and punctual in returning, and then you can with a better face demand similar treatment.

Do not refuse your neighbors in their hour of need, for you also may be glad of a similar favour. In the Backwoods especially, people cannot be independent of the help and sympathy of their fellow creatures. Nevertheless do not accustom yourself to depend too much upon any one.

Because you find by experience that you can borrow a pot or a pan, a bake-kettle or a washing-tub, at a neighbour's house, that is no good reason for not buying one for yourself, and wearing out Mrs. So-and-so's in your own service. Once in a while, or till you have supplied the want, is all very well; but do not wear out the face of friendship, and be taxed with meanness.

Servants have a passion for borrowing, and will often carry on a system of the kind for months, unsanctioned by their mistresses; and sometimes coolness will arise between friends through this cause. In towns there is little excuse for borrowing: the same absolute necessity for it does not exist.

If a neighbour, or one who is hardly to be so called, comes to borrow articles of wearing apparel, or things that they have no justifiable cause for asking the loan of, refuse at once and unhesitatingly.

I once lived near a family who made a dead set at me in the borrowing way. One day a little damsel of thirteen years of age, came up quite out of breath to ask the loan of a best night-cap, as she was going out on a visit; also three nice worked-lace or muslin collars—one for herself, one for her sister, and the third was for a cousin, a new-arrival; a pair of walking-boots to go to the fair in at —————, and a straw hat for her brother Sam, who had worn out his; and to crown all, a small-tooth comb, "to redd up their hair with, to make them nice."

I refused all with very little remorse; but the little damsel looked so rueful and begged so hard about the collars, that I *gave* her two, leaving the cousin to shift as she best could; but I told her not to return them, as I never *lent clothes*, and warned her to come no more on such an errand. She got the shoes elsewhere, and, as I heard they were worn out in the service before they were returned. Now against such a shameless abuse of the borrowing system, every one is justified in making a stand: it is an imposition, and by no means to be tolerated.

Another woman came to borrow a best baby-robe, lace-cap and fine flannel petticoat, as she said she had nothing grand enough to take the baby to church to be christened in. Perhaps she thought it would make the sacrifice more complete if she gave ocular demonstration of the pomps and vanities being his to renounce and forsake.

I declined to lend the things, at which she grew angry, and departed in a great pet, but got a present of a handsome suit from a lady who thought me very hard-hearted. Had the woman been poor, which she was not, and had begged for a decent dress for the little Christian, she should have had it; but I did not respect the motive for borrowing finer clothes than she had herself, for the occasion.

I give these instances that the new comer may distinguish between the use and the abuse of the system; that they may neither suffer their good nature and inexperience to be imposed upon, nor fall into the same evil way themselves, or become churlish and unfriendly as the manner of some is.

One of the worst points in the borrowing system is, the loss of time and inconvenience that arises from the want of punctuality in returning the thing lent: unless this is insisted upon and rigorously enforced, it will always remain, in Canada as elsewhere, a practical demonstration of the old adage—" Those who go borrowing, go sorrowing;" they generally lose a friend.

There is one occasion on which the loan of household utensils is always expected: this is at "Bees", where the assemblage always exceeds the ways and means of the party; and as in country places these acts of reciprocity cannot be dispensed with, it is best cheerfully to accord your help to a neighbour, taking care to count knives, forks, spoons, and crockery, or whatever it may be that is lent carefully, and make a note of the same, to avoid confusion. Such was always my practice, and I lived happily with neighbours, relations and friends, and never had any misunderstanding with any of them.

I might write an amusing chapter on the subject of borrowing; but I leave it to those who have abler pens than mine, and more lively talents, for amusing their readers.

CHOICE OF A VESSEL.

In the choice of a vessel in which to embark for Canada, those persons who can afford to do so, will find better accommodations and more satisfaction in the steamers that ply between Liverpool and Quebec, than in any of the emigrant ships. The latter may charge a smaller sum per head, but the difference in point of health, comfort and respectability will more than make up for the difference of the charge. The usual terms are five or six pounds for grown persons ; but doubtless a reduction on this rate would be made, if a family were coming out. To reach the land of their adoption in health and comfort, is in itself a great step towards success. The commanders of this line of ships are all men of the highest respectability, and the poor emigrant need fear no unfair dealing, if they place themselves and family under their care. At any rate the greatest caution should be practiced in ascertaining the character borne by the captains and owners of the vessels in which the emigrant is about to embark ; even the ship itself should have a character for safety, and good speed. Those persons who provide their own sea-stores, had better consult some careful and experienced friend on the subject. There are many who are better qualified than myself, to afford them this valuable information.

LUGGAGE.

As to furniture, and iron-ware, I would by no means advise the emigrant to burden himself with such matters ; for he will find that by the time he reaches his port of destination, the freightage, warehouse room, custom-house duties, and injury that they have sustained in the transit, will have made them dear bargains, besides not being as suitable to the country as those things that are sold in the towns in Canada. Good clothing and plenty of good shoes and boots, are your best stores, and for personal luggage you will have no freight to pay. A list of the contents of each box or trunk, being put within the lid, and showed to the custom-house officer, will save a great deal of unpacking and trouble. Any of your friends sending out a box to you, by forwarding an invoice and a low estimate of the value of the goods, the address of the party, and the bill of lading, properly signed by the captain to whose care i is assigned, to the forwarder at Montreal, will save both delay and expence. Macpherson, Crane & Co., Montreal, or Gillespie & Company, with many others of equal respectability, may be relied upon. For upwards of twenty years I have had boxes and packages forwarded through Macpherson, Crane & Co., Montreal, without a single instance of loss: the bill of lading and invoice being always sent by post as soon as obtained : by attention to this advice much vexatious delay is saved, and the boxes pass unopened through the custom-house.

I now copy for the instruction of the emigrant, the following advice which was published in the "Old Countryman", an excellent Toronto bi-weekly paper :

EMIGRATION TO CANADA.—The arrangements made by the Government of Canada for the reception and protection of emigrants on their arrival at Quebec contrast in a remarkable manner with the want of such arrangements at New York, and the other ports of the United States, to which emigrants are conveyed from Europe. On the arrival of each emigrant ship in the river St. Lawrence, she is boarded by the medical officer of the Emigrant Hospital at Grosse Isle, situated a few miles below Quebec, and, whenever disease prevails in a ship, the emigrants are landed, and remain at the hospital, at the expense of the Colonial Government, until they are cured.— On the ship's arrival at Quebec, Mr. Buchanan, the government agent of emigrants, proceeds at once on board, for it is his duty to advise and protect each emigrant on his arrival. He inquires into all complaints, and sees that the provisions of the Passenger Act are strictly enforced. This he is enabled to do in a most effectual manner, as under an arrangement sanctioned by the Commissioners of Emigration in Great Britain, whenever an emigrant vessel leaves any British port for Quebec, the emigration officer of that port forwards to Mr. Buchanan, by mail steamer, a duplicate list of her passengers, with their names, age, sex, trade, &c. This list is usually received by him two or three weeks before the vessel reaches Quebec, so that he is not only fully prepared for her arrival, but is furnished with every particular which may be useful to him in protecting the emigrants.— If just cause of complaint exist, he institutes, under a very summary law of the Province of Canada, legal proceedings against the master: but so thoroughly are the value and efficiency of this officer felt, that since a very short period subsequent to his appointment, it has very rarely been found necessary to take such proceedings. In cases where emigrants have arrived without sufficient funds to take them to places where employment is abundant and remunerative, their fares have been paid by Mr. Buchanan, out of the funds in his possession for the purpose. Emigrants from other than British ports experience precisely the same protection at the hands of Mr. Buchanan.— In 1853 about one-sixth of the emigration to Canada was German and Norwegian.

IMPORTANT TO EMIGRANTS.—The many fatal cases of cholera which have taken place on board emigrant vessels, will impress upon all who contemplate emigrating the propriety of adopting the salutary precautions set down by orders of her Majesty's Land and Emigration Commissioners, and widely circulated by placard. These precautions state :—That the sea-sickness, consequent on the rough weather which ships must encounter at this season, joined to the cold and damp of a sea-voyage, will render persons who are not very strong more susceptible to the attacks of this disease. To those who may emigrate at this season, the Commissioners strongly recommend that they should provide themselves with as much warm clothing as they can, and especially with flannel, to be worn next the skin; that they should have both their clothes and their persons quite clean before embarking, and should be careful to do so during the voyage— and that they should provide themselves with as much solid and wholesome food as they can procure, in addition to the ship's allowance, to be used on the voyage, and that it would, of course, be desirable, if they can arrange it, that they should not go in a ship that is much crowded, or that is not provided with a medical man.

EXTRACT FROM MR. VERE FOSTER'S ADVICE TO EMIGRANTS AS TO SHIP STORES AND OTHER ESSENTIALS FOR THE VOYAGE.

I have been allowed by the author of a most useful and comprehensive little pamphlet on emigration, written for the use of poor emigrants by Vere Foster, Esq., and circulated at the low price of one penny, to make the following extracts, which I think must be of much value to families preparing to embark for this country, and contains some points of information which I was not able myself to supply :—

Mr. Foster says :—

The lowest prices of passage from Liverpool to the different Ports in America, are much as follows :—

Quebec	£3 0 0	to	£4 10 0
Philadelphia	3 0 0	to	4 10 0
New Orleans	3 5 0	to	4 10 0

To the United States 10s. less is charged for any passenger under fourteen years of age; to Canada one-half less is charged; under twelve months often free of all charge.

From London £1 higher is charged than the above rates.

The rates of passage are higher than they were last year, on account of the high prices of provisions and increased expenses in the fitting up of ships, caused by the regulations of the late acts of parliament.

Some steamers take passengers from Liverpool to Philadelphia for £8 8s. 0d. Others go in summer from Liverpool to Montreal, in Canada, for £7 7s. 0d., including provisions. In the winter months they go to Portland in Maine, where the fare, including railway fare, also is £7 7s. 0d. : to New York it is £8 8s. 0d.

PURCHASE OF PASSAGE TICKETS.

I would recommend emigrants to employ *no one*, but purchase for themselves at the Head Agency Office of the ship at the port of embarkation; or from the master of the ship in which they are about to sail; where they will be more likely to be charged the market rate. This ticket should be given up to *no one*, but should be kept till after the end of the voyage by the passenger, in order that he may at all times know his rights.

Ships with but one sleeping deck are preferable to those with two, on account of health; and the less crowded with passengers the better for comfort. *

As to those who wish to buy land, let them see it first, and avoid the neighbourhood of marshes, and rivers, where sickness is sure to prevail. † In the States of America, the price of Government land is One dollar and a quarter per acre. In Canada the government land is 7s. 6d. per acre.

OUTFIT OF PROVISIONS, UTENSILS AND BEDDING.

The quantities of provisions which each passenger, fourteen years of age and upwards, is entitled to receive on the voyage to America, including the time of detention, if any, at the port of embarkation, are according to

---

* The humane writer of the "Advice to Emigrants" from which the above remarks are taken, though a person of education and refinement, and in delicate health, voluntarily chose to come out to Canada as a steerage passenger, that he might test in his own person the privations and discomforts to which the poorer emigrant passengers are exposed, and be enabled to afford suitable advice respecting the voyage-out to others.

† This rather belongs to small lakes and slow-flowing waters with low flat shores. Rapid rivers with high steep banks are not so unhealthy.

British Law,

3 quarts of water daily.	1½ lb sugar............ weekly.
2½ lbs of bread or biscuit weekly.	2 oz. tea, or 4 oz. coffee or
1 lb wheaten flour........ "	cocoa............ "
5 lb oatmeal .... "	2 oz. salt .... "
2 lb rice................ "	

American Law.

3 qts. of water daily.	½ lb sugar............... weekly.
2½ lb navy bread ....weekly.	2 oz. tea............... "
1 lb wheaten flour ...... "	8 oz. of molasses and vin-
6 lbs oatmeal .... "	egar................ "
1 lb of salt pork......... "	
(free from bone.)	

According to an act of Parliament which came in force on 1st October, 1852, certain articles may be substituted for the oatmeal and rice, the option of the master of the ship.

In every Passenger ship issues of provisions shall be made daily before two o'clock in the afternoon, as near as may be in the proportion of one-seventh of the weekly allowance on each day. The first of such issues shall be made before two o'clock in the afternoon of the day of embarkation to such passengers as shall be then on board, and all articles that require to be cooked shall be issued in a cooked state. This excellent Parliamentary regulation is often evaded.—Each passenger is entitled to lodgings and provisions on board from the day appointed for sailing in his ticket, or else to 1s. per day, for every day of detention, and the same for forty-eight hours after arriving in America.

EXTRA PROVISIONS FOR THE VOYAGE.

As respects extra provisions, as great a quantity as heretofore will probably not be required, if the ship's provisions are issued according to law, cooked.

In my recent voyage in the Washington from Liverpool to New-York, which voyage occupied thirty-seven days, I took out the following extras, which I found quite sufficient. 1½ stone wheaten flour; 6 lbs bacon ; 2½ lbs butter ; a 4-lb loaf, hard baked ; ¼ lb tea ; 2 lbs brown sugar ; salt, soap, and bread soda for raising cakes. These extras cost 10s. 6d. I also took the following articles—the prices as follows :—

	s.	d.
Tin water-can holding six quarts		8
Large tin hooked-saucepan		6
Frying pan		8
Tin wash-basin		6
Tin tea-pot		4
Tin kettle		9
Two deep tin-plates		3
Two pint-mugs		3
Two knives, forks and spoons		9
Barrel and padlock for holding provisions	1	0
Straw mattrass	1	0
Blanket, single	2	0
Rugs	1	3
Sheets, each		10½

The handles and spouts of the tin-ware should be rivetted as well as soldered. Families would do well to take out a covered slop-pail and a broom. The bottoms of the chests and trunks should have two strips of wood nailed to them to keep them from the damp floor. In addition to the extra stores, a cheese, a few herrings, with some potatoes and onions may be added. [The eyes or shoots can be destroyed by drying the roots in an oven after the baking heat is off, for a few minutes ; or they may be rubbed off with a coarse cloth from time to time.] Preserved milk is also a good thing ; it can be kept good for some time. *

As little luggage as possible should be taken, as the carriage often comes to as much as the first cost : woollen, and shoes, however, are cheaper at home, and therefore it is advisable to bring a good supply.

Fruits and green vegetables should be eaten very sparingly at first: the free indulgence in fresh meat is also apt to bring on diarrhœa.— Many deaths happen in consequence of want of prudent attention to temperance in meats and drinks on first coming ashore.

EMIGRANTS ON LANDING, should not linger about the suburbs of the ports and large towns, but go at once into the interior, for it is one hundred chances to one against their getting employment at these seaports. There is a great propensity in the poorer sort of emigrants to linger idling about the cities, spending their time and their little means, often refusing work when it is offered them, till their last penny is spent, when the trunks and other property are seized to pay for lodging. It is best to get work as fast as possible, and it is unreasonable to look for the highest rate of wages till a little experience in

---

* Fresh milk put into a close jar and set in a pot of water, kept boiling for six or eight hours, and when cool bottled and corked with waxed corks, will keep some time. An ounce of white sugar boiled with the milk or cream will help to preserve it ; and just before bottling, a small quantity —half a tea-spoonful—of carbonate of soda, may be added.

the work of the country has made them expert in the handling of the tools, which are often very different to those with which they have been used to labour.

Intoxicating drinks are unfortunately very cheap in America and Canada. They are a great curse to the emigrant, and the main obstacle to his bettering his condition. Emigrants would do well to take the temperance pledge before sailing; as no liquors are allowed on board ship, they will have a beautiful opportunity of breaking themselves in to total abstinence of a practice which is injurious to health, expensive and selfish, as it robs them of the power of maintaining their families and adding to their comforts."—*Abridged from "Emigration to America" by Vere Foster, Esq.*

I have given you the substance of this valuable advice to emigrants, with here and there a few words added or omitted as the case might be.

I have omitted saying that the most eligible part of Canada for emigrants desiring to buy wild land, is the western portion of the Upper Province, or that peninsula that lies between the great waters of Lakes Ontario, Erie, Huron and the smaller lake Simcoe. Railroads and public works are being carried on in this part of the country; the land is of the richest and most fertile description, and the climate is less severe. The new townships afford excellent chances for mechanics settling in small villages, where such trades as the shoemaker, blacksmith, carpenter, wheelwright and others, are much needed, and in these new settlements labour of this kind pays well, because there is less competition to regulate the prices. It is a good thing for those who grow up with a new place; they are sure to become rich men.

I will also add a piece of additional advice. Let the immigrant on landing at any of the frontier towns ask for the Government agent, but if none be resident in the place, and he is at a loss for advice as to the best mode of proceeding, let him then enquire for the clergyman, the mayor or one of the head gentlemen or merchants of the town. These persons have no interest to deceive or mislead in any way, and will give you all the information that you may need as to the best way of lodging and disposing of your family, and also the most likely persons to afford you employment.

In Toronto Mr. Hawke, the Crown Agent, will give all attention to you: he is a man whose knowledge is only surpassed by his uprightness and benevolence. You have only to ask his address; any one will direct you to his office.

One more piece of advice I would give to mothers who have young girls whom they may think proper to put to service; or to servant girls who come out without parents to act for them. Be careful how you enter into low families such as the keepers of low boarding houses or taverns, without endeavouring to learn something of the character of the parties, and by no means let relations or friends separate in a strange place without making some written note of their place of abode or future destination: by such carelessness many young people have lost all trace of their fathers and mothers, sisters and brothers, or of the friend under whose care they were placed by their relatives, and have suffered the most painful anxiety. Negligence of this kind is very much to be condemned and should be avoided. This is an error that often arises from ignorance and want of proper consideration. Perhaps you who read this book may deem such advice uncalled for, and so it may be in the case of all careful and thoughtful persons; but these may come out in the same vessel with others who are of a reckless, improvident nature, on whom they may impress the value of the advice here given. Among the Irish and even more cautious Scotch emigrants I have met with many many instances of children being left in a strange land without a trace of their place of residence being preserved,—the children in their turn having no clue by which to discover their parents.

POSTAGE.

In Canada the rates of postage are not high, though still they are greater than in the old country. Three-pence will pay a single letter to any part of the Province, and 7½d. to Great Britain, if marked Via Halifax: if sent unmarked it goes through the United States and costs 10d. postage.

In every large town once or twice a month a printed list of unclaimed letters lying at the Post Office is published in one of the newspapers, by which regulation very few letters are lost.

Owing to the rapid progress made in the Province during the last few years in population, trade, agriculture and general improvement, lands have increased in value, and it now requires as many pounds to purchase a farm as formerly it cost dollars.

The growth of towns and villages, the making of roads, gravel, plank and now rail-roads; the building of bridges, the improvement of inland navigation, mills of all sorts, cloth factories, and the opportunities of attending public worship have, under a peaceful government, effected this change; and wise men will consider that the increased value of lands is a convincing proof of the flourishing condition of the people and the resources of the country, and feel encouraged by the prospect of a fair return for capital invested either in land or any other speculation connected with the merchandize of the country.

The crown lands to the Westward, in the newly surveyed counties, are selling at 12s. 6d. currency per acre. The soil is of great fertility; and to this portion of the Province vast numbers are directing their steps; certain that in a few years the value of these bush farms will be increased fourfold; but let none but the strong in arm and will go upon wild land. The giants of the forest are not brought down without much severe toil; and many hardships must be endured in a backwoodsman's life, especially by the wife and children. If all pull together, and the women will be content to bear their part with cheerfulness, no doubt success will follow their honest endeavours.— But a wild farm is not to be made in one, two or even five years.— The new soil will indeed yield her increase to a large amount, but it takes years to clear enough to make a really good farm, to get barns and sheds and fences and a comfortable dwelling-house: few persons accomplish all this under ten, fifteen and sometimes even twenty years. I am speaking now of the poor man, whose only capital is his labour and that of his family; and many a farmer who now rides to market or church in his own waggon and with his wife and children, well and even handsomely clad, by his side, has begun the world in Canada with no other capital. It is true his head has grown grey while these comforts were being earned, but he has no parish poor-house in the distance to look forward to as his last resource, or the bitter legacy of poverty to bequeath to his famishing children and broken-hearted widow. And with so fair a prospect for the future, wives and mothers will strive to bear with patience the trials and toils which lead to so desirable an end, but let not the men rashly and unadvisedly adopt the life of settlers in the Bush, without carefully considering the advantages and disadvantages that this mode of life offer over any other; next his own capabilities for successfully carrying it into effect, and also those of his wife and family: if he be by nature indolent, and in temper desponding, easily daunted by difficulties and of a weak frame of body, such a life would not suit him. If his wife be a weakly woman, destitute of mental energy, unable to bear up under the trials of life, she is not fit for a life of hardship—it will be useless cruelty to expose her to it. If the children are very young and helpless, they can only increase the settler's difficulties, and render no assistance in the work of clearing; but if on the contrary the man be of a hardy, healthy, vigorous frame of body, and a cheerful, hopeful temper, with a kind partner, willing to aid both within doors and without, the mother of healthy children, then there is every chance that they will become prosperous settlers, an honor to the country of their adoption. The sons and daughters will be a help to them instead of a drawback, and the more there are from six years old and upwards to lend a hand in the work of clearing, the better for them: they will soon be beyond the reach of poverty. It is such settlers as these that Canada requires and will receive with joy To all such she bids a hearty welcome and God speed; and I trust the intelligent wives and daughters of such settlers may derive some assistance in their household labours from the instruction conveyed to them as well as to others in the pages of this book, which is not intended to induce any one to emigrate to Canada, but to instruct them in certain points of household economy, that they may not have to learn as many have done, by repeated failures and losses, the simple elements of Canadian housekeeping.

Among the many works most particularly valuable for affording the best information for Emigrants, I would point out "Brown's Views of Canada and the Colonists, Second Edition, Edinburgh, 1851," and Major Strickland's "Twenty-seven years' residence in Canada." The former supplies all necessary statistics, written with much good sense judgment and ability, while the latter, besides being very amusing, contains the best practical advice for all classes of settlers; but unfortunately is published at a price that places it out of the reach of the "People." It is a pity that the plain, practical portion of the work is not issued in a pamphlet form, at a rate which would place it at once within the means of the poorer class of emigrants, to whom it would be invaluable, as it gives every possible instruction that they require as back-woods settlers.

DESCRIPTION OF A NEW SETTLEMENT.

Extracted from Major Strickland's " Twenty-seven years' Residence in Canada West."

"On the 16th of May, 1826, I moved up with all my goods and chattels, which were then easily packed into a single-horse waggon, and consisted of a plough-iron, six pails, a sugar-kettle, two iron pots, a frying-pan with a long handle, a tea-kettle, a few cups and saucers,* a chest of carpenter's tools, a Canadian axe, and a cross-cut saw.

"My stock of provisions comprised a parcel of groceries, half a barrel of pork, and a barrel of flour.

"The roads were so bad (in those days when there were no roads) that it took me three days to perform a journey of little more than fifty miles. [This was twenty-eight years ago, let it be remembered, when travelling was a matter of great difficulty.] We, that is my two labourers and myself, had numerous upsets, but reached at last the promised land.

"My friends in Douro turned out the next day and assisted me to put up the walls of my shanty and roof it with basswood troughs, and it was completed before dark. [This shanty was for a temporary shelter only, while working on the chopping, and preparing for the building of a good log-house.]

"I was kept busy for more than a week chinking between the logs, and plastering up all the crevices, cutting out the doorway and place for the window-casing, then making a door and hanging it on wooden hinges. I also made a rough table and some stools, which answered better than they looked.

"Four thick slabs of limestone placed upright in one corner of the shanty, with clay packed between them to keep the fire off the logs, answered very well for a chimney, with a hole cut through the roof above to vent the smoke.

---

* Instead of crockery, the old bush-settler's plates and dishes, cups, &c. were of tin, which stood the rough travel of the forest roads better than the more brittle ware.

"I made a tolerable bedstead out of some ironwood poles, by stretching strips of elmwood bark across, which I plaited strongly together to support my bed, which was a good one, and the only article of luxury in my possession.

"I had foolishly hired two Irish emigrants who had not been in Canada longer than myself, and of course knew nothing of either chopping, logging or fencing, or indeed of any work belonging to the country. The consequence of this imprudence was that the first ten acres I cleared cost me nearly £5 an acre—at least £2 more than it should have done. *

"I found chopping in the summer months very laborious. I should have underbrushed my fallow in the fall before the leaves fell, and chopped the large timber during the winter months, when I should have had the warm weather for logging and burning, which should be completed by the first day of September. For want of experience it was all uphill work with me.

* * * * * *

"A person who understands chopping can save himself a good deal of trouble and hard work by making what is called a *Plan* heap. Three or four of these may be made on an acre, but not more. The largest and most difficult trees are felled, the limbs only being cut off and piled. Then all the trees that will fall in the same direction should be thrown along on the top of the others, the more the better chance of burning well.

"If you succeed in getting a good fallow, the chances are, if your plan-heaps are well made, that the timber will be for the most part consumed, which will save a great many blows with the axe, and some heavy logging. †

"As soon as the ground was cool enough after the burn was over, I made a Logging Bee, at which I had five yoke of oxen and twenty men. The teamster selects a large log to commence a heap—one which is too ponderous for the cattle to draw : against this the other logs are drawn and piled : the men with handspikes roll them up one above the other, until the heap is seven or eight feet high and ten or twelve broad—all the chips, sticks, roots, and other rubbish are thrown up on the top of the heap. A team and four men can pick and log an acre a day if the burn has been good.

---

* The usual price for chopping, logging and fencing an acre of hardwood land is from eleven to twelve dollars ; but if the pine, hemlock and spruce predominate, fourteen dollars is given.

† I have been told that in the western townships where the land is very heavily timbered, the usual plan now adopted by the settlers is to chop one year and let the timber lie till the following year when it is fired. The fire burns all up, so that a few charred logs and brands which are easily logged up is all that remain. This lightens the labour I am told very much ; it is practised in the "Queen's Bush."

"My hive worked well, for we had five acres logged and fired that night. On a dark night a hundred or two of such heaps all on fire at once have a very fine effect, and shed a broad glare of light over the country for a considerable distance.

* * * * * *

"My next steps towards my house-building was to build a lime heap for the plastering of my walls and building my chimneys. We set to work, and built an immense log heap: we made a frame of logs on the top of the heap to keep the stone from falling over the side. We drew twenty cart loads of limestone broken up small with a sledge hammer, which was piled into the frame, and fire applied below. This is the easiest way in the bush of getting a supply of this useful material.

"I built my house of elm logs, thirty-six feet long by twenty-four feet wide, which I divided into three rooms on the ground floor besides an entrance-hall and staircase, and three bed-rooms above. I was busy till October making shingles, roofing, cutting out the door and windows, and hewing the logs smooth inside with broad axe." [Then follows a description and direction for making shingles.]

In the XII chapter we have an excellent passage about the choice of land, but I must refer my reader to the work itself for that, and many other most valuable hints, and go on to select another passage or two on building &c.

"The best time of the year to commence operations is early in Sept. The weather is then moderately warm and pleasant, and there are no flies in the bush to annoy you.

"A log-shanty twenty-four feet long by sixteen feet wide is large enough to begin with, and should be roofed with shingles or troughs.* A cellar should be dug near the fire-place commodious enough to contain twenty or thirty bushels of potatoes, a barrel or two of pork or other matters.

"As soon as your shanty is completed, measure off as many acres as you intend to chop during the winter, and mark the boundaries by a blazed-line [notched trees] on each side. The next operation is to cut down all the small trees and brush—this is called under-brushing. The rule is, to cut down every thing close to the ground from the diameter of six inches and under.

"There are two modes of piling, either in heaps or windrows. If your fallow be full of pine, hemlock, balsam, cedar and the like, then I should advise windrows; and when hardwood predominates, heaps

---

* This is a chopper's shanty: a good shelter for those who are clearing in the bush or lumbering. It should be chinked, and made wind and water tight.

are better. The brush should be carefully piled and laid all one way, by which means it packs and burns better.

"The chopping now begins, and may be followed without interruption until the season for sugar-making commences. The heads of the trees should be thrown on the heaps, or windrow; this a skilful chopper will seldom fail to do.

"The trunks of the trees must be cut into lengths from fourteen to sixteen feet, according to the size of the timber.

* * * * * * * *

"The emigrant should endeavour to get as much chopping done the first three years as possible, as after that time, he will have many other things to attend to. [It is a mistake to clear more wild land than a man and his family can work, as it is apt to get overrun with a second growth of brush and the fire-weed, and give a great deal of trouble, besides making a dirty-looking, slovenly farm.]

"In the month of May, the settlers should log up three or four acres for spring crops, such as potatoes, (which are always a great crop in the new soil,) Indian corn and turnips, which last require to be pitted or stored from the effects of the severe winter frost.

"The remainder of the fallow should be burnt off and logged up in July; the rail-cuts split into quarters and drawn aside ready for splitting up into rails. After the log-heaps are burned out, rake the ashes while hot into heaps, if you intend to make potash.*

"As soon as the settler is ready to build, let him if he can command the means, put up a good frame, rough-cast, or a good stone-house. With the addition of £150 in cash, and the raw material, a substantial family-house can be built which will last a vast number of years."

So far my brother. I will now add a few remarks myself. There are many very substantial dwellings now seen on the old clearings, built of stone collected from the surface of the field. These are faced with a proper instrument into form, and in skilful hands are used as a proper building material. They have rather a motley surface, unless the building is rough-cast, but are very warm in winter and cool in summer. I like the deep recesses which the windows form in this sort of building; they remind one of some of the old-fashioned houses at

---

* See chap. xiii. page 170, "Twenty-seven years residence in Canada West."

I could, with great advantage to the emigrant, have made more copious extracts from my brother's useful work, but I must content myself with such as more especially bear upon the subject of the first settlement. It is much to be regretted that the high price of these volumes places the work out of the power of the poorer class of the settlers, who would have found much that was practically useful to them, as well as to the reader to whom it is more particularly addressed. A cheap abridgment would be very useful to all classes of emigrants, and I hope may be published soon.

home, with low window seats. I enjoy to sit in these gossiping corners. A good verandah round takes off from the patchy look of these stone-houses. Then there is the strip-house, and the vertical clapboard, or plank-house, and the block-house, either upright or horizontally laid; all these are preferable in every respect to the common log-house or to the shanty; but persons must be guided by their circumstances in building. But those who can afford a hundred or two pounds to make themselves comfortable, do so at once, but it is not wise to expend all their ready money in building a frame house at first. Among other reasons I would urge one, which is :—in building on wild land, owing to the nature of the forest land, it is very difficult to select a good site for a house or the best; and it is mortifying to find out that you have selected the very least eligible on the land for the residence: it is better to bear with cheerfulness a small evil for a year or two than have a ceaseless cause of regret for many years. It is always necessary to have water both for household purposes and near the cattle-yard. Good chain pumps can now be bought at a cost of a few dollars; and for soft water, tanks lined with water-lime can be constructed to any size. This is a great comfort if properly finished with a pump—the coldest water can be obtained; the expense is proportioned to the size.

In building a house a cellar lined with stone or cedar slabs or vertical squared posts, and well lighted and ventilated, is a great object: it will be found the most valuable room in the house. The comfort of such an addition to the dwelling is incalculable; and I strongly commend the utility of it to every person who would enjoy sweet wholesome milk, butter or any sort of provisions. A good house is nothing, wanting this convenience, and the poorest log-house is the better for it; but the access to the under-ground apartment should not be in the floor of the kitchen or any public passage: many limbs are broken yearly by this careless management. An entrance below the stairs or in some distant corner, with a post and rail to guard it, is just as easy as in the centre of a floor where it forms a fatal trap for the careless and unwary.

An ice-house in so warm a climate as the summer months present, is also a great luxury. The construction is neither expensive nor difficult, and it would soon pay itself. Fresh meat can be hung up for any time uninjured in the ice-house, when it would be spoiled by the ordinary summer-heat in any other situation. A lump of ice put into the drinking water, cools it to a delightful temperature, and every one who has experienced the comfort of iced butter, and the luxury of iced creams, will agree with me it is a pity every housewife has not such a convenience at her command as an ice-house.

I have placed my notice of this article in the chapter that is more particularly addressed to the men, because it depends upon them and not upon their wives, having these comforts constructed. A little attention to the conveniences of the house, and to the wishes of the mistress in its fitting up and arrangements, would save much loss and greatly promote the general happiness. Where there is a willingness on the husband's part to do all that is reasonable to promote the internal comfort; the wife on hers must cheerfully make the best of her lot—remembering that no state in life, however luxurious, is without its trials. Nay, many a rich woman would exchange her aching heart and weary spirit, for one cheerful, active, healthy day spent so usefully and tranquilly as in the Canadian settler's humble log-house, surrounded by a happy, busy family, enjoying what she cannot amid all her dear-bought luxuries, have the satisfaction of a hopeful and contented heart.

REMARKS OF SECURITY OF PERSON AND PROPERTY IN CANADA.

There is one thing which can hardly fail to strike an emigrant from the Old Country, on his arrival in Canada. It is this,—The feeling of complete security which he enjoys, whether in his own dwelling or in his journeys abroad through the land. He sees no fear—he need see none. He is not in a land spoiled and robbed, where every man's hand is against his fellow—where envy and distrust beset him on every side. At first indeed he is surprised at the apparently stupid neglect of the proper means of security that he notices in the dwellings of all classes of people, especially in the lonely country places, where the want of security would really invite rapine and murder. "How is this," he says, "you use neither bolt, nor lock, nor bar. I see no shutter to your windows; nay, you sleep often with your doors open upon the latch, and in summer with open doors and windows. Surely this is fool-hardy and imprudent." "We need no such precautions," will his friend reply smiling ; " here they are uncalled for. Our safety lies neither in bars nor bolts, but in our consciousness that we are among people whose necessities are not such as to urge them to violate the laws ; neither are our riches such as to tempt the poor man to rob us, for they consist not in glittering jewels, nor silver, nor gold."

" But even food and clothes thus carelessly guarded are temptations."

" But where others possess these requisites as well as ourselves, they are not likely to steal them from us."

And what is the inference that the new comer draws from this statement?

That he is in a country where the inhabitants are essentially honest, because they are enabled, by the exertion of their own hands, to obtain in abundance the necessaries of life. Does it not also prove to him that it is the miseries arising from poverty that induce crime.— Men do not often violate the law of honesty, unless driven to do so by necessity. Place the poor Irish peasant in the way of earning his bread in Canada, where he sees his reward before him, in broad lands that he can win by honest toil, and where he can hold up his head and look beyond that grave of a poor man's hope—the parish work house—and see in the far-off vista a home of comfort which his own hands have reared, and can go down to his grave with the thought, that he has left a name and a blessing for his children after him:— men like this do not steal.

Robbery is not a crime of common occurrence in Canada. In large towns such acts will occasionally be committed, for it is there that poverty is to be found, but it is not common in country places. There you may sleep with your door unbarred for years. Your confidence is rarely, if ever, abused ; your hospitality never violated.

When I lived in the backwoods, out of sight of any other habitation, the door has often been opened at midnight, a stranger has entered and lain down before the kitchen fire, and departed in the morning unquestioned. In the early state of the settlement in Douro, now twenty years ago, it was no uncommon occurrence for a party of Indians to enter the house, (they never knock at any man's door,) leave their hunting weapons outside, spread their blankets on the floor, and pass the night with or without leave, arise by the first dawn of day, gather their garments about them, resume their weapons, and silently and noiselessly depart. Sometimes a leash of wild ducks hung to the door-latch, or a haunch of venison left in the kitchen, would be found as a token of gratitude for the warmth and shelter afforded them.

Many strangers, both male and female, have found shelter under our roof, and never were we led to regret that we had not turned the houseless wanderer from our door.

It is delightful this consciousness of perfect security: your hand is against no man, and no man's hand is against you. We dwell in peace among our own people. What a contrast to my home, in England, where by sunset every door was secured with locks and heavy bars and bolts; every window carefully barricaded, and every room and corner in and around the dwelling duly searched, before we ventured to lie down to rest, lest our sleep should be broken in upon by the midnight thief. As night drew on, an atmosphere of doubt and dread seemed to encompass one. The approach of a stranger was beheld with suspicion; and however great his need, we dared not afford him the shelter of our roof, lest our so doing should open the door to robber or murderer. At first I could hardly understand why it happened that I never felt the same sensation of fear in Canada as I had done in England. My mind seemed lightened of a heavy burden; and I, who had been so timid, grew brave and fearless amid the gloomy forests of Canada. Now, I know how to value this great blessing. Let the traveller seek shelter in the poorest shanty, among the lowest Irish settlers, and he need fear no evil, for never have I heard of the rites of hospitality being violated, or the country disgraced by such acts of cold-blooded atrocity as are recorded by the public papers in the Old Country.

Here we have no bush-rangers, no convicts to disturb the peace of the inhabitants of the land, as in Australia. No savage hordes of Caffres to invade and carry off our cattle and stores of grain as at the Cape; but peace and industry are on every side. "The land is at rest and breaks forth into singing." Surely we ought to be a happy and a contented people, full of gratitude to that Almighty God who has given us this fair and fruitful land to dwell in.

NATURAL PRODUCTIONS OF THE WOODS.—HOW MADE AVAILABLE TO THE SETTLER.

When the Backwoodsman first beholds the dense mass of dark forest which his hands must clear from the face of the ground, he sees in it nothing more than a wilderness of vegetation which it is his lot to destroy : he does not know then how much that is essential to the comfort of his household is contained in the wild forest.

Let us now pause for a few minutes while we consider what raw material is there ready to be worked up for the use of the Emigrant and his family.

Here is timber for all purposes ; for building houses, barns, sheds, fencing and firewood.

The ashes contain potash, and the ley added to the refuse of the kitchen is manufactured by the women into soap, both hard and soft: or if spread abroad in the new fallow, it assists in neutralizing the acid of the virgin soil, rendering it more fertile and suitable for raising grain crops. From the young tough saplings of the oak, beech and ironwood, his boys by the help of a common clasp knife, can make brooms to sweep the house, or to be used about the doors.— The hickory, oak and rock-elm supply axe handles and other useful articles. From the pine and cedar he obtains the shingles with which his log-house is roofed. The inner bark of the bass-wood, oak and many other forest trees can be made into baskets and mats. Dyes of all hues are extracted from various barks, roots and flowers. The hemlock and oak furnish bark for tanning the shoes he wears. Many kinds of wild fruits are the spontaneous growth of the woods and wilds.

The forest shelters game for his use ; the lakes and streams wild fowl and fish.

The skins of the wild animals reward the hunter and trapper.

From the birch a thousand useful utensils can be made, and the light canoe that many a white settler has learned to make with as much skill as the native Indian.

Nor must we omit the product of the sugar-maple, which yields to the settler its luxuries in the shape of sugar, molasses and vinegar.

These are a few of the native resources of the forest. True they are not to be obtained without toil, neither is the costly product of the silkworm, the gems of the mine, or even the coarsest woollen garment made without labour and care.

A FEW HINTS ON GARDENING.

Owing to the frosts and chilling winds that prevail during the month of April, and often into the early part of May, very little work is done in the garden excepting it be in the matter of planting out trees and bushes ; grafting and pruning, and preparing the ground by rough digging or bringing in manure. The second week in May is generally the time for putting in all kinds of garden seeds : any time from the first week in May to the last, sowing may be carried on. Kidney beans are seldom quite secure from frost before the 25th. I have seen both beans, melons, and cucumbers cut off in one night, when they were in six or eight leaves. If the season be warm and showery early sowing may succeed, but unless guarded by glass, or oiled-paper frames, the tender vegetables should hardly be put in the open ground before the 18th or 20th May : corn is never safe before that time. The coldness of the ground and the sharpness of the air, in some seasons, check vegetation, so that the late sowers often succeed better than they who put the seeds in early. Having given some directions in various places about planting corn, potatoes, melons, and some other vegetables, I shall now add a few memoranda that may be useful to the emigrant-gardener. If you wish to have strong and early cabbage-plants, sow in any old boxes or even old sugar-troughs, putting some manure at the bottom, and six or eight inches of good black leaf-mould on the top, and set in a sunny aspect. The plants thus sown will not be touched by the fly. If sown later in May, set your trough on some raised place, and water them from time to time. Or you may sow on the open ground, and sprinkle wood-ashes or soot over the ground : this will protect the plants.— The fly also eats off seedling tomatoes, and the same sprinkling will be necessary to preserve them.

In sowing peas, single rows are better in this country than double ones, as unless there be a good current of air among the plants they are apt to be mildewed.

Lettuces sow themselves in the fall, and you may plant them out early in a bed, when they will have the start of those sown in the middle of May.

Those who have a root-house or cellar usually store their cabbages in the following way : they tie several together by the stem near the root, and then hang them across a line or pole head downwards : others pit them head downwards in a pit in the earth, and cover them first with dry straw and then with earth above that. The stem with the root should be stored by till spring, when if planted out, they will afford good, early, tender greens at a season when vegetables are not to be had.

There are many substitutes for greens used in Canada. The most common one is the Wild Spinach, better known by its local name of Lamb's-quarter. It grows spontaneously in all garden grounds, and may be safely used as a vegetable. It is tender, and when thrown into boiling water with a little salt, and cooked for five minutes, and drained, and sent to table like spinach, is much esteemed by the country people.

The Mayweed, a large yellow ranunculus that grows in marshy wet places, is also freely used: but be careful to use no wild plant unless you have full assurance of its being wholesome and that no mistake has been made about it. There is another wild green called Cow-cabbage that is eaten, but this also requires an experienced settler to point it out.

It is always well to save your own seeds if you can. A few large carrots should be laid by to plant out early in Spring for seed. Onions the same, also beets, parsnips, and some of your best cabbages.—Seeds will always fetch money at the stores, if good and fresh, and you can change with neighbours.

If you have more than a sufficiency for yourself do not begrudge a friend a share of your superfluous garden seeds. In a new country like Canada a kind and liberal spirit should be encouraged; in out-of-the-way, country places people are dependent upon each other for many acts of friendship. Freely ye will receive, freely give, and do not forget the advice given in the scriptures, "Use hospitality one to another," and help one another when you see any one in distress; for these are opportunities cast in your way by God himself, and He will require the use or abuse of them at your hands.

Rhubarbs should always find a place in your garden; a cool, shady place and rich soil is best: throw on the bed in the Fall a good supply of long dung, and dig it in in the Spring. A barrel without a bottom put over a good plant, or a frame of an old box, will make the stalks very tender and less acid. The Giant Rhubarb is the best kind to plant.

A bed of Carraways should also find a place in your garden; it is always useful, and the seeds sell well, besides being valuable as a cattle medicine.

A good bed of pot-herbs is essential. I would bring out seeds of Balm, Thyme, and Sweet Basil, for these are rarely met with here.—Sage, Savoury, Mint and Peppermint, are easily got.

Sweet Marjoram is not commonly met with. I would also bring out some nice flower-seeds, and also vegetable seeds of good kinds, especially fine sorts of cabbage. You should learn to save your own seeds. Good seeds will meet with a market at the stores.

The following plain, practical hints on the cultivation of ordinary garden vegetables, taken from Fleming's printed catalogue, will be found useful to many of our readers.—

Most kinds of seeds grow more freely if soaked in soft water from twelve to forty-eight hours before sowing; seeds of hard nature such as blood-beet, mangel and sugar beets, nasturtium, &c., often fail from want of attention to this circumstance. Rolling the ground after sowing is very beneficial, and will assist in making the seeds vegetate more freely; when a roller is not at hand, it may be done with the back of the spade, by flattening the earth and beating it lightly.— Kidney or French beans, may be planted any time in May in drills two inches deep, the beans two inches from each other, the drills about eighteen inches apart. If a regular succession is required, sow a few every few weeks from the first of May, to the first July. For climbers the best sorts are the white Lima, dwarf white haricot, bush bean and speckled red. Broad or Windsor beans, do not succeed well in this climate, the summer heat coming on them before they are podded, which causes the blossoms to drop off.

The best soil to grow them in is a rich, stiff clay, and on a northern border shaded from the mid-day sun: sow in drills two feet apart, two inches deep, and the seed three inches asunder.

Blood Beet, Long and Short Turnips, may be sown in a good, rich, deep soil, about the first week in May. Draw drills about one foot apart, and one inch deep; sow moderately thick: when the plants are up strong, thin them out the distance of six inches from each other in the rows. Brocoli and Cauliflower require a deep rich soil of a clayey nature, and highly manured. To procure Cauliflower or Brocoli the seed ought to be sown in a hot-bed early in March; when the plants are quite strong and healthy, they may be planted out in the garden about the middle of May. Plant in rows two feet square. The kinds that will do well in this climate are the Early London, and French Cauliflower, Purple Cape and Walcheren Brocoli.

Cabbage, both early and late, may be sown any time in May. The best situation for raising the plant is a rich, damp piece of ground, shaded. Seed sown in a situation of this kind is not so likely to be destroyed by the fly. When the plants are strong they may be planted in rows, and managed the same as directed for cauliflower.

The best kinds for summer use are the Early York, Battersea and Vannack: for winter use the Drumhead, Large Bergen and Flat Dutch.

Cucumbers may be sown in the open ground any time in May.—They require a good rich soil. Sow in hills four feet apart, leaving only four plants on each hill. The cucumber and melon vines are liable to be attacked by a yellow fly or bug. Soot, charcoal-dust or soap-suds, applied to the plants, will assist in keeping them off. Musk cantaloupe, nutmeg and water melons may also be sown at the same time, taking care to sow the different kinds a good distance apart from each other, as they are apt to mix. Plant in hills three feet square, leaving only three plants on each hill. When the plants have grown about six inches, stop or pinch the leading shoot, which will make the plants throw out side shoots, on which you may expect to have fruit.

CARROTS.—The most suitable ground for growing Carrots, is a deep rich soil, that has been well manured the previous year. Sow any time in May, in drills one foot apart, and one inch deep.

When the Carrots are up, thin them out, four inches apart, and keep them free of weeds. The kinds that are generally sown in the garden are, the Early Horn, Long Orange, and Red Surrey: for field culture the white Belgian and Altringham. The produce of one acre of field carrots, when properly cultivated, may be rated at from five hundred to eight hundred bushels. In cultivating them on the field system the drills ought to be two feet apart, and the carrots thinned out at least twelve inches asunder.

CELERY.—This vegetable is much esteemed as a salad. To have early Celery the seed should be sown in a hot-bed, in the month of March; for winter celery, the seed may be sown any time before the middle of May. Sow on a small bed of fine rich earth; beat the bed a little with the back of the spade; sift a little fine earth over the seed; shade the bed with a matter board till the seeds begin to appear. Celery plants ought to be picked out into a nursery-bed, as soon as they are two or three inches high. Cut their roots and tops a little, before planting: water them well, and shade them from the sun, until they begin to grow. Let them remain in the nursery-bed for one month, after which they will be fit to transplant into the trenches.—*(Fleming's Printed Catalogue.)*

As a corrective to the sourness of very damp rich new soil, a light sprinkling of wood ashes is very useful. Leeched ashes are very good on some soil. The most splendid cabbages I ever saw were raised on ground where the spent ashes from a leech barrel had been ploughed into the soil. The kinds grown were the Conical cabbage and Portugal ivory-stemmed. The plants were from new seed from the Chiswick gardens, and my cabbages caused quite a sensation among the country gardeners.

HOPS.—This most useful plant no settler's house can dispense with: they are generally grown about the fences of the garden, around the pillars of the verandah, or porch, of the dwelling-house ; or in hills in the garden. When in open ground, the hop must be supported with poles at least ten or fifteen feet high, set firmly in the ground.— The hop must be planted in very rich mould, and early in the Spring, that is before the sprouts begin to shoot above the ground. Two good buds at least are required for every root that you set. The Hop seldom is of much benefit the first year that it is planted, though if the ground be very rich, and the roots strong, the vines will produce even the first year. A little stirring of the mould, and a spadeful or two of fresh manure thrown on the plant in the fall, when the old runners have been cut down, will ensure you a fine crop the second year. Hops will always sell well if carefully harvested. In another part of the book I mention that they should be gathered fresh and green : dull, faded, frost-bitten hops are of little worth. When plucked they should be carefully picked from leaves and stalks, and spread out on a clean floor in a dry chamber ; and when quite dry packed closely into bags and hung up in a dry place. Many persons content themselves with cutting the vines long after they are ripe for gathering, and throwing them into a lumber room, there to be plucked as they are required ; but this is a very slovenly way. Children can pick hops at the proper season, and store them by when dry, without much labour, and just as well as the mother could do it herself.

The following article I have selected from the *Old Countryman*, a popular and useful Canadian paper :—

"GARDENING.

"We feel bound constantly to urge upon the attention of our readers the profit and importance of a good garden. Its influence is good every way. It spreads the table with palatable and nutritious food, and fills the dessert dishes with luxuries, and thus saves the cash which must otherwise be paid for beef, ham, veal, and lamb ; besides promoting the health and spirits more than the meat would. Then a good garden is a civilizer. The garden and orchard beautify the home wonderfully and kindle emotions which never die out of the heart.

But we must say a word or two on individual plants, and first of—

ASPARAGUS. This is a delicious vegetable. What the old bed requires in the Spring is to cut off the last year's stalks just above the ground, and burn them ; loosen the earth about the roots, and clean up the whole bed. As the sweetness and tenderness of this plant depends upon its rapidity of growth, the soil should be made very rich.

BEANS should be planted as soon as you feel secure from frost.— They are ornamental when planted in hills two or more feet apart, with birch sticks stuck about the edge, and tied together at the top.

Then there are peas and beets of two or three kinds, parsnips, carrots, lettuce, radishes, cucumbers, rhubarb, pepper-grass, spinach, salsify, parsley, tomato, turnips, celery, early corn, early potatoes, melons, onions, summer squash, and cabbage, all affording the proper summer nutriment, and requiring a similar soil for their production. Sow and cultivate well a few of each, and you will find your account in it.

SMALL FRUITS.—Set red and white raspberries, thimbleberries, black and white, also currants and gooseberries. They are cheap and wholesome food, and as easily raised as potatoes. Any home will have charms for children where these are plentifully grown.

ORNAMENTAL. Do not allow the lusty teams and the broad acres,—the grass, the grain, and the tree to occupy all your time, but give a thought and an eye occasionally to the beautiful. Spread out a sunny space for the daughters, where the boys will cheerfully assist them with the spade. What a charming spot! Here are the mixed balsams and carnations; the mignionette, mourning bride, and columbine; there, love-lies-bleeding, and, in the corner, love-in-a-mist, the candy-tuft, and Canterbury bell. Why, you resume your youth here. Time almost ceases to make its mark. Old scenes come thronging to the soul, such as when you sat on the rustic seat in the garden, and dissected flowers with her who is now the mother of these beautiful and happy daughters. Such are the influences of the flower garden. We need not go to the books for poetry, it is nature everywhere, but especially in such a group as this,—

" There's beauty all around our paths,
If but our watchful eyes
Can trace it midst familiar things,
And through their lowly guise."

We insist upon it, that there is time with all to be given to the ornamental. It will make you richer, better, happier, more cheerful, and enable you to die easier, and will have the same influences upon your family, by creating something of the beautiful around you.—*New-England Farmer.*"

The new settler will be surprized at the facility with which in the open ground, he can raise the finest sorts of melons, with as little labour bestowed upon the plants as he has been accustomed to give to cabbages, lettuce or any of the commonest pot-herbs. The rich black mould of the virgin soil, and the superior heat of the sun in a climate where the thermometer often ranges from 80° to 95° for many days together during the summer months, brings both vegetables and fruit to perfection very rapidly. In the Western part of the country, or that portion lying between the great lakes Ontario, Erie and Huron, fruit is grown and ripened that is with difficulty perfected east of Toronto, where the heat is not so ardent, and late and early frosts nip the fair promise of the wall fruit. The peach, apricot and grape, with many other kinds are rarely met with in the eastern portion of the Province, unless trained on south walls, and protected during the cold season. Pears, however, will grow well : Apples of the finest quality, and many other fruits in the townships between Toronto and Montreal. I have heard that the apples of the Lower Province are considered by horticulturists to be of the finest quality. There are several sorts of apples in great repute in our orchards, and should be cultivated by those who are planting trees—" Pomme-gris," " Canada-red", " St. Lawrence" and " Hawley's Pippin", with some others of excellent reputation ; but as I have devoted a separate section to Apples and the Orchard, I need say no more on this head in this place.

With a little attention and labour, the vegetable garden may be carried to great perfection by the women and children, with a little assistance from the men at the outset, in digging the ground, and securing the fences, or any work that may require strength to effect. In the new ground the surface is often encumbered with large stones, and these must either remain a blot on the fair features of the garden plot, or be rolled away by the strong arm of the men, aided by the lever. These surface stones may be made very serviceable in filling up the lower part of the fence, or, piled in large heaps, be rendered ornamental by giving them the effect of rockwork. I know many gardeners whose rustic seats, overarched by climbing plants, have been made both useful and ornamental with these blocks of granite and limestone forming the seat. Stone-crop, orpine, and many other plants, set in a little soil among the crevices, have transformed the unsightly masses into an interesting and sightly object. The Wild Cucumber, Orange Gourd, Wild Clematis, and a number of other shrubby climbing-plants, will thrive and cover the rocky pile with luxuriant foliage. Thus by the exertion of a little ingenuity, the garden of the settler may be rendered not only highly useful, but very ornamental. A little taste displayed about the rudest dwelling, will raise the inmates in the eyes of their neighbours. There are very few persons totally insensible to the enjoyment of the beautiful, either in nature or art, and still fewer who are insensible to the approbation of their fellow men ; this feeling is no doubt implanted in them by the Great Creator, to encourage them in the pursuit of purer, more intellectual pleasures than belong to their grosser natures. As men cultivate the mind they rise in the scale of creation, and become more capable of adoring the Almighty through the works of his hands.— I think there can be no doubt but that whatever elevates the higher faculties of the soul, brings man a step nearer to his Maker.

How much pleasanter is the aspect of a house surrounded by a garden, nicely weeded and kept, than the desolate chip-yard, unrelieved by any green tree or flower, that is so often seen in the new settlements in Canada. What cheerful feelings can such a barren spot excite; what home affections can it nourish in the heart of the emigrant wife? Even though she may have to labour to rear it with her own hands, let her plant a garden.

APPLES.

The planting of an orchard, which is a matter of great importance to the future comfort of the settler's family, is often delayed year after year, and that is done last, which should have been attended to at the outset.

Not only are apples valuable as a most palatable and convenient article of diet, but also as one of the most wholesome. In a climate where great heat prevails during the summer months, and even later in the fall, the cooling acid of fruit becomes essentially necessary for the preservation of health.

During the first years of the emigrant's life, this want is painfully felt by those who settle down in the backwoods; and a supply should be provided for as early as possible, by planting trees in the first or second year of the settlement.

I cannot too forcibly impress upon the emigrant the advantage he will derive from thus securing to his household, the comforts, I might almost say the blessing, of an orchard.

I would therefore advise him to fence in securely the first acre, or even half acre, of cleared ground about his house, and plant it with young apple-trees. In all the towns now he will find nurseries, where the choicest and best sorts of apples, pears, cherries, and plums, can be bought.

For good root-grafted apples of good character, which will begin to fruit in three years from the planting, the usual price is 1s. 3d. (a quarter dollar.) Pears, plums, and budded cherries, of good sorts, are dearer, say 2s. 6d. the tree. Ungrafted apple-trees, or seedlings of three years growth cost 7½d. (or a York shilling). These last will bear good kitchen fruit, and by chance, if well cared for, a very fine table-apple may be found among them; but those who can afford to lay out a few dollars in securing apples of the first quality, will be wise to do so. But there may be some who are unable to make even this small outlay, and can hardly venture to purchase the ungrafted trees. Let such sow every apple-pip they can obtain, on a bed, set apart in the garden enclosure for that purpose. The fall is the best time to put the pips into the ground; they will come up in the following Spring: but if you sow them in Spring they rarely come up till the following season, while those sown in the Fall come up in the ensuing Spring.

When these nurslings are well up in six or eight leaves, weed them carefully by hand, or with an old knife. The pips should be sown in drills, a foot apart ; the seeds six or eight inches apart ; but as ground is no object, and the young trees will be twice as strong and straight with room allowed to grow in, I would rather weed them out so that each sapling stood eighteen inches apart each way ; you may plant out those you remove, and they will be none the worse for the re-setting.

By the third year these young trees may be grafted, or else they may be removed to the situation in the garden or orchard they are meant to occupy ; and after this removal good well-formed branches may be encouraged, but spurs and sprouts are better kept from filling up the middle of the tree. Seedlings thus managed, and the roots kept well worked about at the surface with the hoe, will stand a fair chance of becoming a valuable orchard. You will be surprised at the rapid advance of these trees in a few years time. A scattering of wood-ashes on the ground, or a little manure, well worked in with the hoe in the Fall, will do great things for your plantation. Many persons grow young nurseries for the sake of grafting on the young vigorous stocks. In Canada root grafting is very much practiced.

My female readers will say, these directions are all very well, but this is men's work ; we women have nothing to do with nurseries, except in the house ; but let me now say a few words on this head.

In Canada where the heavy labour of felling trees and cultivating the ground falls to the lot of the men, who have for some years enough to do to clear ground to support the family and raise means towards paying instalments on the land, little leisure is left for the garden and orchard : the consequence is that these most necessary appendages to a farm-house are either totally neglected or left to the management of women and children. That there is a miserable want of foresight in this, there can be no doubt, for the garden when well cultivated produces as large an amount of valuable crop as any part of the farm.— In any of the towns in the Fall or in Winter, a head of good cabbage will fetch 3d or 4d., onions a dollar a bushel, carrots from 3s. to 4s. a bushel, and other vegetables in like manner ; and as food for the household consumption, they cannot be too highly valued, even for the sake of preserving the health. Nevertheless if the men will not devote a portion of time to the cultivation of the garden, and orchard, the women must, or else forego all the comfort that they would otherwise enjoy.

After all, when the enclosure is made, and the ground levelled and laid out in walks, and plots, the sowing of the seeds, and keeping the crops weeded and hoed, is not so very heavy a task : with the aid of the children and occasional help of one of the elder boys, a good piece of garden may be cultivated. The tending of a nursery of young trees from the first sowing of the seeds in the ground, is rather a pleasure than a labour; and one which I have taken a delight in from my earliest years.

When I was a child of eight years old, I assisted one of my sisters two years older than myself, under my father's direction, in planting a nursery of walnuts. Those trees now form a fine avenue, and have borne fruit for many years.

Little children can be made to sow the stones of plums, cherries, and apple-pips, in the nursery; these in time will increase and bear fruit in due season: they will all bear fruit without grafting or budding, and they are growing while you are sleeping. In a few years they will be a source of comfort and luxury to your family, and you will not then lament the care that you bestowed upon them.

In the early years of our infant settlement on the banks of the Otonabee river, above the town of Peterboro', all the ladies worked in their gardens, raised their own vegetables, and flowers, and reared the fruit trees which in after years almost overshadowed their dwellings. They felt this work as no disgrace to them, but took pride and pleasure in the success of their labours.

My own garden was full of stumps, and stones, roots and wild bushes, and it cost some trouble to reduce it to smooth working order. I got some help to overcome the first difficulties. The stones, some of them of large dimensions, were removed with a handspike, and built up into a heap. Around the stumps, turf and rubbish of all kinds were heaped, and finally covered with a depth of fine black mould, on which gourds, cucumbers, or melons, were planted, the grass roots and weeds nourishing them as well as a regular hot-bed would have done: by this simple contrivance we got rid of much rubbish, which by degrees was converted into the best of manure, and hid many an unsightly object; the vines of the cucumbers &c. running down the steep sloping sides of the mound, and also covering the stumps with their leaves and fruit.

As I disliked the rough unsightly look of the rail fences, I got an old English settler to enclose my garden (which swept in a bold curved line from each corner of the house) with a wattled fence: this looked very picturesque, but did not last more than three years good. I then collected wild gooseberry bushes, currants, bush honey suckles, hawthorns, wild cherry and plum trees, with all sorts of young bushes, and planted them within side my fence, to make a living fence, when the other should have decayed; and had I remained long enough to complete my plans, I should have had a nice hedge. If we could have procured the proper sort of wands, fit for the purpose, I have no doubt my fence would have proved as lasting as it was pretty to look at. It was the admiration of all my neighbours, and many came to look at "Mrs. Traill's fence."

Next to a picket fence made of split cedars, with cedar posts, a log fence is the best in situations where sawn lumber is not easily procured, but the logs should be secured from rolling by stakes and riders. These fences are only suitable to bush settlements, but as my book is intended for emigrants of all sorts, and conditions, and especially for the working hands, I have dwelt more minutely on such things as may suit their particular circumstances, though I trust it may also contain matter of valuable instruction to all classes.

I must now return to the subject from which I first started, Apple-Orchards and Apples.

I again repeat my advice to buy grafted trees if you can afford to do so. There are agents who travel the country, and penetrate even to the verge of the forest, to collect orders for trees, from different nursery-gardens in the United States, and also from the large towns in Canada. I recommend you to deal with the latter, for this reason; your trees are likely to reach your hands sooner after being taken out of the ground : give your strict orders to have the trees well rooted, and the roots matted ; and deal with men of good character, who are well known, and have an established reputation. I will give you a list of the most approved and valuable Apples, at the end of this article.

In planting your trees do not be afraid to make the hole wide enough ; it is better to dig the soil well, and let every part be thoroughly worked till it be fine and mellow : this is better than putting manure to the roots, which gardeners do not recommend. With a sharp knife cut the bruised roots, and if the top be large, and the roots small, reduce the branches : if the roots be large and spreading, little pruning is requisite : the young trees that have thriven best have been uncut when planted.

The careful planter will make holes deep, that a good bed of friable, sandy loam may be spread at the bottom to set the trees on. It makes a great difference on what soil the roots are bedded.

Let the tree be held up by one person, while another carefully arranges the roots, so that they lie in a natural way in contact with the soil ; then lightly strew in the earth, with the hands, and fill up the hole with good soil, pressing the earth down : when planted, a quantity of half-decayed litter should be placed round the tree, as far as the roots extend : this is called by the gardeners mulching, and serves to keep the ground moist and mellow. If you think it needful to support the tree from the action of the wind, tie it to a stake, but place a bit of old cloth between the stake and the young tree, to keep the bark from being rubbed. "In most cases," says a skilful American horticulturist, "it is better to thin out, than to shorten the branches of the newly taken-up trees ; leaves are necessary to the formation of roots, and if you deprive the young tree of all its boughs, you stop its resources for root-growth."

APPLES 71

There are two seasons for orchard planting; in the Fall, and the Spring. Now I am myself rather in favour of the Fall planting, if it be not put off too late. * Many persons plant late, and lose their trees. October is the usual time, and I think it should be done as early in the month as possible. My own idea is that just at the season when the leaf begins to turn yellow, is the safest time for transplanting. If it be put off till the frosts harden the ground, injury to the tender nurslings must follow. In Spring the ground is often too wet, and cold, and the trees get too forward to be removed safely.— April is the Spring month for transplanting, and October in the Fall.

I will now, as well as I can, give you some simple directions about grafting, which is an art often practised by the female hand, as well as that of the professed gardener.

Cut the stock or branch which you design to graft upon, smooth and even, with a sharp knife, or if too large for the knife, with a small fine-toothed pruning saw; with your knife make a cleft of about an inch deep through the crown of the stock, dividing it clean through the bark on either side, into which cleft insert the handle of a budding-knife, which is smooth, and wedge-shaped; or if you are without this useful instrument, have ready a narrow wedge of wood, which will answer all the purposes; this is to keep the cleft open, while you insert the scions or grafts. Select your grafts from any good sorts, from healthy trees, the new, or youngest, growth of wood being chosen. Most grafters cut the scions some days or even weeks before. With a sharp knife pare away the wood on each side, taking care to leave a ridge of bark on your scion, as on this simple circumstance depends the life of the graft. The graft should be about a finger's length, with three distinct buds, one from the base of which you begin to shape the lower part or wedge, which is to be introduced into the cleft. Two grafts, one on each side of the stock, are generally inserted, unless it be in seedling apples, when one will be sufficient. I have seen as many as four scions on the large limbs, but one or two good grafts are better than more.

With your grafting wax at hand, (for clay does not answer in this country as in England,) insert your scions at the edge of the cleft, so that the strip of bark left on it, fills up the opening like a slender gore let into the stock, taking care to bring the edges of the bark of the cleft and the bark of the graft close together, and even, so that neither one shall project beyond the other. Proceed in like manner to your other graft, and then remove the wedge from the centre of the stock; the crack will close, and hold your scions tight: then apply the wax to the sides, covering every part of the seam and a little below, where you see the cracking of the bark; also round the part

---

* Fall planting is now getting more into favour than it was, and earlier planting, say the last week in September.

where the lowest bud rests on the stock : do this effectually, and spread the wax over the crack on the crown of the stock, bringing a little of it all round the edge of the bark, to keep it from drying up. Some wind a strip of cloth, or thread, round, to secure the graft from being moved by any accident : others leave it to chance. You can do so if you like, only there is an old proverb in favor of the binding:

" Safe bind, safe find."

I have only described one method of grafting, but there are many equally simple and safe, which any one conversant with the practice of grafting, will describe, or what is still better, cut a branch, and a scion, and show you the process. I learned to graft from a Canadian lady in her own parlour. I will now give you the receipt for preparing the grafting wax.

GRAFTING WAX

is made in the following proportions : one part of common beef-tallow; two parts bees' wax ; and four parts resin. Melt the whole together, pour into a pail of cold water; rub a little of the grease on your hands, to prevent the wax from sticking, and then as it cools work it well with your hands, first in the water and then on a bit of board, till it is thorougly kneaded, and will be soft and plastic, without adhering to the fingers or running thin. This wax is spread over the sawn limb and round the graft, and down the wounded bark, so as to exclude the air and moisture ; if too soft add a little more wax, or if too hard a little more tallow.

Some use cobbler's wax, some apply pitch, and the common turpentine from the pines ; but the wax is neatest, cleanest, and best.— Clay is of little use, as it either dries with the sun, or cracks with the frost. Some use bass bark to bind round the grafts.

The tools used by those persons who make grafting a business, or have large orchards, are a grafting saw, a pruning knife, a wedge-handled knife, a small hammer with an axe at one end, for making clefts in the large boughs, and a bag for the tools, with a strap to pass about the shoulder, and a box for the wax, with string, or a coil of wet bass or cedar bark for binding ; but many trees are grafted with only a knife, a saw, and the wax.

Those who know how to graft should early sow the seeds of apples, pears, plums and cherries in a nursery bed, that they may have good vigorous stocks to graft upon.

Not long since I met with an old-fashioned book on orchard-planting, where the following direction was given :

" Sow apple-seeds in a ring, at distances of twenty-five feet from ring to ring, on a space intended for an orchard. When your young trees are up, thin out, to two feet apart, keeping them stirred with the hoe, and free from weeds. At the end of three years graft your young stocks. The following year remove all but one healthy tree from each ring, choosing the very best to become your standard.— The rest of your young grafted trees may be set out in suitable places or sold, but you will find the advantage of never having transplanted your seedling, by the superior growth, and vigour, of your graft over the young stocks that have been checked by transplantation from the native soil."

As a manure for orchard-trees, wood soot, wood ashes, and a small quantity of lime is strongly recommended, especially in wet soil. A dead level, unless drained, is not so favourable for apple trees, as the side of a hill facing south or west. Soap-suds are recommended to wash or scrub the bark of apple and pear trees, to prevent scaly bark, and remove moss. In the Fall, a careful person should examine all the trees, and remove the nests of the caterpillars, which will be found adhering to the young twigs, like a gummy swelling of the bark. These are easily taken off like a brittle, varnished crust. Early in Spring search the trees again ; if any escape they will show themselves in the leafing time, and unless the webs which they spin for a shelter, are removed in time, these caterpillars will injure the crop and tree, by devouring the foliage and blossoms.

Having given you some directions for the management of your orchard-trees, I will now furnish you with a list of the most highly approved sorts to select for planting, as the names differ much from those you have been accustomed to see in the English orchards.— America is famous for the excellence of her apples, and those that are the natives of the climate, are always most hardy, prolific, and best adapted for orchard planting in Canadian soil.

SUMMER APPLES.

Early Harvest, Yellow Harvest, Early Joe, Summer Queen, Sweet Bough, Summer Bellflower, (good cooking apple,) Summer Pearmain, Canada Red, Snow Apple ; this last is not ripe till September, but can be used for pies or puddings much earlier ; it is a great bearer, and the thinning out is no real sacrifice, as it improves the size of those left to ripen. It is known in the Lower Province as La Fameuse ; it is a great bearer, and a fine, sweet, juicy apple.

AUTUMN APPLES.

Autumn Strawberry*, Fall Pippin*, Holland* (kitchen apple), Red Astracan*, Hawley's Pippin*, Twenty-ounce Apple*, Burassa* (late Fall), Baldwin, St. Lawrence, Nonpareil Russet, Golden Russet*, York Quiney, Hawthornden*, Gravestien*.

WINTER APPLES.

Winter Strawberry*, Northern Spy*, Rambo, Baldwin*, Roxbury Russet*, Swaar*, Winter Pippin*, Rhode Island Greening*, Ribstone

Pippin*, Newtown Pippin*, Pomme Grise, Spitzenburg*, White Winter Pearmain, Yellow Bellflower, Ladies' Sweeting. These are all choice sorts.

There are many other capital apples, but these are the most celebrated, and therefore I have selected them. Those marked with a star are of the best quality, but all are good. The mulching the trees as before noticed, is of great utility, but not too deeply. Or if much litter be laid round in the Fall, remove it in the Spring, and stir the ground with the hoe : covering the roots too thickly keeps the sun from warming the earth about them.

Having done with the planting, I will now give some good recipes for the cooking, and end with some remarks on the storing of Apples.

APPLE-PIE

Every one knows how to make a common apple pie or pudding.—But in case there may be a few among my emigrant friends, who have been unused even to this simple process in cooking, I will say : peel and core your apples ; good acid cooking-apples are better than sweet ones ; drop them into a pan of c ean water as you pare them; in the pie-dish place a tea-cup, turned bottom upwards ; put in a large table-spoonful of sugar, and two or three cloves, or a bit of lemon peel, if you have these things at hand ; fill your dish with the cored apples ; a very small quantity of water—a large table-spoonful will suffice ; add two or three more cloves, and more sugar ; cover with your paste, rolled thin ; finely crimp the edge, and scallop with your finger and the edge of the knife. A few delicate leaves, cut and marked to resemble apple leaves, placed in the centre, give a pretty look to the dish; but this is a mere matter of taste. If you have any cause to think that the fruit is not quite soft, when the crust is baked, set the dish on the top of one of your stove griddles, and let it simmer a while. Some persons stew the apples first, season and put them into the dish, and when cool, cover and bake ; but I think the apples never taste so well as when baked in the old way.

The reason for inserting a cup in the pie is this : the juice and sugar draws under the cup, and is thus kept from boiling out : paring the apples into the dish of water preserves them from turning brown or black, and the moisture they imbibe renders no other water necessary, or very little. The Canadians season their pies with nutmeg and allspice, making them sickly tasted ; they stew the apples till they are an insipid pulp, and sweeten them till the fine acid is destroyed. A good, juicy, fine-flavoured apple-pie is a rare dish to meet with in hotels and among the old Canadian and Yankee settlers.

DRIED APPLES.

The drying of apples is a great business in the houses of the Canadian farmers, where they have orchards, or live near those who have large orchards, who will sell the inferior fruit very cheap, as low as

7½d. a bushel, if you gather them yourself. Those who revel in an abundance of this useful fruit, often call their young friends together to an Apple-paring "Bee". Bushels and bushels of apples are pared, cored and strung on Dutch thread, by the young men and maidens, and the walls of the kitchen festooned round with the apples, where they hang till dry and shrivelled. They should be dipped into boiling water as they are hung up; this preserves the colour. Some expose them to the action of the sun and wind, on the walls of the house, or spread them on clean boards or trays; when thoroughly dry, they are stored in bags, and hung in a dry place, out of the dust. These dried apples find ready sale at 1s. 6d. per lb., and even higher, if the season be far advanced, and apples scarce. When required for use, they are steeped for some time in hot water. Stewed till tender, with a seasoning of cloves, these apples form a delightful preserve, and rarely need any sugar; but if too sour, a small quantity is easily added.— Some add molasses. Tarts, pies and many pleasant dishes are made with these dried apples: a delicious fever drink is made by pouring off the liquor after the apples have boiled a few minutes. By this simple process of drying, you may have apples to make use of all the year round, long after the fruit has decayed, and lost its flavour, in the apple chamber. In England this process of drying apples might be adopted to advantage.

PRESERVED APPLES.

Take equal quantities of good brown sugar and of good boiling apples; i. e. a pound to a pound; cut the apples up fine, put on your skillet, and to every three pounds of sugar allow a pint of water; scum the syrup as it boils up, add the apples, with a little essence of lemon, or lemon peel; a few cloves, or a bit of ginger: boil till the apples are tender and look clear.

The small American crabs will be excellent done the same way.— For common everyday use, half the quantity of sugar will do.

APPLE JELLIES.

Allow a pound of crushed sugar (this is an inferior sort of loaf sugar, which sells at 7½d. a pound) to a pound of chopped apples, boil the sugar to a syrup, with a few cloves and a stick of cinnamon; throw in the apples, and boil till the fruit is dissolved. If you wish to have it coloured, add in, while boiling, a slice or two of blood beet; this will give a beautiful rich tint to the jelly; or a little saffron steeped in a cup of boiling water, which will tinge it a deep yellow; strain the jelly through a coarse sieve of net or fine canvas. When potted, cut paper dipped in spirits, and lay on the top, the size of the inner rim of the jar: have a larger round cut, so as to cover the outer rim: beat up the white of an egg, and with a feather brush this paper over; press the edges close to the jar: to do this well, snip the edge with the scissors, which will make it form to the shape of the jar.

Preserves thus secured from the air, do not mould as in the ordinary mode of tying them up, and the trouble is not more than tying with string.

APPLES IN SYRUP.

Make a thin syrup with sugar and water, season with spice or lemon peel; pare some small-sized apples, whole, and let them boil till tender, but do not let them break if you can help it. Set the apples and syrup by in a deep dish till cold. This makes a cheap dish to eat with bread at tea. It is easily prepared, and is very agreeable, besides being very wholesome.

APPLE BUTTER, OR APPLE SAUCE.

This is often made in the houses of settlers where there is an abundance of apples, on a large scale; several bushels of pared apples being boiled down, either in cider or with water, for several hours, till the whole mass is thoroughly incorporated. Great care is needful to keep it stirred, so as to prevent burning. There are several ways of making this apple-butter: some make it with cider, others without, some use sugar, others do not; and some boil sliced pumpkin with the apples, if the latter are very acid. It is a standing dish in most American houses, and is very convenient.

ANOTHER METHOD.

Take three pails of cider, and boil down into one; have ready a quantity of sweet apples pared, and quartered, with the peel of one or two lemons; throw the apples into the cider, and as they boil down, add more, till your cider will boil down no more; keep the apples stirred well from the bottom of your skillet, to prevent burning: it will take some time to boil down quite smooth, say three or four hours: when done put it into a clean wooden or stone vessel, and keep covered in a dry place.

You may take out some of this pulp and spread on dishes or tins, and dry in the sun or before the fire, and pack away: it makes a nice dry sweetmeat, or, steeped and boiled up, a delicious wet preserve.—The Canadians who have large orchards, make as much as a barrel of this apple sauce for daily use.

CIDER.

Some persons have cider presses, which forms a part of their business in the Fall. The usual charge for making cider is 1s. per barrel for the use of the press, you finding the labour, &c., and, of course, the barrels and fruit.

Cider sells at from $2½ to $3, if good. Where a farmer has an extensive orchard, the house should be well supplied with this cooling beverage. In harvest time it supplies a valuable drink: in a country where beer is not brewed in private families, and where the exhaustion, and waste on the system, by excessive heat and labour, must require a supply of moisture, cider is very useful. The grateful acid must be preferable to the spirits, which are often mixed with the water, or drunk in fiery drams in the harvest field.

RED APPLE JELLY.

Take the small scarlet American crab apples, and boil down with a small quantity of water. The best plan is to put the apples with a little water, into a jar with a lid to it, and set it into a pot of boiling water; let it remain in this water-bath till the apples are quite soft; pulp them through a sieve; and add one pound of fine sugar to each pint of the apple-pulp, with a stick of cinnamon and a few cloves; boil for half an hour, or till the jelly will stiffen when cooled on a plate; put in jars or glasses, and when cold, pour a teaspoonful of spirits on the top. Wet a paper with white of egg, and fasten down so as to cover the edges of the jar quite tight. When well done, this jelly has the most beautiful transparency and lovely scarlet color.

The nice dishes that can be made with apples would fill in description a small volume; such as puddings, pies, tarts, puffs, turnovers, dumplings, &c., &c. I will only add one more, which is very simple, agreeable and cheap.

APPLE RICE.

Wet a pudding-cloth; place it in a basin or colander, having previously well washed and picked a pound of rice, if your family be large: half the quantity will be sufficient if small: place some of the wetted rice so as to line the cloth in the mould all round, saving a handful to strew on the top; fill the hollow up with cored apples, and a bit of lemon peel shred fine, or six cloves; throw on the remainder of the rice; tie the bag, not too tight, as the rice swells much; and boil a full hour, or longer if the pudding be large. Eaten with sugar this is an excellent, and very wholesome, dish: acid apples are best, and are so softened by the rice as to need very little sugar to sweeten them.

APPLE-PARING MACHINE.

This useful invention saves much time and labour: it is an American invention, and can be bought in the hardware stores for 7s. 6d.

Note.—I strongly recommend to the attention of any one who takes an interest in orchard culture, a small volume called The American Fruit Book: it contains the best practical advice for the management of all the common fruits of Canada and the States. It is to be found in most of the district libraries. A small book and a cheap one, but a treasure to the inexperienced fruit grower.

Apple trees are subject to a disease of the bark, which is produced by the small scaly insect called bark-louse (or cocus) : it resembles a brown shell, or a seed of flax, though hardly so large ; young seed-apple trees are rendered sickly and stinted by this affection : to remedy the disease and destroy its cause, use—one part soft soap, four of water, and a little fresh slacked lime : apply in the month of June, or indeed at any season ; it may be used without injury to the tree. For removing the webs of caterpillars situated on high branches, tie some woollen rags to a tall staff ; wet this mop in water or suds, and apply it to the branch, and by giving a twirl to the stick, you will remove the nest and its contents.

Apples for making cider should be well ripened and picked, free from decay, wood and leaves ; if left in a heap to sweat for a week, they are the better, as they mellow and ripen ; but they must not lie long enough to decay.

I copy a few directions for preserving and gathering apples, from the "American Fruit Book," which may be useful :

"The fruit" (says the author) "is of a finer quality for remaining on the tree till well ripened, though it will often keep better by gathering before quite or over ripe. Some in the warm parts of the country gather in the last week in September, others in October.—

"Gather your apples in dry weather, and pick winter or keeping fruit and dessert fruit by hand carefully. Some persons are so careful as to line the fruit baskets with cloth, or cotton, to prevent bruising. Do not let your fruit lie out in heaps, exposed to the weather, nor yet stand in barrels in the sun.

"In packing in barrels, settle the fruit gently, and head up full, pressing the head in carefully, so as not to injure the fruit.

"After barrelling, apples are generally left in an open shed on their sides, till the frost is beginning to set in, when they may be removed to a cool dry cellar. Apples will bear any degree of cold above freezing point ; and headed up in barrels, even ten or twelve degrees below freezing point."

Some pack apples in bran, sawdust, dry sand, moss, fern, and many other substances. I have generally preferred laying very light layers of dry straw, and layers of apples, alternately.

I have not tried it, but I think fresh wood-ashes would preserve apples from frost. Heat and moisture, united, are destructive to apples, inducing bitter rot. I lost several barrels of lovely apples, by allowing them to remain in a warm kitchen for a month after gathering.

PEARS.

Pears are beginning to be largely cultivated all through the country, and though some sorts are more tender than the apple, others will thrive well, and in good situations produce abundance of delicious fruit. A good, deep, yellow loam, on an inclined plane, sheltered from the north, may be considered the best situation for planting pear-trees.

Like the apple, the ungrafted seedlings well cared-for will bear fruit. The seedling pear and the quince are the best adapted to grafting upon, though the native thorn is sometimes used for grafting the pear upon. It would be advisable to buy good grafted trees to begin with, of the most approved kinds. After they have been proved, you can increase your stock by grafting, yourself.

I will now select a few of the most approved pears for you to choose from. 2s. 6d. is the price usually charged for grafted pears, cherries and plums, of the best varieties: this is double the price of the best apples.

For Summer Pears:—Madeline, Bartlett, Summer Frankreal, Belle of Brussels. Fall:—Belle Lucrative, Flemish Beauty, Seckel, Louise. Vin de Jersey, Vngalien, Maria Louisa, White Dozeune, Vicar of Winkfield, Beurre Diel.

Winter Pears:—Easter Beurre, Winter Nelis Charmontel.

Many of these are very beautiful both to eye, and taste, and if you are at any loss which to select, consult the salesman, or some honest nursery-gardener, to choose for you. The names should be cut on a lead, or a tin ticket, fastened to a limb of the tree by a copper wire, as it is provoking not to know the name of a favourite fruit.

If insects, as the slug, attack the leaves of the pear, dust with ashes or sulphur, which will kill them.

CHERRIES.

The cherry thrives well in Canada, in spite of the frosty winters.— There are many excellent sorts, sold at the nursery gardens, as Tartarian Black, Black-heart, Bigaroux, Maydake, and many others.— There is a red cherry that grows and bears very freely from seed: it ripens in July, is middle sized, of a full dark red, not black, but rather crimson; sends up a vast number of shoots, which will bear in a few years abundance of fruit, if set out, trimmed up, and kept in order.— Suckers should be removed from the roots, as soon as they appear, as they weaken the larger trees, and absorb the nourishment that is required to perfect the fruit.

PLUMS.

The native or wild plum, if introduced into the garden, and kept in order, produces a very useful fruit for preserving, but is not so good for general purposes as the Gages, and Damascenes, Orleans, or several other of the cultivated sorts ; it will, however, grow where the better sorts will not—in wet marshy ground, in hollows, and near water courses.

Owing to some causes which I am not able to explain, the plum is short-lived, and often perishes from diseases that attack the sap-vessels, or from insects that cause blight to the blossom, rendering the fruit useless, or utterly preventing its forming. Still, with care, much of this may be prevented, and in some situations plums are healthy, and yield abundantly. The Green-gage, Blue-gage, Yellow-gage, Golden-drop, Egg Plum, Imperial Gage, Washington, and the common Blue Damson Plum are among the best sorts. The soil may be light rich loam, not too dry.

WILD FRUITS.

In the long cultivated districts of Canada, especially in townships lying west of Toronto, where the seasons are warmer, and the winters compartively mild, great pains are now taken in planting orchards of the choicest fruits. Apples, pears, plums, cherries, peaches, and even grapes ripen and come to perfection, as well as the small summer fruits. Extensive orchards of all these fruits, are attached to most of the old farms, west of Toronto ; but in the more northerly portions of Canada this is not yet the case. Orchards are, it is true, now generally planted, and gardens are more cared for than they were some years ago, but those who settle down in newly-surveyed townships, and far from the vicinity of large towns, which the hardy and adventurous emigrants, eager to secure a larger quantity of land, still do, must secure this advantage by early planting. The absence of fruit from their diet would be most severely felt, were it not that Nature has bounteously scattered abroad some of these blessings in the shape of wild fruits, which are met with in many situations, and often brought as it were almost miraculously, to the settler's very door, springing up without his care or culture.

The year or two after a fallow has been chopped, and logged, and cropped, in all the corners of his rail fence, and by the rude road that he has hewed out to his dwelling, spring up the red raspberry, black raspberry, the blackberry, and often the strawberry. The wild gooseberry, both smooth and prickly, is seen on upturned roots, at the edge of the clearing. Wild currants, both black and red, are found in moist swampy spots : here also are often to be found wild plums and choke-cherries, (the last not very fit to eat ;) and a tangled growth of wild grapes, near creeks and lakes; fox and frost grapes entwine the trees, near the shores of lakes and rivers; while the high-bush cranberry shows its transparent clusters of scarlet berries, from among the fading foliage, or on the utterly leafless bough. On open lands, as on those parts called Plains, the abundance of wild fruits is yet greater than on the forest clearings. Here the ground is purple with the sweet and wholesome fruit of the huckleberry, the luscious bilberry; and strawberries of the most delicious flavour carpet the ground.— The May-apple in moist rich soil springs up, both in the bush and on any shady lands. On summer fallows on these plains, and in the first and second years' ploughed lands, the strawberries attain a size that is remarkable for wild fruits of this kind, and quantities are gathered for home consumption, and also carried into the towns for sale.— There are besides the eatable fruits that I have named, many other small berries, that are wholesome, and eaten freely by the Indians, but which require a knowledge of their nature and growth, to be ventured upon by any but the natives, and botanists whose knowledge of the structure of plants enables them fearlessly to venture upon using the wild fruits, and roots and leaves of plants, that would be dangerous to be used as food by the unlearned. This is indeed the main use of botany as a study, though many persons foolishly despise it, because they are really not aware of the value of the science, and the benefit that mankind has derived from it. It is easy to see how useful these wild fruits are to the settler, in the absence of the cultivated sorts; and though the earliest efforts should be made for planting a garden and orchard, yet supposing circumstances should have prevented the obtaining of good trees, and bushes, something may be done towards improving the wild fruits by cultivation. The wild gooseberry, planted in good soil, and in a *shady, cool* part of the enclosure, will thrive well, and in time the thorns that beset the outer coat of the berry, will disappear. There are smooth red gooseberries, as well as those so appropriately called *Thornberries*, that can be found. On old neglected clearings; by forest roads and wastes; in open spots, and the edges of beaver-meadows, you may procure many varieties. If you have a straight fence, plant the wild bushes near it, as it serves to shelter them, not from the cold, for that they prefer, but from too much heat. The cultivated gooseberry is liable to mildew, which often destroys the promise of a fine crop.

The wild raspberry I do not advise you to cultivate: it grows too weedy, and there is no rooting it out; besides you will find it in all your fields, fences, and even in the very forest. But the grape is much improved by cultivation, and if you have an unsightly upturned root, or tall jagged stump, near the house, plant the vine beside it, or plant a small dead tree firmly in the ground, with all its branches on, (a sapling, of course, it must be,) for the vine to climb up. Thus you will have a beautiful object, and fruit, which after the frost has softened it, will make a fine rich jelly, or wine, if you like it.

The wild red plum is greatly improved by garden culture: it is, when ripe, a valuable fruit: skinned, it makes good pies, and puddings, and, boiled down in sugar, a capital preserve. The bush settlers' wives boil down these plums in maple molasses, or with a proportion of maple sugar. This is one of the comforts of having a good store of maple sugar: you can have plenty of preserves from wild raspberries, strawberries, plums, and wild gooseberries. The wild plum loses much of its astringency by cultivation; it is so hardy that it can be moved even when in flower; though early in Spring, or Fall, is better. This plum is not subject to the disease called black canker, or black knot, which destroys the cultivated sorts soon after they arrive at maturity; indeed it destroys even young trees, where the disease is unchecked. The wild plum forms the best and most healthy stock for grafting or budding the finer sorts upon, and is less liable to disease. Of late, nursery-men have greatly recommended this stock as producing healthier trees. While upon the subject of plums, let me strongly recommend to emigrants coming out, to bring with them small canvas-bags containing the stones of all sorts of plums—damsons, bullace cherries, and nuts of various sorts: even the peach will produce fruit from seed in the western parts of Canada: seeds of apples, pears, quinces, medlars, and indeed of all fruits that you can collect. If these grow you may obtain something for your surplus trees; and, if well treated, they will amply repay your trouble, and you will enjoy the great satisfaction of watching them come to perfection, and regarding them with that affectionate interest which those only experience who have raised seedlings from fruit grown in their beloved native land, and, perhaps, from the tree that they played under, and ate the produce of, when they were little children. In enumerating the blessings that awaited the returning Jews from their captivity, the prophet says—" And every man shall eat of the fruit of his own vine, and sit under the shadow of his own fig-tree." He could hardly promise them a greater blessing.

I also recommend you to bring out the seeds of raspberries, gooseberries, currants, and strawberries. Pulp the ripe fruit into cold water; wash away the fruity part, and drain dry; expose the seed in a sieve turned bottom upwards, or on a dry clean board, in the sun and wind, till well assured that all moisture is removed; mix with a little dry white sand; put the seeds into vials or dry paper bags, writing the name on each sort; and let a good bed be prepared in your new garden, by stirring well with the hoe if in quite new soil; or trench-in good rich earth in old; keep your nurslings, when up, well weeded, and thinned, so as to leave each plant room to grow.

The high bush cranberry, or single American Guelder-rose, is a very ornamental shrub in your garden; it likes a rich moist soil and a shady situation. The flowers are handsome in Spring, and every period of ripening in the fruit, is beautiful to see, from the pale orange tint, to the glowing scarlet when fully ripe, and, after the frost has touched them, to a light crimson. The berry when fully ripe is almost transparent. The flat, hard seeds in this juicy fruit make it unsuitable for jam but as a jelly nothing can be finer, particularly as a sauce for venison or mutton. The native soil of the high bush-cranberry is at the edge of swamps, or near rivers and lakes, where the soil is black and spongy; but they also thrive in shady flats in dry ground in our gardens.

The large spurred hawthorn, also, may be found near creeks, and on the banks of rivers, on gravelly soil. This is if anything, more beautiful than the common English white thorn, the "May" of the poets. The Canadian hawthorn will grow to a considerable height, bears abundance of fragrant flowers, and is followed by fruit as large as a cherry, and when ripe very agreeable to the taste. The thorns are so large and so strong that it would make a formidable hedge, if any one would plant it ; but few will take the time and trouble.— Some of our English labourers from the wooded counties in the East of England, where the culture of the thorn hedges is much attended to, might try the plan for a garden hedge. The long winter in Canada, the great value of labour, and the continued pressure of work in the open seasons of the year, are bars to many experiments of this kind being carried into effect. But hedge or no hedge, I recommend the hawthorn as an ornament for your garden.

On old grassy clearings, which have once been burned and cropped, strawberries spring up in abundance, of several kinds ; among which may be found a very pretty, delicate, trailing plant, with light crimson berries, in grains of a fine acid : these are known by the name of creeping raspberry :—they are thornless, and trail in delicate wreaths upon the ground.

The black raspberry makes fine pies : it is richer and sweeter than the red ; the branches are long and weak ; the bark red, with a whitish bloom on them. They are something between the raspberry and blackberry of the English hedges. The Canada blackberry or thimble-berry, is not so deadly sweet as the fruit of the common bramble, but is a very pleasant berry, and lately has been cultivated in gardens, and made to produce a fruit superior in quality to the mulberry.

The huckleberry is, among all the wild fruits, one of the most wholesome, eaten as they come from the bush, or stewed with, or without sugar, they are a nice dish ; but with a few red currants added, they are much better, the tartness of the currant improving the sweetness of the huckleberry. A pudding, or pie, or preserve, made with equal parts of red currants, huckleberries, and the fruit of the bush bilberry, is delightful, the bilberry giving an almond-like flavor, and increasing the richness of the other fruits.

The bilberry grows on high bushes, the large fruited from six feet to ten feet high, the fruit being the size and colour of small smooth red gooseberries : the dwarf kind seldom exceeds three or four feet in height, and the tall bilberry, or Juneberry, is a beautiful-growing shrub, with reddish bark, elegant white blossoms, and rose-coloured fruit, smaller in size than the other two, though the bush attains the height of fifteen and twenty feet. These bushes grow chiefly on dry gravelly, or sandy soil ; seldom in the rich black soil of the dense forest.

I am particular in noticing these peculiarities of soil, and habits, in describing the wild fruits, that you may not look for them in situations foreign to their natures, and feel disappointed if you do not find on your own immediate locality every one of the native fruits that I have described and recommended to your notice. Every spot has its peculiar vegetables, flowers, and fruits, and we must recollect in counting our blessings, what an old poet says :—

" Who least has some, who most, has never all."

It is our wisest part to receive with gratitude that which our Heavenly Father has prepared for us, and not weary him by discontented repinings, remembering in humbleness of heart, that we are unworthy even of the least of his mercies.

Of wild cherries there are many different species, but they are more medicinal than palatable : steeped in whiskey, with syrup added, the black cherry is used as a flavour for cordials ; and the inner bark made into an extract, is given for agues, and intermittents, and also in chest diseases. All these wild cherry trees are beautiful objects, either in flower or fruit, especially the red choke-cherry, with its bright transparent fruit ; but the excessive astringency of the juice causes a spasmodic contraction of the throat, which is painful, and to delicate persons almost dangerous, from whence its name of choke-cherry.— The bark is tonic and bitter : when steeped in whiskey it is given for ague. No doubt it is from this that the common term of "taking his bitters," as applied to dram-drinking, has been derived. Bitter indeed are the effects of such habits upon the emigrant.

The reason why the native plants often fail to grow and thrive when removed to the garden, arises from the change in the soil and situation : to remove a plant from deep shade and light rich soil, to sunshine and common earth, without any attention to their previous habits, is hardly reasonable. A fine leaf mould, water, and shelter should be afforded till the tender stranger has become inured to its change of soil and position : those that neglect to observe the habits and natures of wild plants, rarely succeed in their attempts to naturalize them to the garden, and improve them by domestic culture.

I will now give some recipes for drying and preserving the native fruits :—

DRIED APPLES.
(See that article.)

DRIED GREEN GAGES, OR ANY KIND OF PLUMS.

Gather your plums when not too ripe; split with a knife, and remove the stone: put a little fine sugar into the cavity, and set your plums on a dish, or tray, to dry in the sun, or below the kitchen-stove. At night put them into a *cool* stove, or into a brick oven, after the bread has been withdrawn. If you have neither stove nor oven let them dry in a sunny window of a warm room.

When quite dry, pack in paper-bags or boxes. In some stores, there are sold nice round white wooden boxes, with a lid and handle, which are excellent for keeping cakes, sugar or dried fruits: they are cheap, and very convenient.

These dried plums are very little, if at all, inferior to the dried Portugal plums, and are excellent either as a dry sweetmeat, or, steeped and boiled up, as a preserve. Plums or any other fruit, crushed and spread out on a flat pan to dry, with a little fine white sugar sifted over them, are also good, and economical, as they take little sugar.

HUCKLEBERRIES, RASPBERRIES, CHERRIES, OR ANY SMALL FRUIT,

may be dried either in a cool stove, or before the fire, or in a warm, sunny window; but fire-heat is the best, as the sun is more apt to draw the flavour from the fruit, and increase the acidity.

Boil huckleberries, currants, and bilberries for half an hour, or longer; spread them out on tin pans, and let them dry in the oven, or below the stove, or out of doors; cut into squares, when dry enough to move; turn the pieces and let them dry on the under side; sift a little white sugar upon each piece, and pack by pressing the fruit-cakes closely: keep in dry bags or boxes: stew down one or more of these cakes as you want them for use. These dried fruits are very useful in sickness: a portion of one of the cakes put into a jug, and boiling water poured on, makes a delightful acid drink: black currants cured this way, are very good. The drink taken warm is a fine remedy for a cold or sore throat.

Many persons use the dried fruit of currants or huckleberries, as a substitute, in cakes and puddings, for the Zante currants.

WILD GOOSEBERRIES.

These are not often dried, as they become hard and flavourless; but either green or ripe, they can be used as pies or puddings, or boiled down to jam.

The wild green gooseberry, or thornberry, is often beset with real sharp thorns; not on the branches, for they are generally smooth; but on the berry itself: to avail yourself of the fruit, you must pour boiling water on them : let them lie in it a minute ; then rub them in a coarse clean dry cloth on the table : this will remove, or soften the spines so that their roughness will be taken away : make into pies, and sweeten with maple-sugar or molasses.

To make either the unripe or ripe gooseberries into jam, boil them down till soft, in a water-bath first, closely covered : when quite soft, add half a pound of sugar to each pint of fruit, and boil one hour longer. Some allow to eight pints of fruit, six pounds of sugar.

RASPBERRIES.

This fruit is most abundant in Canada where a clearing has once been made. The birds sow the seeds. The raspberry seems to follow the steps of the settler, and springs up in his path as if to supply the fruit which is so needful to his health and comfort. Ripening in July, the raspberry affords a constant and daily supply for his table, till the beginning of September. Large quantities of this fruit are sold in the towns by the bush-settlers' wives and children, who get from 4d. to 5d. a quart for the berries.

A dish of raspberries and milk, with sugar, or a pie, gives many an emigrant family a supper. The black raspberry makes the best pie, and this fruit dries better than the red, as it is sweeter and richer in quality : it can be greatly improved by culture.

Raspberry vinegar, too, is a cheap luxury to those who have home-made vinegar and home-made sugar.

RASPBERRY VINEGAR.

To every quart of good vinegar put two quarts of raspberries : let them stand for twenty-four hours ; drain them off through a sieve, but do not squeeze them ; add the same quantity of raspberries to the strained vinegar a second time ; let them stand as before ; drain and add a third quantity : when you have drained the fruit off a third time, measure the liquor into a stone covered-jar, and to each pint of juice add a pound of lump sugar : set the jar in a pot of boiling water, and let the vinegar boil for ten minutes, stirring it to mix the sugar well through : when cold, bottle it for use : it is all the better for standing for some months before being used.

A cheaper sort might be made with fine moist sugar, or with crushed sugar, but must be well scummed. Raspberry vinegar makes an excellent fever drink, a small quantity being mixed in a tumbler of cold water : it is very refreshing in hot weather, and is made in considerable quantities by those who have wild raspberries growing near the clearings, and plenty of sugar at command.

PLUM JAM.

Take any quantity of the red plums, and put them into a stone jar: set this into a pot of water, having first tied a piece of clean cloth over the top of the jar ; bladder is best if you have it at hand. Let your fruit-jar remain till the fruit is soft ; remove all the stones that you can find ; measure your pulp into a preserving pan, and to every six pints of fruit add four pounds of good soft sugar : break some of the stones, and add the kernels to the fruit : boil all up for nearly an hour, and put by in jars ; cover when cold with papers dipped in white of egg.

ANOTHER WAY.

To each pound of fruit, either blue, green or red plums, add a pound of sugar : boil till the fruit begins to sink, and the juice looks thick and ropy. Some open the fruit with a sharp knife, and remove the stone, before boiling ; but many do not take that trouble, but allow somewhat less sugar.

There is not a finer preserve, or one that keeps better, than plum jam : it may be made with maple-sugar, or the plums boiled in molasses.

For Dried Plums see that article. The red plum will not answer so well for drying, being too acid and juicy.

I recommend the emigrant to bring out stones of all varieties ; even the hedge-bullace and damson, which are not found here, and would thrive well.

PEACHES. *

This delightful fruit cannot be grown in every part of the Province. The Peach orchards begin to be cultivated westward of Toronto, where all kinds of fruit grow and flourish, the climate being warmer, and the winters not so long or so severe. With the culture of the peach I have had no experience ; but there are many excellent directions given in a charming work, published in Rochester, entitled "The Horticulturist," a magazine on rural art and rural taste, † in which the cultivation of the Peach is much attended to. To any one who can afford to buy it, this beautifully embellished work would afford much excellent information on the cultivation of fruit and flowers: it comes out monthly. It is to be regretted that so few plain practical gardening-books have as yet been published in Canada, devoted to vegetable and fruit culture, suited expressly for the climate and soil of Canada.

Ripe peaches are brought over during the season, from the States, in large quantities : they sell high, and are often in bad order. By and by, I trust that Western Canada will supply the home market.—

---

* The Peach has been improperly introduced here, among the Wild Fruits of Canada.—EDITOR.

† The price of this work is two dollars per annum, the uncoloured, and four dollars the coloured numbers.

Peaches are dried in the same way as green gages. They also make a delicious wet preserve.

CRANBERRIES.

The low-bush cranberry is not to be found about your clearings, or in the woods : it is peculiar to low sandy marshes, near lakes and river-flats. The Indians are the cranberry gatherers : they will trade them away for old clothes, pork or flour. This fruit is sometimes met with in stores ; but it is of rare occurrence now : formerly we used to procure them without difficulty. The fruit is, when ripe, of a dark purplish red ; smooth and shining ; the size of a champaigne gooseberry ; oblong in form. I have never seen the plants growing, but have a dried specimen of the blossom and leaves : they are very delicate and elegant, and must be beautiful either in flower or fruit, seen covering large extents of ground known as cranberry marshes.— At Buckhorn-lake, one of the chain of small lakes to the northwest of Peterboro', they abound ; and at the back of Kingston, there is a large cranberry marsh of great extent. It is in such localities that the cranberry in its native state is to be looked for. The cranberry will keep a long time just spread out upon the dry floor of a room, and can be used as required, or put into jars or barrels in cold water. This fruit is now cultivated to some extent in the United States : directions for the culture are given in " The Genesee Farmer," published in Rochester at one dollar per annum.

CRANBERRY SAUCE.

A quart of the ripe picked berries, stewed with as much water as will keep them from drying to the pan, closely covered : a pound of soft sugar must be added when the fruit is burst ; boil half an hour after you add the sugar, and stir them well. When quite stewed enough, pour them into a basin or mould : when cold they will be jellied so as to turn out whole in the form of the mould.

This jam is usually served with roasted venison, mutton and beef. It makes rich open-tarts, or can be served at tea-table in glass plates, to eat with bread.

The Indians attribute great medicinal virtues to the cranberry, either cooked or raw : in the uncooked state the berry is harsh and very astringent : they use it in dysentery, and also in applications as a poultice to wounds and inflammatory tumours, with great effect.

HIGH-BUSH CRANBERRY.

This ornamental shrub, which is the single guelder-rose, is found in all damp soil near lakes, and creeks, and rivers : it is very showy in blossom, and most lovely to behold in fruit ; it bears transplantation into gardens and shrubberies, but a low and shady situation suits its habits best, and in this only it will thrive and bear fruit to perfection. The flat seeds render the fruit less proper for jam; but it is so fine as jelly, and so little trouble to make, that I shall give directions for it as follows:—

CRANBERRY JELLY.

Gather the fruit as soon as the frost has touched it, any time in October or November: pick the berries into a jar, and set the jar on the stove, or in a vessel of boiling water, covered down, till they burst; pass the fruit through a sieve or colander: the seeds being large, will not go through: boil the juice up, with a pound of sugar to a pint of juice: if you want it for immediate use, a smaller quantity of sugar will be sufficient, as it jellies very readily; but any fruit jelly that has to be kept for weeks and months, requires equal quantities of sugar and fruit to preserve it from fermentation.

STRAWBERRY JAM.

Boil as many pounds of sugar as you have pints of ripe fresh fruit, with a pint of water; boil and scum the sugar; then add your fruit, and boil well for an hour: if you use white sugar, three-quarters of an hour will do.

The fine colour of the fruit, and its delicate flavour, are injured by coarse sugar, and too long boiling.

I have lately heard that adding a pound of sifted sugar to every pint of whole fruit, merely strewing the sugar with the fruit as you pack it in the jars, will make a fine preserve, without boiling at all.

RASPBERRY JAM.

Pursue the same plan as directed for strawberries; but for family use, raspberries may be boiled into jam, with brown or even maple sugar: boil an hour after adding them to the syrup. Some persons mix currants and raspberries together; this improves both.

CURRANT JAM.

String the currants and boil with equal parts of sugar, as directed for raspberry jam.

ANOTHER WAY.

Stew the currants till they burst; then add three-quarters of a pound of sugar; boil till the seeds begin to sink, and the jam is thickened, so that it stiffens when cold.

A MIXED-FRUIT JAM.

Take equal parts of bilberries, huckleberries, and red currants; stew well with half a pound of sugar to each pint of fruit, when burst. This is a fine preserve, most excellent in flavour. These fruits boiled in a crust, or baked as a pie, are very delicious.

CURRANT JELLY.

To every pint of clear juice add a pound of lump sugar: boil together for an hour, or till the mixture will jelly when cold. Raspberry-jelly is made in the same way. Cold currant-jelly is made by mixing one pound of juice, and merely stirring well together. The process of jellying commences at the bottom of the vessel, and of course is slower, but equally effectual as boiling would be. Try it!

CURRANT VINEGAR.

Gather ripe red or white currants, string them, and put them into a vessel: to four quarts of the fruit allow a gallon of water; let them stand in a warm kitchen to ferment for some days, stirring the fruit with a stick to prevent mould gathering on the surface: when the fermentation has continued for some time, strain off the liquor from the fruit: bruise the latter, or squeeze it well with your hands, while straining it. Add two pounds of coarse sugar to each gallon of liquor, and put it into a cask or any suitable vessel, and let it remain in a warm room. I had in six weeks strong fine-coloured vinegar, fit for pickling, with only one pound of sugar to the gallon.

BLACK CURRANTS.

This useful fruit may be dried whole, or boiled down and spread on tin plates and dried, with or without sugar; made into jam or jelly, or merely stewed with a little sugar, sufficient to sweeten, not preserve them. The convenience of this method is very apparent. In Canada, preserves are always placed on table at the evening meal, and often in the form of tarts. This method enables any one who has ripe fruit to prepare an agreeable dish at a small expense, and very little trouble, if a party of friends arrive unexpectedly to tea.

CURRANTS AND SUGAR.

This is a favourite dish to set on at tea-time—ripe currants strung into cold water, from which they are drained immediately, and sugar, brown or white, strewn over them. A rich natural syrup is thus formed, which improves the acidity of the currants, besides giving a bright fresh look to the dish of fruit which is very agreeable to the eye.

CURRANTS AND RICE.

Prepare rice as in the directions for apple-rice pudding, using ripe currants instead: boil in a cloth or mould, and serve with sugar and butter.

BAKED CURRANT PUDDING.

Make a fine batter with eggs and milk and flour sufficient to thicken to the consistency of cream: throw in a pint of ripe red currants, and a little finely shred suet, or some small bits of butter, on the top of the pudding: bake, and serve with soft sugar.

An Indian-meal pudding, with ripe currants, either baked or boiled, is very nice: if boiled and tied in a cloth, it requires long boiling—two or three hours, if large.

MANDRAKE, OR MAY-APPLE. (*Ripe in August.*)

This was the first native fruit that I tasted, after my arrival in Canada. It attracted my attention as I was journeying through the woods to my forest-home. The driver of the team plucked it for me, and told me it was good to eat, bidding me throw aside the outer rind, which he said was not fit to be eaten. The May-apple when ripe is about the size of an egg-plum, which it resembles in shape and colour. The pulp of the fruit is of a fine sub-acid flavour, but it is better not gathered too ripe: it should be allowed to ripen in a sunny window. The time of its ripening is in August: the rich moist lands at the edge of the forest, and just within its shade, is the place where the May-apple abounds. In the month of May, it may be seen breaking the black soil, the leaves folded round the stem like a closed parasol. The fruit-bearing plant has two large palmated leaves, i. e., leaves spread out like a hand; the stalk supports the leaf from the centre; in the fork formed by the leaves a large rose-shaped flower, of a strong scent, rises. Very fragrant at a little distance it is, but rank and overpowering when held too near. The colour of the blossom is a greenish white.

The May-apple makes a delicious preserve. Gather the fruit as soon as it begins to shew any yellow tint on the green rind: lay them by in a sunny window for a day or two; cut them in quarters and throw them into a syrup of white sugar, in which ginger sliced, and cloves, have been boiled: boil the fruit till the outer rind is tender: take the fruit out, lay them in a basin, sift a handful of pounded sugar over them, and let them lie till cold. Next day boil your syrup a second time, pour it over the fruit, and when cold put it into jars or glasses, and tie down. It should not be used till a month or six weeks after making: if well spiced this preserve is more like some foreign fruit. It is very fine. Some only make use of the soft acid pulp, but though the outer part is not fit to be eaten in a raw state, it is very good when preserved, and may safely be made use of, boiled with sugar and spices.

This fruit might I think be introduced into garden-culture, and prove a valuable addition to our tables; but in event of planting it in the garden, a very rich light mould must be given to feed the plant, which grows by nature in the rich vegetable leaf-mould.

FERMENTATIONS FOR BREAD.

The making and baking of good, nourishing, palatable bread, is perhaps one of the most important duties of the practical housewife: so much of the comfort and health of a family depends on the constant supply of this most essential article of diet, that I shall give it a first place in the instructions that I am about to furnish to my female readers.

Many of the settlers' families for whom this little volume is intended, may have emigrated from large towns or cities, where the baker's shop supplies all the bread that is daily consumed by the inhabitants: or it may be placed in the hands of one, who from her position in life has been totally unacquainted with labour of any kind, and who may be glad to profit by the directions I am about to give. Even to the active, industrious wife, or daughter of the labourer, well skilled in the mystery of making bread, both brown and white, something new may be gleaned from these pages, for there is a great difference in the materials she will have to make use of, and in the managing of them.— First then I shall say something about the different modes of fermenting, or raising the bread, and give directions for making the various kinds of barm that are used in Canadian houses; that in circumstances where one fails, another may be adopted. To those who reside in towns, and have no garden of their own in which hops can be cultivated, it is better, if they wish to make their own rising, to buy hops at the store, which can be got good at from 1s. 6d. to 2s 6d. per lb., varying in price as the previous season has been good or bad for the supply. Country people will often sell hops as low as 1s. or 1s. 3d., but they are not so good as those you buy at the stores, few persons knowing the right time to gather them. This should be done when the hop is full blown, and when the yellow dust, at the base of each of the fine thin leaves that make the blossom, is well formed, of a bright yellow colour, and a little glutinous to the touch. If the hop begins to lose its colour and fade, much of the fine bitter flavour is gone: it is over ripe.

Some persons prefer having recourse to brewer's yeast or distiller's yeast; the latter is not so good or sure, and obtaining the former is uncertain, as the demand is often greater than the supply; while if you make your own hop-rising, you are not subject to disappointment, unless you are careless and let your stock run out. For a penny or three half-pence you may obtain about half a pint of fresh beer-yeast at the brewer's.

CURING BREWER'S YEAST.

This yeast is very bitter, and those who do not relish the bitterness that it is apt to impart to the bread, should remedy the defect by pouring about half a pint or more of lukewarm water on the yeast, and letting it stand a few hours previous to using it: this draws a portion of the bitterness away. Pour off the water clear from the yeast, then stir the yeast up, adding a little warm water, and a tablespoonful of flour, mixing it well; let it stand a short time, till it begins to rise in bubbles. A large cupful of this will raise you about

FERMENTATIONS FOR BREAD.

ten pounds of flour. The residue may be bottled and set by in a cool place for a second baking. This sort of yeast does not keep so well as the hop-rising; for the making of which I will now give you directions.

HOP-RISING.

Boil down two large handfuls of hops, in three quarts of water, till the hops begin to sink to the bottom of the vessel, which they do after an hour's fast boiling. Put about a quart of flour in an earthen pan, or any convenient vessel, not too shallow, and strain the liquor, boiling off the fire, into the flour, stirring the batter quickly as you do so. The flour will thicken up like paste: stir it as smoothly as you can, then let it stand till blood warm; mix in a tea-cupful of the old stock of barm, and let the vessel stand covered up near the fire till it begins to show that fermentation has taken place. In summer you need only cover the jar or pan; it will rise in a few hours; but new barm is not so good as after it has worked for some days. A large earthen pitcher tied down from the air, or a stone jar with a cover, is best for keeping the rising in. The vessel should be well cleaned before refilling.

ANOTHER SORT.

Boil your hops for two hours. With a pint of the liquid cooled down to moderate heat, mix a pint-basinful of flour to a batter, very smoothly; next strain in the remaining scalding hop-liquor, stirring the whole till it is about the thickness of cream: set this mixture on the stove, or some hot coals on the hearth, in a clean pot; the one you have just used for boiling the hops, well rinced and wiped clean, will do; keep the mixture stirring till the whole begins to thicken and assume the appearance of a thick gruel. Some do not think it necessary to boil it after it thickens, but it keeps better if it remains on the fire a few minutes after it comes to the boil: if it be too thick to stir easily, thin with a little boiling water: add a large tea-spoonful of salt. Pour this hop-gruel into your jar, and when cooled down so that you can bear a finger in it comfortably, add a cupful of rising, and set it by. Some add a table-spoonful of brown sugar.

This sort of barm keeps longer without souring than the common sort. Remember that for keeping yeast in summer, a cool dairy or cellar is best; and in winter some warm closet or cellar, which is too close to admit of frost, is most advisable. A teaspoonful of soda or salaratus, dissolved in a little water, and stirred into yeast that is a little sour, will reclaim it, but it must be done just at the time you are going to make use of the yeast, or it will lose its good effect.

HOP-YEAST WITH POTATOES.

Pare and wash a dozen good-sized potatoes; set them on with about a quart or three pints of water, with a heaped tea-spoonful of salt; boil till they are soft enough to mix through the water like gruel. Pour into your rising-jar or pan, and mix in, as smoothly as you can, flour enough to make a thick batter; have your hops boiling, as in the former receipts, stir the strained liquor into your potato and flour batter, add a large spoonful of sugar, and mix all smoothly; when cooled down, add a couple of large spoonfuls of rising, to work it. After it has worked, it is strained into a bottle, and set by for use.

A large cupful will raise about ten pounds of flour. Some persons give the preference to this potato-barm, but either of the recipes is good for fermenting bread.

SUGAR-YEAST.

Boil two handfuls of hops in a gallon of water for an hour; strain off and add two table-spoons of salt; mix in one pound of flour and two pounds of soft sugar; stir all together when milk warm; add two spoonfuls of good yeast; let it rise for two days, then bottle and cork lightly, and put in a cool cellar: a large cupful will raise about ten pounds of flour, or more.

This recipe I have not tested myself, but I am told it is good, and has the advantage of fermenting itself, without the addition of other barm to set it to work.

LEAVEN CAKES.

Boil three ounces of hops in three gallons of water, till reduced to a quart: while boiling-hot strain the liquor into one quart of rye-meal, stirring it well. Let it cool: add a cupful of good yeast: when it has begun to work well, stir in as much Indian-meal as will thicken the mass to a stiff dough; knead it upon a board well, roll it into cakes about an inch in thickness, and let them dry on a clean board in the sun, for two or three days: do not leave them out after sunset. Two inches square of this yeast-cake dissolved in warm water, and thickened with a table-spoonful of flour, will raise one or two good-sized loaves. If hung up in bags in a dry room, this leaven will keep good for many months.

The above is from an American receipt-book, and I have been told it is a good receipt.

ANOTHER AMERICAN-YEAST.

Boil very soft and mash four large potatoes; mash them very fine; pour over them one pint of boiling water; when only warm, stir in two large spoons of flour, two of molasses, a tea-spoonful of salt, and a cup of good yeast. This must be used fresh: the above will raise a baking of bread for a family. Set in a sponge over night.

BUTTER-MILK CAKES.

You may raise nice light cakes, to be eaten hot with butter, by putting into a quart of buttermilk as much soda or saleratus as will make it effervesce or foam up like new yeast. It is better to dissolve the soda in a cup of hot water; and bruise the lumps well, before you put them into the water, so that the whole be thoroughly dissolved; any bits that are left unmelted will make a distasteful spot in your cake; mix your dough very lightly, kneading it only just stiff enough to roll out into cakes about an inch in thickness: put them at once into a hot oven: the oven should be pretty hot, or your cakes will not be so light. This sort of bread is very convenient; it needs no shortening, nor any other seasoning than a little salt with the flour.

A teaspoonful of sal volatile in powder (that is the ammonia used as smelling salts), with two teaspoonfuls of cream of tartar, mixed very thoroughly with the flour, before it is wetted, will raise nice light plain buns, to be eaten hot.

I will also recommend "Durkee's Baking Powder": it is sold in all Canadian stores and drug-shops, at 7½d. the sealed packet, on which are printed directions for using it. This powder imparts no ill taste to the bread or cakes; producing a very light cake with no trouble.— Emigrants should provide an article of this kind among other sea-stores, as a convenient and wholesome substitute for raised bread, for the use of themselves and little ones.

The use of these acid and alkaline salts in fermenting flour food, has become very general of late years; they have the advantage of convenience in their favour, and are regarded by many persons as being more wholesome than bread raised with yeast, which has a tendency to turn sour, especially on the stomachs of young children and persons of weak digestion.

Owing to the superior dryness of the atmosphere in Canada, bread seldom turns mouldy, or takes a fermentation, after it has been kept many days, as is often the case in moist hot weather in the old country. During my long sojourn in Canada, I have never seen or tasted a piece of mouldy bread.

SALT-RISING.

This sort of barm is much used among the old Canadian and Yankee settlers. It has this advantage over other kinds of rising; it requires no addition of any other yeast to stimulate it into active fermentation. Those who are in the constant habit of using it, make excellent bread with it. I dislike the peculiar flavour it imparts, and if it is not really well managed, it is neither pleasant nor wholesome; but many persons prefer it to all other modes of fermenting bread, so I shall furnish the instructions for making it.

Take one teaspoonful of salt, one pint of warm water or new milk, rather more than blood-heat; thicken with as much flour as will make a batter the thickness of good cream; mix in a jug that will hold about a quart; set the jug in a pan or pot half filled with water, warm, but not too hot; cover your mixture close, and set it in a warm place near to the stove or fire: in about four hours bubbles will begin to rise on the surface, and in about two more the yeast will begin to rise in a fine soft creamy head. The nice point in making salt-rising bread, is to know when the yeast is risen enough : after a certain time it goes down, and will not raise the bread, or turns it sour.— Experience will guide you after one or two trials. But we will suppose the yeast is risen nearly to the brim of the jug ; then take as much flour, say four quarts, as will make you two loaves, or one good bake-kettle loaf ; make a hole in the flour, add a little salt, and pour your barm in ; mingle it thoroughly, and knead your dough smoothly and well with your hands, as you would make up any other loaf : let your bake-can be well greased before putting your loaf in ; cover it with the lid. In baking in the bake-kettle, do not fill it much more than half full, that your dough may have room to swell ; many a good loaf is spoiled by being crowded into too small a space. Set the pan with your loaf at a moderate distance from the fire, covered up ; when it rises, which you see by its occupying a larger space, and cracking on the top, you may advance it nearer the fire, turning the bake-kettle round gradually from time to time, till every side has felt the influence of the heat. When within two inches of the top, put a scattering of coals (live wood-embers) below the kettle and on the lid ; or heat the lid on the fire, but not too hot at first, and then add live coals. You must keep your kettle turned gradually, that the sides may brown, and do not put too many hot coals below at once. You will soon learn the art of baking a shanty-loaf : a little attention and care is the main thing. When the crust is hard and bears pressure without sinking in, the bread is done.

Many a beautiful loaf I have eaten, baked before a wood fire in a bake-kettle. The bush-settlers seldom can afford to buy cooking-stoves during the first few years, unless they are better off than the labouring class usually are when they come to Canada.

BREAD

Having given you a chapter on the different modes of making yeast, for the raising of your bread, collected from the best sources, I shall now proceed to the making and baking of the bread. I can hardly furnish a more excellent receipt for good bread, than that which is used in my own house ; which indeed I can recommend to all housekeepers, as fine in quality and appearance, while at the same time it is decidedly economical. It can be made purely white ; or brown, by the addition of two or three handfuls of coarse bran.

Should the quantity here mentioned prove too large in proportion to the number of the family, a little experience will enable the person who attends to the making of the bread, to reduce it one-half or one-third.

MRS. TRAILL'S BREAD.

Wash and pare half a pail of potatoes, taking care to remove all dark specks ; throw them into a vessel of clean water as you pare them, as they are apt to acquire a brownish colour, which spoils the white and delicate appearance of the bread. Boil the potatoes till reduced to a pulp, bruising any lumps smooth with a wooden beetle or pounder : it will then have the consistency of thick gruel : when cool enough to bear your hand in it, stir in as much flour as will make the mixture the thickness of thick batter ; add a good handful of salt, and two cupfuls of your hop barm or any good rising that you may have. A deep, red earthen pot, or a wooden pail, will be a good vessel to contain your sponge. It is a wise precaution to stand your vessel in a pan, as it is apt to flow over. If set to rise over-night, it will be risen time enough to work up in the morning early : in summer we seldom make this potato-bread, on account of the potatoes then not being so fit for the purpose, for, while young, they will not boil down so smoothly ; but from the month of August till May, it may be made with great advantage. The quantity of sponge, above, will raise two large milk-dishes of flour, or about twenty pounds of flour. If you have a large kneading-trough, you can mix the whole at once, and knead it well and thoroughly ; but if your trough be too small for convenience, divide your sponge, and make two masses of dough, working it very stiff on your board, scoring the top with a knife, and cover it up by the fire with a clean cloth ; or you may make only half the quantity, using, of course, less potatoes and water. In about two hours, or may-be longer, you will have a light dough, like a honeycomb, to make into loaves. When baked, take your bread out of the pan, wet the crust of your loaves over with clean water or milk, and wrap them in a clean cloth, setting them up on one side against a shelf till cold. This plan keeps the bread from becoming hard and dry. For lightness, sweetness and economy this is the best bread I know, resembling really-good baker's bread in texture and look. I cordially recommend it to the attention of the Canadian housewife.

INDIAN-MEAL BREAD.

Add six pounds of sifted Indian-meal to six pounds of wheaten flour ; one gallon of water, pour, boiling-hot, on the Indian-meal ; when cool enough to work with the hand, mix in the wheaten flour, and a cup of yeast, with a little salt ; knead the mass, and set it to rise near the fire. This bread has a fine yellow colour, and is best used pretty fresh, as the Indian-meal is of a drying quality.

ANOTHER BREAD WITH INDIAN-MEAL.

Take as much good flour as will fill a good-sized milk-dish ; add to the flour a quart of Indian-meal, and a tablespoonful of salt ; mix the meal and flour well together : make a hole in the midst, and pour in a large cup of good rising, adding warm water; mingle stiff enough to knead on your flour-board; then when your mass of dough is worked smooth, lay it back in the pan or trough that you mixed it in, and let it lie covered near the fire to rise; when well-risen, divide, and bake in your oven or bake-kettle.

Some persons wet the Indian-meal with hot water first, but either way can be tried. I have used any supporne, or Indian-meal porridge, that has been left after breakfast, in making bread, and found it a very good addition. A good bread can also be made of equal proportions of rye, Indian-meal, and wheaten flour; rye alone does not make such good bread, the rye being very glutinous, which a mixture of Indian-meal corrects.

BRAN BREAD.

A sweet and economical, and most wholesome bread may be made by pouring water, either warm or cold, on to bran, stirring it up, and leaving it to steep for an hour; then strain the bran off through a sieve or strainer, pressing all the moisture out. There should be liquor enough to mix your bread, without any water, unless it be too cold, and a little hot water is required to raise the temperature; add the usual quantities of salt and yeast, and mix and knead as in other bread. The most wholesome and nutritive parts of the bran will thus be preserved and added to your bread.

Cobbett recommends this bread, and I have proved its good and wholesome qualities myself. All the fine flour and bran that passes through the sieve, should be put into your bread, along with the liquor, for this constitutes part of its excellence. If you wish for *browner* bread, throw in a handful of dry sweet bran, and mix with your flour, in addition, but not that from which the gluten and fine sugary particles have been extracted by the water.

Many persons who do not use potatoes in their bread, as directed in the first receipt, set a sponge over night, merely mingling the flour, warm water, salt and yeast, and when well risen, (which it is known to be by the air-bubbles that rise on the top,) thicken with flour, and knead well: when the dough is of sufficient lightness, make up into loaves; let them rise a second time in the bread pan or bake-kettle, and bake.

I have now given the best simple receipts for making bread, that I am acquainted with. There are methods of making light bread without using the yeast to ferment the flour.

I will now give an American receipt for unfermented bread, which I have not myself tested :—

EXCELLENT BREAD WITHOUT YEAST.

Scald about two handfuls of Indian-meal, into which put a teaspoonful of salt, and as much cold water as will reduce the mixture of meal to blood-heat; then stir in wheaten flour till it is as thick as hasty-pudding, and set it before the fire to rise. In about half an hour it generally begins to thin and look watery on the top. Sprinkle in a little more flour, and mind and keep the pot turned from time to time, taking care not to let it be too near the fire, or it will bake at the sides before it is risen. In about four hours it will rise and ferment, as if you had set it with hop-yeast; when it is light enough, mix in as much flour as will make it into a soft dough: grease a pan, put in your loaf, and let it rise, covering it up warm, and turning it so that the heat affects it equally; in less than an hour it will be ready for the oven: bake as soon as it is risen. Some bake in a Dutch-oven before the fire.—*From Mrs. Child's Frugal Housewife.*

EXCELLENT HOT TEA-CAKES.

One quart of fine flour: two ounces of butter: two teaspoonfuls of cream of tartar, mixed dry through the flour: one teaspoonful of salaratus or soda: moisten the latter in milk or water till dissolved: mix with sweet milk or cold water.

These cakes to be rolled, and cut out with a tumbler, about an inch in thickness, served hot and buttered.

SHORTS OR CANAILLE.

This is the common name given to the inferior flour which is separated in bolting, at the mill, from the bran and fine flour, and is seldom used as a mixture in bread. This is not economical management: for mixed with fine flour, it makes sweet good bread; and many a loaf made from it I have seen, when other flour was scarce. The bread is closer in texture, and does not rise as light as brown bread with a mixture of bran in it; but still it is by no means to be despised. As unleavened cakes, it is perhaps more agreeable than raised bread. The Irish call these coarse cakes by the odd name of "fudge."

BROWN CAKES.

Mingle a handful of fine flour, with as much of the coarse shorts as will make a baking of cakes for tea, say about three pints of the coarse, to half a pint of the fine: a little fine flour must also be used in kneading on the board, and rubbing the dough from your hands.— Rub a good bit of shortening into your dry flour, as if you were going to make short cakes: dissolve a teaspoonful of salaratus or soda, in a cup of hot water; add this to as much buttermilk, or sour milk, as will mix the flour into a light dough: do not omit salt, and do not knead the mass too stiff; only stiff enough to enable you to roll it out about an inch thick; cut into round or square cakes, and bake in a quick oven.

Eaten hot, with a little butter, these are good, plain, houshold tea-cakes; with molasses and ginger they are very good.

BROWN SUPPORNE.

This is porridge, made entirely with shorts, and eaten with cold butter or new milk. It is made in the same way as Indian-meal supporne (see that article). In the absence of corn-meal or oatmeal, children will eat this dish very readily, and it is often a convenient substitute for bread, when flour runs out, and you are unable to obtain an immediate supply. It is most commonly made with water, but may be mixed with milk, or milk and water, the flour being stirred in as the water or milk boils.

MILK PORRIDGE.

Have your milk boiling, and a basinful of flour, into which a little salt may be mixed: with one hand sprinkle in your flour, and stir with a wooden stick or a spoon, till you have made your porridge as thick as you desire it to be: remove it from the fire to the top of the stove, or place the pot on a few hot embers, not near enough to the fire to scorch, and let it simmer for some time, stirring it carefully. This makes a very satisfying meal for children.

FARMERS' RICE.

Set milk on the fire, in a clean skillet, to boil, with half a tea-spoonful of salt in it. Take dry fine flour in a basin; into this sprinkle cold milk, a few drops at a time, till it is damp, but not wet like dough: rub the damp flour in your hands, which must, of course, be delicately clean. The wetted flour must be rubbed till it adheres in small pieces like grains of rice; if not damp enough scatter in a little more moisture, or, if too wet, add a little flour: when ready, throw this mock-rice into your milk, stirring it in by degrees: let it boil quick while mixing; then set it at a little distance, say outside the griddle of the stove, and let it boil for fifteen minutes or half an hour; a little nutmeg, sugar and butter makes this a nice dish; but some prefer it unseasoned, or with salt and butter.

These are homely dishes; but they are intended for homely people, who have not the materials for luxuries at their command, but who may be glad to learn how to vary the method of dressing such simple food as they can obtain, so as to render it palatable and pleasant.

BISCUITS.

An excellent, cheap, useful biscuit can be made as follows: Rub into a quart of fine flour, about an ounce of butter or lard, and a little salt: mix with cold water into a stiff, smooth paste; roll it out, and strew dry flour on the paste; work this flour well in with the rolling-pin, fold it together, knead it and roll it again, throwing over it more dry flour, working it with the rolling-pin till the flour is incorporated; and do this several times, or as long as you can knead it smooth: break it into small pieces, and roll in your hand, about the size of a large walnut, then roll with the pin into thin biscuits, prick them with a fork, and bake on a flat pan in a brick oven: if the oven be cool, they will be tough: the more dry flour you can work into the dough, the better will be the biscuit. These are useful if you have no cakes at hand, and are good for the sick; rolled fine, make capital pap for weaned babies.

I learned to make them, under the direction of a physician, as food for a delicate infant; many persons I have taught to make these biscuits, and they will be found very useful where the fermented bread causes acidity, and soda-biscuits and American crackers are not at hand, or the housewife too poor to buy them.

ANOTHER SORT.

Instead of cold, use scalding water and roll very thin. The butter may be melted in the hot water: mix and knead very smooth, but without beating in the dry flour, as in the former receipt: roll very thin, and bake quickly.

SODA BISCUITS.

Six ounces of butter: six ounces of sugar: one teaspoonful of soda, dissolved in one pint of milk: flour enough to form a stiff dough: melt the butter in the milk, and also the sugar, which should be white. Knead and roll out several times, till the mass be quite smooth; roll in thin sheets about a quarter of an inch thick, cut into square cakes, and bake in a brisk oven.

ABERNETHY BISCUITS.

Seven pounds fine flour; three-quarters pound of butter, rubbed well into the flour; 1½ pound of loaf-sugar, dissolved in one quart of cold water: half ounce carraways, and a teaspoonful of salt. Well knead this dough; divide, and make four dozen biscuits.

This quantity can be reduced to one-half, at the convenience of the baker.

Biscuits are both a cheap and wholesome bread, and are a very valuable sort of food for invalids or very young children: they are far less expensive than sweet cakes, and by many persons are greatly preferred, as being easier of digestion, but they require more hard labour, and attention in baking.

The American crackers are sold in many of the stores at 7½d. a pound, but they can be home-made almost as well.

Those who have a stone or brick oven, can make their biscuits much finer and crisper, besides giving them the real biscuit flavour, by putting them into the oven after the bread, pie, &c. have been baked, and leaving them for some hours on the oven floor, while any warmth remains. Thus they are twice baked, and will keep for weeks and months. Bread of any kind does not mould, as in the damper climate of Britain; even in very hot weather, bread, cakes and other flour-food will keep uninjured for many days. I have rarely seen mouldy bread or cake, during twenty years' sojourn in Canada. Next to biscuits there is nothing better than rusks: some call them "tops and bottoms," others "twice-baked cakes."

RUSKS.

Half-a-pound of butter or lard (butter is best), or half the quantity of each, dissolved in a pint of hot milk, six eggs well beaten, a little salt, as much yeast as will raise these ingredients; add as much flour as will stiffen into a very thick batter; cover warm, and when risen, stiffen just enough to admit of rolling lightly, about an inch in thickness: cut out with a tumbler or small round cutter: set to rise a few minutes; bake, but not *over*bake, cut them in two pieces, or, if very thick, make three slices with a sharp knife: return to the oven, and bake till each piece is crisp. Some lay on the top of a stove, turning them twice or thrice.

HARD RUSKS.

Dissolve half a pound of butter or lard (the latter will do), in *boiling* water, with a little salt: mix with a spoon as much flour as you can stir into the water and lard smoothly: as the mixture will be scalding-hot, you must wait till it cools down low enough to admit of your hand, working in a tea-cup not quite full of yeast; then knead the mass thoroughly, and cover it down near the fire till it rises.—When light, roll out, and cut into thin cakes, not quite an inch thick; bake and split them; return to the oven, and when dry, lay them out to cool; when cold, put by in a bag or canister for use. These rusks are as sweet as if sugar had been mixed with the flour. They will keep for weeks, and are excellent grated down for pap or panada for the sick, or a gruel made by boiling them, adding a teaspoonful or two of new milk, and seasoning with spice, for a sick person, where bread, however good, would be rejected.

TO MAKE AMERICAN CRACKERS.

One quart of flour, into which rub two ounces of butter; dissolve one teaspoonful of salaratus in a wine-glass or cup of warm water; half a teaspoonful of salt, and milk sufficient to mix it into a stiff, smooth dough: beat it for half an hour, working it well with the rolling-pin; make into thin biscuits, or small round balls flatted in the middle with the thumb, and bake till dry and crisp.

CAKES.

EXCELLENT GINGERBREAD.

Take three pounds of flour, one and a half pound of brown sugar; one pound of butter, six eggs, two tablespoonfuls of ginger, and a teaspoonful of salt: bake on tin sheets rolled very thin.

COMMON GINGERBREAD.

Treacle 1½ lb: seconds flour 2 lb: butter 2 oz: ginger 1 oz: spices 2 oz: of pearl-ash one dessert-spoonful; mix with milk warmed, into a dough; let it stand till it rises, bake on tins, and cut in squares.

GINGER CUP-CAKE.

Five eggs; two large cups of molasses: the same of rolled soft-sugar: two ditto butter: one cup of new milk: five cups of flour: half a cup of ground-ginger: a small teaspoonful of pearl-ash, dissolved in vinegar or cider. Cut up the butter in the milk, warm so as to melt; also warm the molasses, stir it into the milk and butter; stir in the sugar: let it cool. Beat the eggs light; stir in alternately with the flour, add the ginger and other spices, with the pearl-ash: stir the mass well; butter tins to bake it in.

GINGER BREAD.

To a pint of molasses add half cup butter, three eggs, half cup sour-milk, one teaspoonful salaratus, one ditto cream of tartar, two cups flour, two table-spoonfuls of ginger.

PLAIN PLUM-CAKE.

One pound of flour: quarter pound of sugar; quarter pound butter; half a pound currants or raisins; three eggs; half a pint of milk or sour-cream, and a small teaspoonful of carbonate of soda, and spice to taste.

LEMON CAKE.

One tea-cup of butter, three of powdered sugar, beat together to a cream; stir in the yolks of five eggs, well beaten; dissolve a teaspoonful of soda in a tea-cup of milk, and add to the above: also the juice and grated-peel of one lemon, the whites of three of the eggs, beaten to a froth, and four cups of flour. Bake in two pans about half an hour.

COOKIES.

One pound of flour; half pound butter, rubbed well in: ¾ lb sugar: two eggs: half a cup of sour cream: one teaspoonful saleratus: a few carraways: nutmeg or ginger if you like. Roll out thin, and cut in round cakes.

DROP SWEET-CAKES.

Four eggs well beaten: a large cupful of sugar: the same of butter melted: flour enough to thicken to a thick batter; a few currants or seeds, or essence of lemon: beat for a few minutes, drop on tin sheets, and bake in a good hot oven.

If the batter spread too much, add a little more flour.

CHEAP FAMILY CAKE.

To one egg and four ounces of butter, well beaten together, add a teaspoonful of allspice, half a teaspoonful of pepper, a pint of molasses, a teaspoonful of saleratus dissolved in a cup of cream or milk, and flour enough to make it the consistence of fritters; set in a warm place to rise, and when perfectly light, bake moderately.

SILVER CAKE. (*From the "Maple-Leaf."*)

One pound crushed sugar, three quarters of a pound of dried and sifted flour; six ounces of butter: mace and citron; the whites of fourteen eggs. Beat the sugar and butter to a cream; add the whites, cut to a stiff froth, and then the flour. It is a beautiful-looking cake.

GOLDEN CAKE.

This and silver cake should be made together, to use both portions of the eggs. Take one pound of flour dried, one pound white sugar, three-quarters of a pound of butter: the yolks of fourteen eggs, the yellow part of two lemons, grated, and the juice also. Beat the sugar and butter to a cream, and add the yolks, well beaten and strained. Then add the lemon-peel and flour, and a tea-spoonful of sal-volatile dissolved in hot water. Beat it well, and, just before putting in the oven, add the lemon-juice, beating it in thoroughly. Bake in square, flat pans, ice it thickly, and cut it in square, thick pieces. It looks nicely on a plate with silver cake.

CALIFORNIA CAKE.

One cup of butter, three of sugar, one cup sour milk, one teaspoonful saleratus, and two of cream of tartar, six eggs and five cups of flour.

LADY CAKE.

Five oz. butter, half pound sugar, the whites of eight eggs, half pound of flour. Flavour with almonds—one ounce bitter, two sweet.

CAKES.

SODA CAKE.

One pound of flour, four ounces of butter, six ounces sugar, three eggs, one spoonful of sour cream, with one of saleratus, spices and fruit to taste. Bake in a very slow oven at first.

LEMON CAKE.

Six eggs, five cups of flour, three cups of sugar, one cup of butter, one cup of milk, one teaspoonful of saleratus, and the peel and juice of a lemon.

FARMERS' SPONGE CAKE.

One teaspoonful of carbonate of soda dissolved in a tea-cupful of sweet milk, two tea-spoonfuls of cream of tartar, mixed dry into the flour, one egg, one cup of soft sugar, one cup of butter melted : it can be made richer by the addition of a cup of currants, or spice to flavour it. Mix to a thickish batter, and pour into a flat pan ; or bake in tins.

CUP CAKE.

Cup-cake is about as good as pound-cake, and a great deal cheaper. Three cups of flour, one cup of butter, two cups of sugar, and four eggs, well beat in together, and baked in pans or cups.

NOTE.—This is a regular American cake.

DOUGH NUTS.

Three pounds flour : one pound sugar : ¾ lb butter : four eggs : 1½ pint of milk : nutmeg and cinnamon, one teaspoonful : two large tablespoonfuls of barm : knead lightly : cut in strips, and twist and throw into boiling lard ; when they are of a fine light brown, take the dough-nuts out : sift sugar over them while hot.

ANOTHER.

Take one pint of flour, half a pint of sugar, three eggs, a piece of butter as big as an egg, and a teaspoonful of dissolved pearl-ash ; when you have no eggs, a gill of lively yeast will do ; but in that case they must be made over-night. Cinnamon, rose-water, of lemon-brandy, to season, if you have it.

If you use half lard instead of butter, add a little salt.

Do not put them in till the lard is boiling-hot. The more fat they are fried in, the crisper they will be.

COMMON BUSH TEA-CAKES.

Scrape down a large cupful of maple-sugar, and dissolve in warm water, into which also put a teaspoonful of saleratus, well powdered ; rub into two basins of flour, a good bit of butter, or some lard or dripping, and throw in a few carraways, or any spice you may have, and a teaspoonful of salt : knead lightly, cut out with a tumbler, the lid of an old tin tea-pot, or any other convenient cutter, and bake before the fire in the frying-pan, or in the bake-pan. The frying-pan is often used in the backwoods, for baking cakes or bread. In Canada they are generally made with a very long handle, in which there is a loop, through which a strong cord is passed, which is again passed over a nail in the chimney-board ; or a machine called a pan-jack, is placed behind it, with notches which allows the cook to raise or lower the pan to the fire. A few hot embers are placed below the pan, to heat the bottom. This is a shanty-oven, often made use of in the backwoodsman's house.

CANADIAN CROQUETS.

Sift a teaspoonful of white sugar through a bit of muslin ; add to the sugar three or four drops of essence of lemon, or almonds : beat up two eggs with the sugar, and to these add as much very-fine flour as will make the eggs into a stiff paste. It is better to work it with a spoon till it is smooth and stiff enough to handle : knead it, and roll it out as thin as paper. With a sharp penknife cut out leaves and shells, and roses; or, twist narrow slips into braids, cutting the veinings of the leaves and the edgings.

Have ready a clean tin-pan. half full of boiling lard : you can try the heat by throwing in a little bit of your paste ; if hot enough, it will rise directly to the surface, and become stiff in about a minute or two. Throw in your croquets, one or two at a time ; two minutes will cook them : take them out with a slice, drain and lay them on a dish, sift a little fine white sugar on them as you take them out.—From these materials you will have a heaped dish of most elegant-looking cakes, at a very small cost.

SWEET FRUIT-CAKE.

This is made by rolling out a fine short crust very thin, and spreading about an inch thickness of apple-marmalade, made by boiling down dried-apples to a pulp ; over this lay another thin crust of pastry : it should be baked in shallow tin-pans, and, when quite cold, cut into squares, or vandyke-shaped pieces, by cutting squares from corner to' corner. This is sold in the confectioners under the name of mince-pie, and pie-cake.

As this work is not intended for a regular cookery-book, I have limited myself to such cakes as are in common use in the farm-houses. Canada is the land of cakes. A tea-table is generally furnished with several varieties of cakes and preserves. I have given you as many receipts as will enable you to make a selection : if you require more costly luxuries, there are plenty of good receipts to be had, by referring to any of the popular cookery-books.

INDIAN RICE.

Indian Rice is a wholesome and nourishing article of diet, which deserves to be better known than it is at present. It grows in vast beds, in still waters, in a depth from three to eight feet, where there is a great deposit of mud and sand. In many places where there is little current, these beds increase so as to materially fill up the shallow lakes, and impede the progress of boats on their surface.

When the rice begins to shew its tender green blade above the water, you would think the lake was studded with low verdant islands. In the months of July and August, the rice comes in flower, and a very beautiful sight it is for those who have an eye to enjoy the beauties of Nature. The leaves, which are grassy, attain a great length, and float upon the surface of the water; I have seen the leaves of the rice measured to the amazing extent of eleven, twelve and thirteen feet. The deer come down at night to feed on the rice-beds, and there the hunter often shoots them. The Indians track them to their feeding-places, and shoot them by torchlight.

In the month of September is the Indian's rice harvest : by that time it is fully ripe and withered. The squaws collect it by paddling through the rice-beds, and with a stick in one hand, and a sort of sharp-edged, curved paddle in the other, striking the ripe heads down into the canoe, the ripe grain falling to the bottom. Many bushels are thus collected. They then make an enclosure on a square area of dry ground, by sticking branches of pine or cedar close together, to form a sort of hedge ; in the centre of this place they drive in forked sticks, in a square of several feet, across which they lay others, and on this rude frame they extend mats of bass or cedar, for the manufacture of which the Indian women are renowned : they light a fire beneath this frame, and when reduced to hot, glowing coals, the rice is spread on the mats above the fire : the green enclosure is to keep the heat from escaping : the rice is kept stirred and turned with a wooden shovel or paddle, and, after it is dried, the husk is winnowed from it in large open baskets, shaken in the wind. This is the mere drying process of the green rice.

The parched Indian-rice is heated in pots over a slow fire, till it bursts and shows the white floury part within the dark skin. This sort is eaten by the Indians in soups and stews, and often dry, by handfuls, when on journeys, as the parched corn of the Israelites.

Indian-rice is sold in the stores at 10s. a bushel : it affords a great quantity of food. The Indians sow it it up in mats or coarse birch-bark baskets : it is dearer now than it used to be, as the Indians are indolent, or possibly, employed in agricultural pursuits or household work.

In appearance this rice is not the least like the white rice of commerce being long, narrow, and of an olive-green colour outside, but when cooked, is white within. The gathering of wild rice is a tedious process, and one rarely practised by the settlers, whose time can be more profitably employed on their farms ; but I have nevertheless given this description of harvesting it, as it is not devoid of interest, and, should this book fall into the hands of any person, who by accident was reduced to having recourse to such expedients as the wild country afforded, for food to keep themselves from starving, they might be able to avail themselves of the knowledge.

Men who have gone up lumbering, on the shores of lonely lakes and rivers, far from the haunts of civilized men, have sometimes been reduced to worse shifts than gathering wild rice to supply their wants.

I will now give the most approved recipes for cooking the Indian rice.

WILD-RICE PUDDING.

A basinful of Indian-rice carefully washed and picked, should be soaked for some hours ; the water being poured off twice during that time. Put it on in a covered vessel, with plenty of water, which should be drained off after it has boiled for half an hour, as there is a weedy, fishy taste with the rice, unless this is done. Milk may now be added in place of the water, with a little salt, and the rice simmered for an hour or more, till every grain has burst, and the milk is absorbed. Now add, when cool, four eggs, a bit of butter, sugar, and a little nutmeg or cinnamon. This makes an excellent baked or boiled pudding : and, leaving out the sugar, and spice, and eggs, and adding more salt, is a good vegetable dish.

STEWED-RICE THICKENED.

Boil or stew in a bake-kettle your rice, and milk as above, keeping a few hot embers above and below it. When nearly ready, mix a large table-spoonful of fine flour with some cold milk, in a basin, and stir into the rice, and let it boil up for five or ten minutes.

This may be sweetened, or eaten with salt, and is an excellent dish. To make it a savoury dish, put butter, salt and pepper, leaving out the sugar.

INDIAN-RICE IN SOUP.

The Indians use the parched rice in their soups and stews, which are chiefly made of game, venison and wild fowl. As an ingredient in fresh soup it is very good, but must be well soaked and carefully picked. Many persons prefer the wild rice to the white Carolina rice, in venison-soup.

Note.—The wild rice, commonly called Indian Rice, is by botanists called Water Oats (*Zizania aquatica*). The flower-stem comes up sheathed in a delicate green, hollow, membraneous leaf, and displays the elegant awned flowers : from these the anthers depend, of a delicate straw colour and purple, which have a most graceful effect, waving in the wind. The upper or spiked part is the one that bears the seed : as the flowers approach maturity, the green, grassy leaves fall back from the stem, and float upon the surface : they are no longer needed to protect the fruit.

BUCKWHEAT.

This grain is grown in Canada for the fine flour which is used as an article of food in the form of pancakes. It is the same grain that at home is known by the name of French-wheat ; and in some counties of England, by the name of Branck. In England it is chiefly grown for feeding of fowls and game. In France I have heard it is used by the peasants as bread, probably in the way that the Canadians use it, as pancakes. Buckwheat is of easy culture : it is sown late, and cut early. Hogs are fed with it, in the straw : sometimes it is sown by the farmer to enrich the soil, by being ploughed down whilst in flower.

When intended as a crop for harvesting, it is cut and bound in sheaves, thrashed and ground into flour, which must be sifted with a fine sieve, as the husky part is quite black, and any portion mixing with the flour would render it unsightly. I will now give the best receipt for cooking

BUCKWHEAT PANCAKES.

The usual mode of preparing this favourite article of food, which the Americans and Canadians consider a national dainty, is as follows:

Take about a quart or three pints of the finely-sifted flour, mix to a batter with warm milk or water, a teaspoonful of salt, and half a teacupful of good barm : beat it well for a few minutes, till it is smooth, and leave it in a warm place all night, covered in an earthen pot or tin-pail, with a cover. In the morning have ready your griddle or frying-pan, wiped clean, and some lard or butter, made quite hot ; into this drop a large spoonful or small teacupful at a time, of your light batter, till your pan be full, but do not let them touch: if the lard be very hot, the pancakes will set as you pour them in, and be well shaped, and as light as a honey-comb : fry of a light brown, and turn them ; lay them on a hot plate, and serve quite hot, with maple molasses, treacle or butter.

If the batter have worked sour, melt half a teaspoonful of saleratus or soda, and stir in.

The buckwheat pancakes should be served hot and hot to table. Buckwheat pancakes are a favourite breakfast-dish with the old Canadian settlers.

These pancakes may be raised by mixing in three teaspoonfuls of the baking powder, just before frying, instead of using yeast to ferment the batter.

OATMEAL PANCAKES.

Mix one part of flour with three parts of oatmeal, and set with warm water and a little salt, into a thin batter ; add a little barm, and let it rise ; pour your batter on a hot, well-greased griddle or frying-pan, or drop into hot lard, as in buckwheat pancakes.

It is a mistake to suppose that oatmeal or buckwheat-flour will not rise. I believe that the flour of any grain will rise and make leavened bread, and, in scarcity of wheaten flour, a mixture may be made to great advantage, of rye, maize, oatmeal, or barley-flour. At all events, it is well to know how to make good food out of the inferior grains. The English peasantry who live on the best wheaten flour, are not more healthy, and hardly so strong in muscle, as the natives of Scotland and Ireland, whose diet is chiefly oatmeal and potatoes. Most medical men agree in the opinion, that brown bread, or bread with a part of the bran left in, is much more conducive to health, unless to very weakly persons of lax habit, than the pure white bread ; and that were brown bread more common as a staple article of diet, there would be fewer calls upon them for medicines.— Habitually costive persons should adopt the constant use of brown bread, and abstain as much as possible from white bread, especially bakers' bread, in the composition of which alum and other astringents are often introduced.

OAT-MEAL PORRIDGE.

This wholesome dish is prepared as follows :—

Have ready boiling water, as much as will be required for your family ; into this throw some salt ; experience will guide you in the quantity, for it must depend upon taste, and the necessity for a large or small cooking. Have ready your oatmeal in a dish or basin, and a thick wooden round stick, which any boy can make for you with a good knife, and smoothing it off with a spoke-shave or a bit of glass. While you throw the meal slowly into the boiling water with one hand, keep stirring it with the stick with the other, till your porridge is thick and smooth ; then let it boil for about ten minutes, and serve it in plates, with a cup of milk to each person. Some, however, prefer butter to eat with it, others molasses : it is a matter of taste and convenience.

MILK-PORRIDGE WITH OATMEAL

is made as above, only substituting milk for water, and less oatmeal. In making milk-gruel, it is better to mix the meal in a basin, smoothly, with water, and when the milk in the pot boils, pour and stir in the mixture.

Children are fond of this dish for supper and breakfast, and it is nourishing, light and wholesome, unless there be acidity of stomach ; then it is not so good, as oatmeal has a tendency to create heartburn, when the digestion is deranged.

OAT CAKE.

It would seem presumptuous in an Englishwoman to give a recipe for making Oat-cakes. The North of England people know how to make them. The Scots and Irish are famous for them, and the inhabitants of the South, East and West of England would not eat them.

In Canada they are made by all classes of Irish and Scotch—some the plain, old-fashioned way, and others with shortening, as butter or lard. I like them best with a good deal of butter in them ; they are less hard, and, I think, more palatable : and some put soda in the water, which I have been recommended to try. I have seen persons in ague, throw a handful of toasted or fresh oatmeal into a jug of cold water, and take it, not as a cure, but as a drink in the fever. I have seen very good results, in violent pains in the body alleviated, by oatmeal made hot in the oven or pan, slightly sprinkled with water to create a steam, put in a flannel-bag or a coarse cloth, and applied to the sufferer : or an oat-cake toasted and wrapped up in a damp cloth, laid over the stomach. Simple as such remedies are, in case of sudden illness it is well to remember them, especially in a country where doctors are few and far off, besides being very expensive visitors in a poor emigrant's log-house or shanty.

I might enumerate many other uses to which oatmeal can be put, and furnish a long list of dishes in which it figures as a principal ingredient, but these hardly belong to my plan : therefore I leave Oatmeal to more experienced housewives, and proceed to give instructions on the cultivation and uses of

INDIAN-CORN.

With the exception of wheat, there is not a more valuable grain, or one more various and valuable in its uses to man, than Indian-corn. It enters into the composition of many most nourishing and excellent compounds, and is equally palatable and wholesome in its green or ripened state, as food for man or the domestic animals about his homestead : while the wild creatures gather their portion, from the big black bear, down to the active and predaceous chipmunk. It comes amiss to none of God's creatures, and if it costs some labour to plant and harvest, it amply repays the care bestowed upon it. There are seasons when it does not arrive at perfection, as in the cold, wet harvests of 1835, 1836, and 1837, but those were years when the wheat grew in the sheaves, and grain of all kinds was with difficulty brought to perfection.

Even when the Indian-corn does not succeed so well, it still produces a great amount of sweet and nourishing food for animals, and though the grain may not come to its fullest state of perfection, it will be equally good for cattle, and the fattening of swine; so that after all, the loss is really not so great, as the failure in any other of the green crops would be.

CULTURE OF INDIAN-CORN.

The best soil is light, good loam, and lands that have been cultivated for some years, open and sunny, rather than the virgin soil of new lands : in the latter case the plant is apt to be too rank, running more to straw than grain. Indian-corn will bear soil well manured.— The best sort of corn (of which, however, there are many varieties) is the yellow eight-rowed corn, i. e. eight rows of grain on each cob. You will see varieties in the colour of the grain on the same cob ; such as pale straw color, white and yellow, sometimes red, and even bluish green ; but a good unmixed seed is better.

The time of planting is generally from the 20th to the 25th of May, though I have often known it planted as early as the 18th, in very warm dry seasons. The greatest danger the young plant has to encounter, is frost, which often nips the tender, green blade, when it is some inches above the ground.

Some persons steep the grain twelve or sixteen hours before planting, but this should only be done when the sowing has been retarded, to hasten vegetation, and if the ground be very dry. If the soil be wet from recent rains, it is not prudent to steep the seed, as it is liable to rot in the ground, and never come up.

The corn dropper should be supplied with a lap bag, of coarse canvas, tied round the waist, or slung across the shoulders, the mouth being wide enough to admit the hand freely ; or a basket with two handles on one side, and one on the outer side ; through these handles straps are passed, which are slung over the left shoulder, the basket hanging a little under the left arm, which arrangement admits of the readiest access to the corn with the right hand : the outside handle serves for the dropper to steady the basket. One person should open the earth slightly with the hoe, into which four grains of corn are dropped, in a square of about two inches, as near as possible, from each other : the person who hoes, then draws the earth over the corn. Some merely let the grains fall on the surface, while the other covers them with earth, forming a slight hill over them : others again draw a furrow, and plant the corn in rows, at certain distances. These things are better learned by experience, and the advice of old settlers—sound, practical men, who have no interest in misleading the inexperienced emigrant.

The distance in planting corn, when it is the usual hill culture, is three feet from hill to hill, and three feet from row to row. Some allow a few inches more, considering that the plant having more space and air, repays them by an increase of luxuriance. The first hoeing generally takes place when the plant is about a foot high, when the earth is drawn towards the stems of the plants, and stirred well about them. The next hoeing should be before the plant begins to run up to flower. Where the fields are free of stumps, a one-horse plough is generally preferred to the hoe, as being a great saving of labour, and equally efficacious in earthing up the corn. Some cross-plough, but I do not think this is very often practised. Women and children take great part in the culture of the corn-crop, especially in the bush-farms, where the roots and stumps obstruct the plough, and the hoe alone can be made use of. Pumpkins are usually planted along with Indian-corn : the broad leaves of the pumpkin spreading over the ground, serves to shade it, and retain its moisture for the benefit of the Indian-corn, acting as a sort of wet-nurse to the tender plant.

The pumpkin-seed is planted in every other hill, and in every other row ; which allows free space for the plants to run over the ground, without choking each other.

Some farmers remove the unfruitful shoots and suckers from the stem of the plants, that are thrown up ; while others, who regard the fodder for their cattle as a matter of importance, think that they lose more than they gain.

As soon as the grain begins to fill with milk, and has acquired some substance, it is fit for the table ; but the white, sweet, garden-corn is best for cooking, and should be cultivated for that purpose, instead of robbing your field-crop.

The first week in October is the usual time for harvesting Indian-corn, which is done by cutting it near the root, or pulling it : it is then set round in bundles, so as to form a large circular stook, which is tied with a band at the top, and these stooks are left to dry in the field till the farmer has leisure to house them. The common way is then to pull the cobs off the stalk, and throw them in heaps, when they are carted home to the barn or corn-crib.

The corn-crib should be raised from the ground, and made of logs or boards, close enough to keep out squirrels, but so as to admit the air, which is essential to its keeping well. The crib is made small at bottom, and wide at top, and roofed over.

Before threshing, it is necessary to husk the corn, which is simply stripping off the fine sheathing that surrounds the cob or ear ; to effect this, "Husking Bees" are often called. Neighbours and friends, especially young folks, meet and sit round, and pull off the husk.— The meeting usually ends in an evening frolic, a dance and supper.— This is seldom had recourse to excepting by the small farmers.

The choicest cobs should be selected for seed : these are only partially husked ; the husk that remains is turned back, and the cobs are braided together in ropes, and hung across a pole or beam, to be kept against the spring. When rasping your seed-corn, break off about an inch or more from the cob, as the grains at the end of the cob are not so fine, or fit for planting, as the rest.

There are various ways of thrashing Indian-corn, but the usual method is simply with the flail ; some tread it out with horses, on the barn floor. This is an ancient mode of thrashing, practised in the East, and also in Portugal and Spain. The first crop of Indian-corn I ever saw, was rasped by means of a bit of iron-hoop, set in the edge of a barrel ; but this was a slow process. In the States there are machines on purpose for rasping corn, that work very expeditiously, and are a great saving of labour.

Four quarts of good seed will plant an acre of bush land, with the stumps on it : six quarts are allowed for old land, where the ground is not encumbered by stumps or trees.

I have been particular in describing, as minutely as I could, all these things relating to the cultivation of this crop, so universally grown in Canada; for though it is not often left to the management of females, yet such things have sometimes occurred through sickness or accident befalling the head of the family, that the work or the direction of it, has fallen upon the wives and daughters of the farmer.

I have known women in Canada, who have not only planted and hoed the corn, but have also harvested it.

I knew the wife of an officer, who had settled on a government grant in the backwooods: she was a young woman who had never been accustomed to any other work than such light labour as the most delicate female may take pleasure in, such as the culture of flowers, and making pastry and preserves, and such matters; but of laborious work she knew nothing. Well, it so happened, that her female servant, her husband, and also the man-servant, all fell sick with intermittent fever: in a few days both the man and the maid went home to their own friends, and this young wife, who was also a mother, and had a baby of ten months old, was left to nurse her sick husband and the child, and do all the work of the house. At first she was inclined to fret, and give up in despair, but when she looked upon her sick husband and her helpless babe, she remembered that duty required better things from her than to lie down and weep, and lament: she knew that other women had their trials, and she braced up her mind to do what was before her, praying to God to give her strength to do her duty, and she went on cheerfully and with a brave spirit.

The spot where these people lived was very lonely; it was a new clearing in the forest, and there were not many settlers near them: it is now full eighteen years ago, and emigrants were not as well off then as they are now in their new settlements, and often had to put up with great privation, and encounter great hardships.

Besides a few acres of fall wheat, they had half an acre of Indian corn, on which they depended in part for food for the household, and also for fatting some pigs for winter meat.

The corn was just ripe, for it was the last week in September; the great golden pumpkins showed like gigantic oranges on the ground, between the rows of ripened corn; but, alas! the fence was not very secure, and the hogs of a settler about half a mile off, came through the woods and destroyed the corn.

The blue jays, and the racoons from the forest, came to share in the spoil; the grain was fast diminishing, which was to have done so much for the support of the little household. The poor wife looked at her fever-stricken husband, and at her baby boy; neither could help her, and at first she hesitated before she could decide upon which plan to pursue. However she left plenty of cooling drink by the bed-side of her sick partner, and with baby in her arms she set out to the field;

fortunately it was close at hand, just beside the garden. She spread a shawl on the ground at the foot of a pine tree that stood on the clearing, and setting up an umbrella to shade the little one from the heat of the sun, she set to work on her task of gathering the corn. She soon became interested in the work, and though her soft hands, unused to rough labour, were blistered and chafed, in a few hours she had stripped the cobs from a large portion of the corn, and thrown them into heaps, running back from time to time to speak to her baby, and amuse him by rolling towards him the big yellow golden pumpkins, with which in a short time she had effectually fenced him round, while the little fellow, shouting with joy, patted and slapped the cool rind of the orange-coloured fruit with his fat white hands, and laughed with infant glee.

Between gathering the corn, playing with the baby, and going to visit her sick husband, she had enough to do.

She next brought out some large Indian baskets, into which she gathered up her corn. At sunset she dragged her little one home, mounted in great state on the top of one of the loads; weary enough she was in body, but well satisfied in mind, at her day's work.

In this way she harvested and housed her first crop of Indian corn. Her husband was well enough to aid in storing the pumpkins by the time her task was finished.

In after years she has often with honest pride related to her children, how she gathered in the first Indian corn crop that was raised on their bush farm. Possibly this very circumstance gave a tone of energy and manly independence of spirit to her children, which will mark them in their progress in after life.

I will now proceed to giving some improved recipes for the cooking of Indian corn.

HOMINY.

This is the Indian name for a preparation of corn either slightly broken in a crushing mill, or whole. The whole corn is steeped for some hours, twelve at least; it is then boiled in what is commonly called white lye, which is made with a small portion of ashes tied up in a cloth, or a clean bag, but a large tea-spoonful of salaratus, or a bit of pearlash would, I think, answer as well or better than the ashes, and be less trouble. Drain off the water when the corn has boiled an hour or so, and lay the corn on a pan before the fire to dry. When the fine skin begins to strip a little, put it into a clean bag, and beat it till the scales fall off. Sift or fan the bran away, rubbing it through your hands. When clean, return it to the pot, and boil it with plenty of water for six or eight hours, keeping it closely covered till it is quite soft. This dish is eaten with milk, or with meat seasoned with pepper and salt. If to be eaten as a vegetable, a piece of meat may be boiled with the corn; but if too salt, the meat should be steeped and parboiled.

INDIAN-CORN.

When hominy is made of crushed c⟨ ⟩ it may be steeped and then pressed through a coarse sieve : the scales will float, and can be skimmed off. The water must be kept to boil the hominy in, as it contains the flour. This must be boiled many hours, and is eaten with milk.

SUPPORNE.

This is a thick sort of porridge, made from Indian meal, very similar to oatmeal porridge, only it is boiled rather longer. The sifted Indian meal is sprinkled into the boiling water, and stirred quickly,— rather more salt is used than for oatmeal porridge,—and when boiled about twenty minutes, is taken up in a dish, and is eaten with milk, sugar, butter, or any other seasoning that is prepared. If there be any left from the breakfast or supper, it may be cut (for it becomes quite solid when cold) in slices an inch thick, and fried for breakfast, and buttered hot, or eaten with meat gravy.

Supporne to the Americans and Canadians is what oatmeal porridge is to the Scotch and Irish. It is the national dish, and very good and wholesome food it makes. One bushel of Indian meal will go as far as two of flour in puddings and cakes, bread and porridge, as it absorbs a great deal more water or milk, swells in bulk, and satisfies the appetite sooner. Supporne is better for long boiling.

MILK SUPPORNE.

A very nice sort of hasty pudding is made in the following manner : —to three handfuls of Indian meal add one of wheaten flour, and mix them well : set on the fire a quart of sweet milk and a pint of water, with a tea-spoonful of salt. As soon as the milk and water boils, throw in and stir your flour and meal, and let them boil a few minutes, fast. After the meal has been all stirred in, if not quite thick enough, you can throw in a little more meal,—remove from the stove or fire, and let it simmer on a few embers on the hearth, or on the outside of the stove, for a quarter of an hour longer, or even half an hour. This needs no seasoning otherwise than the salt that you put in, and is very delicious, being richer and more satisfying than the common supporne. It makes a good pudding for children, and, if seasoned with nutmeg or cinnamon, four or five beaten eggs, and sweetened, it is an excellent baked or boiled pudding.

GREEN CORN.

Green Corn can be preserved by simply turning back the husk, all but the last thin layer, and then hanging it in the sun or in a very warm room. When it is to be used boil it soft, and then cut off the cob and mix it with butter. The summer sweet corn is the proper kind.

Another is to par-boil sweet corn : cut it from the cobs and dry it in the sun, then store it in a cool dry place, in a bag for use.

GREEN CORN PATTIES.

Twelve ears of sweet corn grated, one tea-spoonful of salt, and one of pepper, one egg beaten into two table-spoonfuls of flour; mix, make into small cakes, and fry brown in butter or sweet lard.

GREEN CORN FRITTERS.

One tea-cupful of milk, three eggs, one pint of green corn grated, a little salt, and as much flour as will form a batter. Beat the eggs, the yolks, and whites separate. To the yolks of the eggs add the corn, salt, milk, and flour enough to form a batter. Beat the whole very hard, then stir in the whites, and drop the batter a spoonful at a time into hot lard, and fry them on both sides, of a bright brown colour.

BOILED CORN.

This is a favourite dish in Canada and the States. When the grains are sufficiently swollen and beginning to harden, but not to become hard, break off the cob, and boil for two hours or till they become tender. Some like corn best boiled with salt at meat, but that is a matter of taste or convenience. As a vegetable it is much admired, especially the sweet garden corn: the grain of this is of milky whiteness, and is very nice even in its corn state, being full of rich, *sugary* milk. It is of green *sweet* corn that the preceding dishes are made.

Some people cut the grains from the cob and boil them like peas, with butter and pepper for seasoning; this obviates the ungraceful mode of eating corn so much objected to by particular persons.

STEWED CORN.

This is a nice dish: cut the corn from the cob, boil for an hour and a half, reducing the liquid that you boil it in to a quart; cut some slices or steaks of any fresh meat, adding young onions, carrots, and sweet herbs, with pepper, salt, and a couple of tomatoes cut up; stew till the vegetables are tender. Should the gravy be too much reduced in quantity, add a little boiling water or cream.

FRIED CORN.

Green sweet corn fried in butter and seasoned is excellent: the corn should be boiled first till tender.

INDIAN MEAL PANCAKES.

Make a batter with one part flour, and three parts Indian meal, a little salt, and some warm (not hot) water or milk, half a tea-spoonful of salaratus dissolved in butter-milk if you have any, if not, milk will do, if sour so much the better; stir into your bowl or pan with the batter, and beat it a few minutes; heat your griddle or frying pan quite hot, with butter or lard, and drop in your pancakes. As soon as browned on one side turn them : keep them from burning by adding a little more fat or melted butter. Strew sugar on the surface as you lay them on the dish. Some butter them hot, and sift sugar also. These pancakes are far lighter for the stomach than flour pancakes.

It is a simple dish—easily made—very economical—and makes a wholesome variety at dinner or supper. A handful of currants strewn in, or a few ripe garden currants makes them nicer, or eaten with preserved apples where you have an orchard, and fruit of this kind is plentiful.

INDIAN MEAL PUDDING WITH MEAT.

This is a good substantial dinner when you have fat meat in the spring, and no vegetables. Mix Indian meal, seasoned with salt, to a thick batter with hot water or cold milk, add a little tea-spoonful of soda, but it is not indispensable ; grease your bake-kettle or stove-pan, pour in your batter, stirring it well, slice some ham or fat bacon, pepper them, (a grate of nutmeg is an improvement if you have it at hand,) and lay them on the batter. Your slices of meat must not be very thin : half an inch thick at least. When the meat is brown on one side, turn the slice, and if done too quickly, remove to a hot dish and keep them covered up till the pudding is done. Some do not put the meat in till the batter is well set, but the pudding is best when both are done together. The Indian meal absorbs the fat from the meat without tasting greasy, and a very savoury and relishing dish is made out of very homely ingredients. Fresh meat, a small joint of mutton or beef, can be thus cooked, the pudding making an excellent addition to the dinner ; and by this mode of cooking a small portion of meat will give an ample provision for a large family.

INDIAN POUND CAKE.

8 eggs, beaten, 1 pint of powdered sugar, 1 pint of sifted Indian meal, ½ a pint of fine flour, ½lb. of butter ; stir the butter and sugar to a cream, beat the eggs apart, stir the meal and flour to the eggs and sugar and butter, add nutmeg and lemon peel, or essence of lemon, with a glass of wine and brandy ; butter a flat pan or little tart tins, and bake. This may be eaten the same day or as soon as cold.

INDIAN TEA-CAKE.

A pint basinful of Indian-meal sifted, four well-beaten eggs, a tea-cupful of butter melted, a cupful of sugar, and a table-spoonful of treacle or molasses, (but if you have none, this last can be omitted ; the cake will be good without, though it looks richer,) a table-spoonful of carraway seeds, or a cupful of currants ; a teaspoonful each of ginger and nutmeg grated, and half a teaspoonful of salt. Dissolve a teaspoonful of soda or salaratus, in some milk, and mix these ingredients to a pretty thick batter; bake in a stove pan, in a brisk oven. When done, cut the cake into squares: it should be about two inches thick when baked.

This is a very nice cake, quickly made, and is rich and light, without injuring the digestion.

A fine cake can be made of Indian-meal, eggs, butter, molasses and ginger, with soda and sour milk or cream.

Allspice makes a good seasoning for a plain cake; and dried garden-currants or huckleberries are good put in.

INDIAN-MEAL BREAKFAST-CAKES.

One quart of sifted Indian-meal, one handful of fine flour, three eggs well beaten, a cup of yeast, one teaspoonful of salt, one quart of milk made pretty hot; put in the yeast, eggs and salt, and then stir in your meal. Mix into a batter overnight, adding in the morning a little pearl-ash, or soda or saleratus, just before baking, but be careful to roll and dissolve before putting it to your batter, and stir it well through.

Pour the batter on a hot, buttered griddle, and turn when browned on the under side: serve hot.

JOHNNY-CAKE.

One quart of Indian-meal: two tablespoonfuls of molasses, or a cup of coarse sugar; one cup of butter melted, a teaspoonful of salt, and one of ginger; two eggs: make these ingredients into a batter with scalding water or milk: pour the batter into a flat pan, and bake brown: cut in squares, and serve hot with butter or preserves.

PLAIN JOHNNY-CAKE.

Take a quart of sour milk or buttermilk, to which add as much soda or pearl-ash as will make it froth up well; thicken this milk with Indian-meal; add a little salt; pour the batter into a flat pan, and bake it brown; cut in pieces, and eat it hot with butter or molasses. A few seeds are an improvement to Johnny-cake.

BAKED INDIAN MEAL PUDDING.

Scald a quart of milk, and stir in seven or eight table-spoonfuls of Indian meal, a little salt, sugar or molasses to sweeten it, a cup of beef or veal suet, nicely shred, a teaspoonful of ginger or any spice you prefer, a tea-cupful of currants or chopped apples, and four eggs beaten to froth; sprinkle a little fine suet on the top and grate a little nutmeg.

PLAIN INDIAN PUDDING.

The same as above, only omitting the eggs and fruit. The same pudding may be boiled instead of baked, but the cloth must be tied so as to allow of the meal swelling, and requires to be boiled two or three hours.

INDIAN PUDDING TO EAT WITH MEAT.

This is simply a batter, made with Indian meal, a little salt, and scalding milk or water, tied up, not too tightly, and boiled three hours.

INDIAN-MEAL YORKSHIRE PUDDING.

Make a batter of Indian meal, with milk and two or three eggs, and pour into the pan, when you are roasting beef, pork, mutton, or any fresh meat: it absorbs the gravy, and is very nice. It is as well to pour off some of the gravy before you put your batter in with the meat, as it is apt to rob the meat of all that runs from it. When you serve the meat, pour over it the reserved gravy, made hot.

INDIAN FRUIT PUDDING.

Make your batter with hot milk, a little suet, shred fine, or butter rubbed with the meal, six eggs, and a pint of any green or ripe fruit, (as currants, gooseberries, cherries, huckleberries, or apples chopped fine,) a little sugar, and a tea-spoonful of salt; boil for two hours, or longer if your pudding be large.

CORN STARCH.

This is a most truly valuable article of diet, as well as being used in the dressing of fine linen. It is prepared in the United States, and sold in all Canadian stores, in packets, on which are printed directions for using it.

It is quite as palatable as arrow-root—much cheaper—and as easily prepared. As diet for the sick, it is very valuable; and also for young children. It would form a most admirable sea-store for emigrants.—A half pound packet of this fine light powder costs 7½d., or a York-shilling. It makes delightful custards and puddings.

CORN-STRAW BEDS AND MATS.

The sheathing which envelopes the grain of the Indian corn is often used for filling beds, or loose mattrasses, to put below feather beds; and is preferred by many people to straw or any other material. The best method of preparing it is this:—after the corn has been husked, or the cob stripped of the dry sheath that protects it, take a few nails and drive them quite through a piece of board,—the bottom of an old box will do for the purpose: the nails must project so as to present the points an inch or two beyond the surface, and several, say six or eight, must be driven in so as to form a sort of comb, having a double row of teeth. Gather up a handful of the dry husks, and draw them quickly across the nails so as to tear them into strips: with a little practice this work can be carried on very quickly. A bag of coarse brown linen, with an opening in the middle seam, large enough to admit of a person's hand, and furnished with strings or large buttons, is the best receptacle for the straw. The persons who makes the beds stirs the contents of these mattrasses by putting in her hand. Mats for laying under beds are also made by braiding the sheathing into thick ropes, and sewing them together with a wooden needle or a large iron needle, with an eye large enough to admit of a single blade of the husk being threaded through it. This is then tied ; but those who do not care for the trouble of constantly threading and tying, use twine, or the tough inner part of the cedar tree.

Round and oval mats are made for the doors, of the corn sheathing. The rough ends of the husk are left projecting about an inch. The braid is made in this fashion :—you take nine blades of the sheathing and tie them at the top, to keep your work from coming undone : the braid is the simple three ply ; but you use three blades together, instead of one. To make it thick enough, every time you come to the left side, insert there a fresh blade, leaving a little bit of the end to project at the edge. About twenty yards is sufficient for a door mat : it is sown together with the big needle, and twine or bark. Children can be taught to make these things ; and they cost nothing but the time, and can be made of an evening or on wet days, when other work cannot be attended to.

This is one among the many uses to which this valuable plant can be applied : even the cobs themselves are of service after the grain has been taken from them. They make excellent corks for bottles ; and a bag of them of all sizes should be kept for such purpose. Burnt slowly in the smoke-house, the corn-cob is in high repute, as affording the finest flavouring for hams and bacon ; and burnt to fine white ashes, they afford a very excellent alkali for raising gingerbread, and other cakes. I have seen Canadian housewives make a pure white ley of the ashes, for that purpose.

POTATOES.

The most common method of planting potatoes in the new soil, is in hills : on the older farms, in ridges, earthed up by the means of a single-horse plough. The potato is set all through the month of May and the early part of June, and even later than this ; but the earlier they are planted, the better chance you will have of a fair crop.

In the bush-farms potatoes are generally planted in hills : the method is simple. One person drops the seed on the ground, at a distance of sixteen or eighteen inches apart, and two feet between the rows : another follows, and with a hoe, draws the earth each way over the set : some flatten the top of the hill with the hoe, and shape them like little mole-hills. When the shoot breaks the ground, and the leaves expand, the earth is again drawn up to the plant. In the fresh virgin soil, once hoeing is all the crop receives ; but in gardens, we give the potatoes a second, and sometimes a third hoeing. The hills are preferred in new clearings, where the roots and stumps would prevent the ridges from being straight, and interrupt the ploughing. The Irish plan of lazy-beds is seldom practised in Canada, unless it be to improve a piece of turfy or weedy soil. The field-crop of potatoes is seldom fit for use before August, but earlier sorts may be planted in the garden for table, which will be fit in July. The sorts usually set are early kidneys, for garden culture. Pink-eyes, the common white and red apple potato; rough-skinned purple, and cups, for the main crop. There are many others that I could name. I would advise any settler coming out early in the Spring, to bring a small quantity of good potatoes for seed, in a box of dry sand. New seed will fetch high prices, and pay well if the crop succeeds. There is always an eagerness to obtain new sorts of an approved potato, especially early kinds.

The month of October is the general one for storing the field potatoes, which should be taken up in dry weather. I feel assured that a vast deal of loss, both in quantity and quality, is caused by storing potatoes wet.

The cellar, the root-house, and pits in the ground, are the storing-places. There are objections to the cellarage, as the cellars, which are, for the most part, pits dug under the flooring of the kitchen-part of the log-house, are often too warm, and the potato heats, or exhausts itself, by throwing out sprouts, besides, in the Spring, causing a bad smell and impure air, very injurious to the health of the inmates of the dwelling.

The root-house is better, but requires to be constructed with due attention for excluding the frost. In pitting potatoes, the mode observed by some of the most careful farmers, is this :—the potatoes are suffered to lie spread on the ground, to dry in the sun and wind, as long as possible, during the day : they are then gathered in large heaps, on a dry spot, sandy, if possible, and the ground slightly inclining towards the south, or east : no pit is dug—the potatoes lie on the ground only: over the heap is spread a good quantity of dry litter or straw; on this earth is thrown, about a foot in depth; on this more straw or the dry stalks of the potatoes, and another banking of earth. A few boards placed slanting, so as to throw off the rain, is sometimes added; but the frost seldom penetrates the second layer of straw. Those who have a good safe root-house, or large cellars, seldom pit : but if it is unavoidable, the way I have recommended is the best, for securing this valuable root from the severe frosts of a Canadian winter.

NOTE.—A highly intelligent Scotchman, in our vicinity, tells me that he has found from long experience, the following plan is the best for preserving the quality of the potato :—when taking up the crop, he lays the roots in heaps of eight or ten bushels on the surface, covers them with dry haum and earth, but leaves a vent or space at the top, with no earth on it, to allow the steam that rises from the potatoes to escape, till the cold weather comes on, when the pits are either removed to the root-house or cellar, or secured by an additional quantity of litter, and an outer banking up of earth.

POTATO BREAD.
(See Bread.)

Every body knows how to cook a potato; but every one does not know that it is better to put them on in cold than in warm water, and also, that cutting a slice off the rose-end—in the end which is beset with eyes, will greatly improve the mealiness of the potato. A cup of cold water thrown in a few minutes before they are done, also is good. After the water has been drained off, and the pot returned open to the fire, to dry them for a few minutes, a sprinkle of salt is a decided improvement; then let them be served up as hot as possible.

After dinner, let any potatoes that remain be peeled while yet warm, and set aside for breakfast; sliced and fried, with pepper and salt to season them, or placed whole in the oven or bake kettle, with a little dripping or butter, and made nicely brown, forms a good dish to eat with meat in the morning, and saves the trouble of boiling. In Canadian farm-houses meat is generally cooked twice and sometimes thrice a day. Or the potatoes may be put on the fire in a frying-pan or spider; (this is a convenient little pan with three legs, that is used to fry or stew in, which accompanys all cooking-stoves: it has a comical name; but the little pan is a very convenient utensil;) a little butter, pepper, salt, and a little chopped onion being added, the cook, as she stirs the potatoes, minces them or mashes them fine with the blade of the knife, keeping them from burning by constant stirring, till they are nicely browned. This is a favourite way of cooking potatoes a second time: I learned it from an American lady.

MASHED POTATOES.

Pare the potatoes very free from spots; throw them into cold salt-and-water as you pare them; when all are done, put them into clean, cold water, and boil till soft, carefully skimming the pot: pour off dry; then mash fine, adding a cup of milk or thin cream, and a little more salt, or you may put in a bit of butter: dish, and smooth the potatoes on the top and sides, and put into the oven or before the fire to brown. Cold mashed potatoes, cut in slices an inch thick, and browned in the oven like toast, and buttered, is a nice dish for breakfast.

POTATO SOUP.

Set on the fire, bones of beef, or any fresh meat, with a gallon of water, into which slice onions, carrots, and turnips; a little salt and pepper: boil till the vegetables are soft. Have ready, potatoes finely mashed—a quart basin full; add them to the soup, from which the bones may now be removed; boil an hour, slowly; pass the soup through a colander; if too thick, add a little boiling water or liquor in which meat has been boiled; return the soup after straining it to the pot; shred in a little green parsley and savory; give it a boil up, and serve it with toasted bread. If you have no meat, a piece of butter rolled in flour, will do to enrich the soup instead.

POTATO FISH-CAKES.

This is an excellent dish. If salt cod, or fish of any kind, salted or fresh, be left cold, remove the bones and skin carefully; pound the fish in a clean pot with the beetle, till every piece is separated; if too dry, add a little hot water or melted butter; when thoroughly reduced, and well picked from the bones, add mashed potatoes, nicely seasoned with pepper—some add cayenne, but as children dislike such hot seasoning, it is better omitted in the mass; pound the fish and potatoes till they are well mixed; throw a little flour on a clean board, and taking out a small portion, *mould* it with your hands into a round cake; flatten on the top, and roll it in the flour. When you have a dishful made, fry the fish-cakes in hot dripping, butter, or lard, on a brisk fire: when neatly made and nicely browned, this is a nice way of cooking fish. If fresh fish is used, you must season with a little salt: some persons add an egg and a little finely chopped parsley, when pounding the potatoes and fish. The same preparation put in a deep dish, and browned before the fire or in the oven, is, I believe, called Chowder by the American cooks: it is less trouble, but the fish-cakes both look and eat better.

POTATO-CAKES.

A very favourite cake with the Irish. They are simply made with potatoes boiled very soft, and kneaded with flour and a little salt, rolled thin; cut in squares, and baked quickly. The goodness of this cake depends on the making and baking: some persons use twice as much flour in making them as others. A nicer potato-cake is made by adding a little cream to moisten the potatoes and flour, making the dough stiff and rolling it thin, and working a piece of butter in, as in making pastry; bake lightly in the oven, or fry, and sift over them a little fine sugar.—All potato-cakes are best eaten hot.

POTATO-DUMPLINGS.

Make a dough with mashed potatoes and flour, wetting the mass with a very little milk, to enable you to knead it smooth; make dumplings, and boil in milk. Some boil the dumplings in milk, till the dough is boiled down, and the milk thickened like hasty pudding. This should be done in a bake-kettle placed over a few hot embers, and the lid heated on a clear fire; but it requires great care to keep the milk from scorching : when nicely done, it is a good sort of pudding for children : with the addition of sugar, eggs, and spice, it is as good as custard.

IRISH MASH.

This is not the dish commonly known as Irish stew, but a more economical one ; though certainly very inferior in goodness. It is made with a large quantity of potatoes, seasoned with onion and pepper ; cold meat chopped up and mixed through the potatoes : there is no gravy, or very little, and the dish is rather recommended for its satisfying than its delicate qualities ; nevertheless it is a useful sort of dish where the meat is scarce in a large family.

Many a savoury dish can be made with potatoes and a small portion of meat, either as pie or stew ; but I think it better to confine my recipes to dishes that are more peculiar to the cookery of Canada.

POTATO-STARCH.

As I have before observed, it is a great object with the Canadian settlers to manufacture everything they consume, if it be practicable. The careful emigrant's wife buys no starch ; but makes all she uses, either from potatoes or bran.

Potato starch is the fine flour that is obtained from the potato by grating it down in water.

Pare some large potatoes ; white skinned are preferable to red or purple ; grate them down to pulp on a coarse rasp, or the large-holed side of a bread grater ; let the pulp fall into a pan of clean cold water. When you have reduced all your potatoes by grating, stir the mass well up with your hand ; lay a clean coarse cloth in your colander over a vessel, and strain the whole mass ; squeezing it till the pulp is quite dry. The liquor that remains after the straining must then be left to settle for an hour or more, or till it looks clear, and shows a sediment at the bottom. It may then be poured off, and a second water put on ; stir this, and leave it again for some hours. A third water should be added ; pouring off the former one as before : three waters is generally sufficient. The last time you pour the water off, you will perceive a slightly discoloured crust on the top of your starch, or some of the fine fibrous matter that has passed through : remove it with a clean spoon, and the pure, spotless, white substance below is the starch. This must be taken out, and spread to dry in a warm, sunny place, stirring it very frequently, till the whole is perfectly dry. It may then be put in paper bags, and hung up in a dry room.—Be sure that it is quite dry before bagging it.

Not only does this make the clearest and best of starch for muslins and linens ; but is a good substitute for arrow-root, boiled in milk, either for invalids or babes ; and is valuable in places where delicacies for sick persons cannot easily be procured.

CORN STARCH.

This is an American preparation of Indian corn, which is sold in small packets, in most of the Canadian stores. It is used not only for starching clothes, but as an article of diet; for puddings, custards, and mixed with milk for pap, for very young children. I should think a similar preparation could be made by steeping corn, till it be swelled and fermented; bruising it, and pouring off the white floury sediment, as in potato starch; bleaching it, and drying.

BRAN STARCH.

A large supply of good starch can be made by the following process: steep half a bushel of bran in a clean tub or barrel, pouring over it several pailfuls of water. Let it stand in the sun or in the warm kitchen, till it begins to ferment: this is known by the bran swelling, and throwing up bubbles. At the end of a week, if the weather be very warm, it will ferment; but sometimes it will take a fortnight to sour. Stir the mass well up several times; then strain off squeezing the bran through a canvass cloth, coarse, but quite clean. When the liquor that has been strained has settled, pour off the top, and throw on more fair water; stir up, and again leave it to settle. After repeating the washing process three times, strain once more through a fine sieve or canvass cloth; and when you pour off again, remove the brown, discoloured starch from the surface of the cake that remains in the bottom of the vessel: dry thoroughly, as for potato starch, and tie it in bags for use. Cows or hogs will eat the refuse bran. If you like to blue your starch, it must be done by bluing the last water that you put on, and stirring well; but it is better to blue the water you boil your starch with.

Those who understand the art of dying, use the sour, fermented water that is poured off, in colouring red and scarlet, which are brightened by acid.

PUMPKINS.

This vegetable, or rather fruit, is extensively grown in Canada; being always planted with Indian corn. It is given in the fall of the year to the cattle and swine, which feed upon it eagerly: it is fattening and nourishing, and imparts no bad flavour to the milk, as turnips are apt to do.

Among the old-fashioned settlers, the pumpkin is much esteemed for pies, and a sort of molasses, which they prepare from the fruit by long boiling. When properly made, there is not a better dish eaten than a good pumpkin-pie. Now I must tell you, that an English pumpkin-pie, and a Canadian one, are very differently made, and I must give the preference, most decidedly, to the American dish; which is something between a custard and a cheese-cake, in taste and appearance. I will now give you a recipe or two for

PUMPKIN-PIE.*

Select a good, sweet pumpkin, fully ripe: to ascertain if it be a sweet one, for there is a great difference in this respect, cut a piece of the rind and taste it, or cut several, and then you can judge which is best. The sweetest pumpkins require less sugar, and are much richer.

Pare and cut the fruit into slices, removing the seeds and also the fibrous, spongy part, next to the seeds. Cut it into small pieces, and put it on the fire with about a pint of water, covering the pot close: you are not to bruise or stir it. Should the water boil away so as to endanger the pumpkin burning to the bottom of the pot, a small quantity more of water may be added. It will take three or four hours to boil quite soft, and of a fine brownish yellow. Some improve the colour and richness by setting the pot on a few embers, near the fire, and keeping the pot turned as the pulp browns at the sides: but this requires to be carefully attended to.

When the pumpkin is as soft as mashed turnips, pass it through a hair-sieve or a colander; then add new milk and two or three eggs well beaten, with grated ginger; as much sugar as will make it sweet enough to be pleasant. Pounded and sifted cinnamon is frequently used as spice or nutmeg; but ginger and cinnamon are preferable to any other spice for pumpkin-pies. The milk must not be sufficient to thin the pumpkin too much: it should be about the consistence, when ready for the oven, of finely mashed turnips: if too thin you will need more eggs to set it; but it absorbs a great deal of milk, and is better to stand some little time after the milk is added, before being baked.

Make a nice light paste; line your dishes or plates, and then put in your mixture. These pies are always open; not with a cover of paste over them.

A very rich pumpkin-pie may be made by adding cream, lemon-peel, the juice of a lemon, and more eggs.

A finer dish, than a good pumpkin-pie, can hardly be eaten: and it is within the power of any poor man's family to enjoy this luxury. If you do not grow this fruit, any neighbour will give you one for the asking.

ANOTHER WAY.

Boil your pumpkin, as before directed, for three or four hours; bruise it fine with a beetle, such as you pound potatoes with; mix with new milk, and two or more eggs, as you like: add a little sugar, and ginger or all-spice, and bake in lined tins for half an hour. Some people grate the raw pumpkin on a coarse grater, boil it with

---

* I had this recipe from a Canadian lady who is celebrated for the excellence of her pumpkin-pies. I can vouch for their goodness from my own experience.

a very little water for an hour or so, then add milk by degrees, as long as it will absorb it, keeping it simmering slowly. When well boiled and swelled, let it cool,—when cold, sweeten and season, and bake as in the other receipt.

DRIED PUMPKIN.

Boil down the pumpkin; and when soft, take it out of the pot, spread it on dishes or tins, and set them in the sun or under the stove to dry. When quite dried, pack in paper bags, and hang up in a dry room. This mode will enable you to make pumpkin-pies at any season, when required. Steep it in milk, till it swells and softens, and make your pies as usual.

Some cut the pumpkin in rings, and hang up to dry in the kitchen; but it is apt to mould and turn black: possibly, if dried at once in the sun outside the house, or at night in the oven, it would keep better.

PUMPKIN-MOLASSES.

This article is made by boiling down a quantity of ripe pumpkin for many hours, expressing the juice, and then boiling it down to molasses syrup.

SQUASH.

This is a vegetable of the gourd tribe of plants, and is in much repute with many of the Canadians. It grows very luxuriantly in the new bush-soil without any need of manure. The seeds are either set in a hollow basin, one or two in a place, or on hills; but hollows are considered preferable, as the loose soil dries too much. The same may be observed with respect to cucumbers and melons in new gardens.

Squashes are of various kinds and qualities, and are boiled green, like the vegetable-marrow, or mashed like turnips, with milk and pepper and salt. Squashes, when ripe, are made into pies, in the same manner as pumpkins.

In old gardens manure is necessary for the growth of all this tribe of plants. A good hot-bed for squashes or cucumbers may be made by piling the weeds and rubbish, dried leaves and stalks of vegetables, and covering the mound with several inches of fine mould. On this set your seeds, and you will have a fine crop; besides covering an unseemly object, and making an excellent bed, of the finest soil, for flowers or vegetables of any sort requiring good, rich, mould.

CUCUMBERS AND MELONS.

(Plant, if in open ground, from 18th to 25th May.)

Both these fruits can be raised in Canada without the trouble of making hot beds, and sheltering them with frames, provided your soil be rich enough, and the young plants are protected from the late frosts, which will sometimes, even in the latter part of May, cut both corn and the tender leaves of the melon. It is not commonly the case, but it has happened even in the early part of June. In general the seeds are put in about the 20th of May, and if you wish to bring them on safely, place a square of bricks about each plant : on this lay a pane of glass. Glass costs very little in Canada. This will serve as a frame-light, and you may open and close it at will. Water your plants, and keep the glass over them at night, or till your plants no longer require such care. Spread a little fine hay over the ground between the plants : this will keep in moisture to the roots, and help ripen the fruit. A bit of slate or glass is sometimes laid beneath the fruit to attract the sun's ray. I have seen splendid melons—musk, cantaloupe, rock, and nutmeg-melons brought to great perfection in the open ground, on new soil. If the summer and fall are fine and sunny, which is generally the case in Canada, you may reckon on having ripe melons in plenty with a little care.

The ends of the shoots, of both melons and cucumbers, should be nipped as soon as the plant shows for bloom, this increases the size of the fruit very considerably.

There is a plan that I have seen recommended in horticultural books for growing cucumbers : this is on a frame of sticks, placed close together, slanting like the pickets of a ha-ha fence. On this the vines are trained, and suffered to grow, stopping the length of the end shoots, to keep them from trailing beyond the frame : or the top of a bush set in the ground for them to climb, has also been recommended : the former plan, if more trouble, is certainly the neatest.

MELONS PRESERVED.

Cut a ripe musk or cantaloupe melon in slices,—remove the seeds,—sprinkle a little white sugar on the fruit, and let it stand for an hour. To every pound of fruit allow three-quarters of a pound of sugar, white, it should be ; a dozen cloves, and some ginger, sliced. Now pour off the juice that has run from your fruit,—put it along with the rest of your sugar and spice into a clean skillet or preserving-pan, and boil it up. When boiling put in your melon and boil for half an hour. The peel of a lemon, thinly pared and cut in strips, may be added. The juice of two, squeezed in, greatly improves the preserve, but it may be omitted. This makes a very beautiful-looking preserve, of a fine apricot colour. It is very rich ; but rather too luscious for some tastes.

The citron-melon is grown especially for preserving; and is a very elegant-looking dish on a supper-table.

TOMATOES.

Canada produces this fruit in great perfection. The culture is simple—a bed of light rich mould should be prepared, on which the seed should be sown in the early part of May; a light dressing of wood ashes sprinkled over the bed saves the young plants from the attack of the fly which is very apt to injure the first seed leaves unless guarded against. The tomato is very hardy and bears transplanting well, as the plant grows very large and bushy in a good soil. You must not set out your tomatoes nearer than three or four feet of each other; a border is best, as the sun and light have better access to them than when planted on a bed. I copy a passage from the "Rochester Horticulturist" which may be useful to the Canadian gardener.

The correspondent of the 'Horticulturist' says, "A trellis on which to train the tomato is easily made my setting stakes behind the row of plants, slanting very considerably backwards; on these laths may be nailed a foot apart, or wires may be stretched. Each branch of the tomatoes will need to be tied at first, but afterwards it will be sufficient to run twine from stake to stake in front of them. Mine have been trimmed and trained in that way for many years. The top buds should be shortened to check their growth. The fruit thus treated is remarkably fine in quality and abundant in quantity."

The tomato is used in many different ways as a dinner vegetable, as a sauce, and even as a tart and wine. I will now add the best receipts for dressing it as a vegetable, and for catsup.

TOMATOES PREPARED AS A VEGETABLE DISH.

Gather ripe tomatoes, remove the stalk, lay them in a deep pan, pour boiling water over them, and remove the skins; put them in a sauce-pan with a little salt, a bit of butter, cayenne pepper, or other pepper if preferred, and one table spoonful of vinegar, stew for half an hour. This is a good sauce for roasted meat.

DRIED TOMATOES.

This is for the convenience of having the benefit of the fruit at any season. The tomatoes are skinned and salted, and set into a vessel in a water bath, and stewed for half an hour; the excess of juice may be drained off, which will do for catsup, then spread the pulp on earthen dishes or plates, and dry them gradually in a cool stove or brick oven; when quite dry hang them in bags in a dry room, and soak when wanted to cook for sauce—but they will require seasoning with pepper and butter.

AN EXCELLENT TOMATO SAUCE.

Wash eight dozen ripe tomatoes, place them in an earthen pan, having divided them in one or two pieces, carefully removing any stalk that may adhere, or any blackened or decayed part; over each layer strew some salt, and let them stand for two days: put them in a preserving pan with the liquor, and boil well for fifteen minutes; then pass the pulp through a colander or coarse sieve to separate the skins from the pulp: to this strained juice add 4 oz. mustard seed, 2 oz. whole pepper, 1 ripe red pepper, having removed the seed; 2 oz. whole ginger, 2 oz. allspice, several cloves of eschalot; boil all together till the pulp is reduced to nearly half the quantity, rub it through the colander and press it with a spoon ; a gill of vinegar to wash the pulp clean through from the spices, at last, may be added ; bottle when cold, and cork tight down. Those who can afford it, put a teaspoonful of white wine into each bottle the last thing.

PRESERVED TOMATOES.

To three pounds of fresh ripe tomatoes, add the juice, and finely cut peeling of two lemons; boil together with some sliced ginger for one hour, then add 4 lbs. of lump sugar, and boil half an hour longer. This looks like a fine West India preserve.

TOMATO CATSUP.

Pick the ripest fruit, break them up, and strew a good handful of salt among them, let them stand by for a day and a night, boil them with black pepper, cloves, allspice, a red pepper, and a little onion, or eschalot ; when the tomatoes are reduced to pulp, let them be poured out to cool in an earthen pan.

When the tomatoes are cold put them through a coarse sieve and bottle them for use. The coarser parts may be put with the spice into a jar, and vinegar poured over them. They will make a good sauce for cold meat, or seasoning for soup and stews.

Fasten down your bottles with paper dipped in white of egg, which will exclude the air.

Green Tomatoes are often put into jars of pickles, and I have been told will make tarts, but I think the rank flavour would not be agreeable, or even wholesome. Tomato catsup is used as a sauce for fish or meat, and also as a seasoning to soups and hashes.

When I make Tomato catsup myself, I allow a table spoonful of strong vinegar to every quart of juice, but most persons make it without vinegar.

Any one who has a good cellar may have a supply of the fresh fruit for use, by taking up the plants before they are ripe, and hanging them on a pole head downwards. They can be ripened in a sunny window, or used green.

PRESERVED GREEN FRENCH BEANS.

This is done by gathering the green beans while tender, and throwing them into strong brine, in which a bit of alum is dissolved: fill the vessel, a small cask is best, with the beans till it will hold no more, and is closely packed; lay some straw on the top to keep the beans from floating, and cover them down from the air. Some make no brine, but strew dry salt between the layers of beans:—they should be steeped for some hours to draw out the salt.

LIMA BEANS. *(Time to sow, 18th to 25th May.)*

There are no beans that are more truly valuable to cultivate than the white lima bean; it is a climber, and requires poles to cling to. It is better to be set in hills three feet apart, about four seeds in each hill; three slender poles, seven or eight feet in height, set so as to meet at the top, should be put in at the same time as the seed. With a small hoe earth up the plants when in six or eight leaves, and your labor is done. This bean bears profusely; the crop continues in succession till the oldest beans are ripe. The green beans are very large, and very tender; in moist rich ground they are excellent. The ripe beans are of a pure ivory white colour, flat and kidney-shaped. These beans form a favorite article of vegetable diet in America. The manner of preparing them is as follows:

STEWED BEANS.

Steep the beans, say a quart, in hot water for twenty-four hours, or even longer; boil them, and remove the skins; the water should be changed, and the beans when soft enough, drained and seasoned with pepper, salt and butter. They take three hours to boil soft. Another way is to par-boil a bit of pork, and put it to boil with the beans; then remove the beans to a deep pan or dish, put the pork in the middle, and brown all together in the oven. Beans are a good ingredient in soup, and also as a pudding, made in a similar manner to pease-pudding.

SUBSTITUTES FOR TEA AND COFFEE.

It sometimes happens to persons living at a distance from towns, that their stores of tea and coffee have been exhausted, before a fresh supply can be procured; or the want of ready-money for purchasing these necessary luxuries, has left the poor emigrant to such resources as the herbs of the field offer. Among the old Canadians there are persons intimately acquainted with the virtues of various plants which they frequently make use of instead of tea, and consider them more wholesome than the more palatable Chinese leaf, which we are so accustomed to regard as indispensable to our comfort.

Necessity, no doubt, has taught the old settlers, both in the States and Canada, to adopt certain leaves, roots and berries, as a substitute for the genuine article ; and habit has reconciled them to the flavour. Some attribute valuable medicinal properties to their simple infusions, and, possibly, not without reason. The Indians boil the chips and bark of the sassafras, or spice-wood tree, as a luxury, as well as a medicine, and bring it from distant parts of the country. I once tasted the decoction, and found it very pleasant, besides tasting the bark, which had a fine aromatic flavour, like the nutmeg.

Tinctures, essences, and fermented drinks are in high repute, I have been told, in the States : the sassafras is regarded as a fine purifier of the blood.

There is a species of fern, known by the country people by the name of sweet-gale, and sweet fern : it is woody, growing in a slight, waving bush, about three or four feet from the ground : when the leaves are rubbed they give out a delightful, aromatic, spicy odour, which soon goes off. When boiled, it has a slightly resinous taste, with a bitter flavour, that is not very unpleasant. This sweet-fern is in high repute among the Yankee and old Canadian housewifes, as a diet-drink : they attribute to it many excellent virtues, and drink it as we do tea.

It grows only on very light, sandy soil, by wastes on the road side, or at the edge of pine woods. At dewfall, at night, or early in the morning, this shrub gives out a delightful perfume : it is very elegant in form, and in quality tonic and astringent: it has been recommended as a specific for ague. The botanical name is Comptonia asplenifolia.

CEANOTHERS.—NEW-JERSEY TEA.—MOUNTAIN SWEET.

These are the names of another very pretty and fragrant shrub, with white feathery flowers, that have the scent of the flower we used to call Meadow-sweet, and, Queen of the Meadows. It does not grow in the thick forest, but on open plain-lands, such as the Rice-Lake, Brantford, Monaghan and other open, shrubby lands.

The natives use the leaves of this plant as a substitute for tea.— There is nothing injurious in this plant ; and like the former one, it is tonic and astringent. I have never tasted the tea made from the leaves of this shrub, but I intend to cure some as a trial of its flavour, adopting the method, as near as I can, practised by the Chinese in drying their teas, heating the leaves in a pan for a few minutes, rolling them with the hand, and letting them cool, and heating them again.

The lumbermen use the New-Jersey tea, when out at their work, and also the Labrador-tea.

LEDUM LATIFOLIUM.—LABRADOR TEA.

This very pretty and singular shrub grows chiefly on the low level banks of swampy, half dried-up lakes. There are two kinds ; one that is called marsh rosemary, the leaves bearing a strong resemblance to the shrub rosemary : it has pale, lilac flowers, and bluish-coloured, hard berries, resinous in taste, not unlike juniper-berries in taste and appearance ; but it is the broader-leaved that is used as tea by the lumberers. The under side of the leaves of this plant, are of a deep rust colour, and soft and cottony : the outer surface is hard and dry, of a deep, dull green : the flowers are white, and very prickly : the whole plant has an aromatic scent, which is rather too powerful in the decoction, for it must be boiled for a few minutes.— Some people highly approve of this beverage. I have tasted it, but disliked the resinous flavour.

PINUS CANADENSIS.—HEMLOCK TEA.

The tops of the hemlock are used by some persons as tea, but I think very few would drink hemlock-tea if they could get a more palatable beverage.

As a remedy for a severe cold, I believe a cup or two of hemlock-tea, drunk quite warm in bed, is excellent, as it promotes perspiration; it is also a powerful diuretic, as well as sudorific. Do not be alarmed at the name of *hemlock*; it is not the poisonous plant known by that name, that is here spoken of; but a very beautiful species of pine tree, called the hemlock-spruce, which grows in Canada, in the forests, on poor, rocky soil : it is very hard to cut down, and difficult to burn up : the wood of the hemlock is not much used, it being full of resinous knots, tough and stringy.

There are many other herbs used as tea, but it is better to obtain information from those who are in the practice of testing their qualities.

For substitutes for coffee, the list is endless. Beans, peas, corn, potatoes raw, cut small, and dried to a brown colour, all through ; rye, wheat, and even bread. The very best that I can recommend, is made from the root of the common dandelion.

DANDELION COFFEE.

Dr. Harrison, of Edinburgh, recommended the use of this root, many years ago. It possesses, he says, all the fine flavour and exhilarating properties of coffee, without any of its deleterious effects.— The plant being of a soporific nature, the coffee made from it, when taken in the evening, produces a tendency to sleep, instead of exciting wakefulness, and may be safely used as a substitute for the Arabian berry, (he adds,) "being equal in substance and flavour to the best Mocha coffee." This is going too far : it is the best substitute that has been found, but certainly not equal in flavour to really fine coffee. I will now give my sister, Mrs. Moodie's, recipe for preparing the dandelion-root, and her method of cooking it. "The roots should be carefully washed, but not so as to remove the fine, brown skin which covers them, and which contains the aromatic flavour. The roots, when dry, should be cut up into small pieces, about the size of a kidney-bean, and roasted either in a Dutch-oven, before the fire, or in the stove, stirring them from time to time, to prevent burning : when they are brown through, and crisp, like freshly-roasted coffee, remove them, and let them cool ; grind like coffee. Put a small cupful into the coffee-pot, and pour over it a quart of boiling water, letting it boil again for a few minutes : drunk with sugar and cream, this preparation is very little inferior to good coffee."

"Experience," she says, "taught me that the root of this valuable plant was not so good in the Spring as in the Fall. In new clearings this herb abounds, and grows most luxuriantly in the fine new soil.— The best season to collect it is in the month of October, when the potato-crop is being taken up. To persons residing in the bush, to whom tea and coffee may happen to be an expensive article of consumption, the knowledge of this valuable property in a plant spread so abundantly over their fields, may be very useful."

I can speak to the excellence of the dandelion-coffee, having often drunk it, though I do not think I ever succeeded in making it myself, so well as my sister did. I believe that I scraped as well as washed the root, and thus injured instead of improving the flavour. The addition of a small quantity of good coffee would be an improvement, and would be very economical, as the difference would then hardly be detected, between the substitute and the genuine article. The small haricot-bean, browned, and a small quantity of coffee added to it, gives a respectable imitation. The acorns of the white-oak, browned and ground, are also used.

Before I leave the subject of the dandelion, let me observe that it is sometimes blanched, and used as a salad, instead of endive ; or boiled as a vegetable.

COFFEE.

The best coffee, or what is here *called so*, sells at 1s. 3d. per ℔, in the country stores ; but a better article may be got at 1s. per ℔, in any of the larger towns, and at 10d., unroasted.

"The reason," says an agricultural journal now before me, "that coffee is seldom well made, is, first, the berries are too hastily roasted, or roasted too much : a light cinnamon is their proper colour. Secondly, the coffee is ground too fine ; and thirdly, it is often boiled too much ; by which the bitter principle is extracted, and the finer flavour flies off ; and fourthly not enough coffee is allowed in the pot."

A FEW REMARKS ABOUT BEER.

There is nothing that the new settler complains more feelingly of than the want of good beer and ale. Nobody brews beer in their own homes in Canada. Beer can be got in all towns, it is true ; but it is not, the emigrants say, like the sweet, well-flavoured, home-brewed beer of the English farm-houses. The reason why so few of the Canadians brew their own beer, arises from several causes : first, that there are so few maltsters ; that barley is not very generally grown as a rotation crop : and then, the want of vessels and conveniences for brewing, is an obstacle which it often takes years to overcome ; and by that time, the taste for beer has often unhappily been superseded by that of whiskey. I feel assured that if there were more private families who brewed beer, there would be a thousandfold less whisky drunk in this colony. As there is no prohibition in Canada, against people malting their own barley, I think it would be wise for every farmer to grow a small quantity of this useful grain, and learn the practice of malting it : they might not perhaps, produce at first, as fine a flavoured malt as what they had been accustomed to purchase at home, from the malster ; but one that would supply them with a very palatable beer, and at a very little cost : the hops they can grow in their own garden ; every one cultivates this plant on account of it being an indispensable ingredient in making barm for raising the household bread, besides shading and adorning their verandahs, by its luxuriant foliage and graceful flowers. The bush-settler has, however, little time to attend to malting and brewing ; but those who reside upon old cleared farms, would find no great difficulty in supplying themselves with beer of their own manufacturing, at a small expenditure of time and trouble. Many of the cotters' wives in Suffolk, used to make a cheap sort of beer for the use of their families, from treacle, hops, bran and water, with yeast to ferment it.— This they might also make in Canada. During the very hot weather, some cooling and strengthening beverage is much required by men who have to work out in the heat of the sun ; and the want of it is often supplied by whisky diluted with water, or by cold water, which, when drunk in large quantities, is dangerous to the health, and should, if possible, be avoided.

Instead of the usual allowance of strong beer and harvest-cakes, at four o'clock in the afternoon ; tea or coffee, with bread and butter, pancakes or cakes, are carried out into the field as a refreshment.— They have supper on their return, at seven or eight at night.

There are no harvest frolics held here, as in England. The practice seems altogether laid aside. No gleaners are ever seen in Canadian harvest-fields. Perhaps this very circumstance will show that the poor man does not require such a means of increasing his store : he reaps his own field, and his own hogs and fowls are the gleaners that gather up that which his own hand has scattered.

TREACLE-BEER.

To a five-gallon cask allow four pounds treacle : boil a large handful of hops in a gallon of water, for an hour : strain the liquor off the hops into your cask : add the treacle : fill up with water, to which put one pint of yeast : in two days bottle it, but do not cork till the third : it will be fit to drink in two days after corking.

MAPLE-BEER.

(See that article.)

BEET BEER.

Clean and well scrape and wash six sugar or white beets: cut them in slices, and boil for two or three hours in six gallons of spring water: when the liquor is as sweet as beer-wort, strain it into a small cask: add to this the liquor in which you have boiled down a good handful of hops: when cooled to blood-heat, add a teacupful of good rising: set your cask in a warm place, till the fermentation takes place: when the beer has worked for two or three days, fill up the cask, and set it in a cool cellar: it will be ready in a week or ten days for drinking.

BEET-VINEGAR.

This is made in the same way; only, instead of stopping, let the fermentation go on, and keep the vessel open in a warm place near the fire, for some weeks, and you will have a beautiful vinegar of a fine colour.

BEET-MOLASSES.

Boil down for some hours, white sugar-beets, with one or two blood-beets to colour the liquor of a fine red. When the liquor is very sweet, remove the beets, and strain through a flannel-bag: beat up two eggs, and pour into the beet-syrup, taking care that it be quite cool: return it to the fire; and when the scum rises, remove it carefully: it must now boil fast, and be reduced to a thick syrup, as in maple molasses. Those who dislike the sweetness of the beet-molasses, may sharpen it by adding a little lemon-juice, or the juice of any acid fruit: it is a lovely colour, and, in the absence of other preserve, is useful and wholesome, and costs nothing but the trouble of boiling down.

MAPLE-SUGAR.

This little volume would be incomplete unless it contained some instruction on the making of maple sugar, though the manufacturing of this Canadian luxury, is no longer considered so important a matter as it used formerly to be: the farmer, considering that his time can be more profitably employed in clearing his land, will not give his attention to it, for maple sugar is less an article of trade than it used to be. The West India sugars are now to be bought at 4d per lb., or if you pay a dollar you can get 14 lbs. of good soft sugar. The price of maple sugar is never less than 3d., but 5d. for many years, was the standard price if it were good; now there is little call for maple sugar, muscovado being quite as cheap. Still there are situations and circumstances under which the making of maple-sugar may be carried on with advantage. There will always be a class of emigrants who, for the sake of becoming the proprietors of land will locate themselves in the backwoods, far from the vicinity of towns and villages, who have little money to expend, and who are glad to avail themselves of so wholesome and so necessary a luxury at no greater cost than their own labour.

With the assistance of the children and the females of the house, a settler may, if he have a good sugar bush, make several hundred weight of sugar in a season, besides molasses and vinegar. Many a stout boy of fourteen or fifteen, with the aid of the mother and young ones, has made sugar enough to supply the family, besides selling a large quantity. In the backwoods the women do the chief of the sugar making; it is rough work, and fitter for men; but Canadians think little of that. I have seen women employed in stronger work than making sugar. I have seen women underbrushing, and even helping to lay up and burn a fallow, and it grieved me, for it was unfit for them.

We will suppose that the settler has resolved upon making sugar. The first thing is to look out for a good sugar bush, where he can be sure of a hundred or two hundred of good trees standing not very far from each other. In the centre of his bush he should fix upon a boiling place: a fallen pine, or any large tree should be chosen: if there be not one ready felled, he must cut one down, as he needs a good lasting back log against which to build his fire at the boiling time; but there are other requisites to be attended to: a certain number of troughs, hollowed out of small pine, black ash, basswood, and sundry other kinds of wood; one or more troughs to each tree; if the trees be large, two, and even three troughs are placed, and so many incisions made in the bark with the axe, into which spills of cedar are inserted; these are made with a hollow sort of chisel; but some do not take much pains, and only stick a flat slip of shingle, slanting from the gash in the bark, to direct the flow of the sap to the trough. The modes of tapping are various: some use the augur and bore a hole, which hurts the tree the least ; some cut a chip out across the bark, and cut two sweeping lines down so as to give the sap two channels to flow in; others merely gash the bark with a slanting cut, and insert the spill.

My brother, Mr. Strickland, in his work on Canada, gives very good instructions on this subject.

There should be a large trough hewed out almost as big as an Indian canoe, or barrels, placed near the boiling place for a store trough ; into this the sap is collected: as fast as the smaller ones fill, the boys and women empty their contents into pails, and the pails into the large receptacle. The boiling place is made by fixing two large stout forked posts into the ground, over which a pole is laid, stout enough to support the kettles ; ironwood is good for this purpose ; on this the kettles are hung at a certain height above the fire. A hoop, with a piece of clean coarse serge or flannel sewed over it, serves for a strainer ; the edge of the pots should be rubbed with clean lard to prevent the sap boiling over. It is a common plan, but I think by no means a nice one, to keep a bit of pork or fat bacon suspended by a string above the sap kettles: when the boiling sap reaches this it goes down: but I think my plan is better, and certainly more delicate. If possible have more than one kettle for boiling down; a constant change from the pots facilitates the work: as the first boiling decreases, and becomes sweeter, keep adding from the others, and filling them up with cold sap. A ladleful of cold sap thrown in at boiling point, will keep it down. Attention and care is now all that is required. The one who attends to the boiling should never leave his business; others can gather the sap and collect wood for the fires. When there is a good run, the boiling down is often carried on far into the night. If heavy rain occurs, it is better to empty the sap-troughs, as the sap would be too much weakened for boiling. The usual month for sugar-making is March, though I have known some years in which sugar was made in February. By the middle of April the sap is apt to get sour if kept many hours, and will not grain. If you have sap kept rather long, put salaratus in till it foams a little ; but it is seldom that good sugar is made from acid sap. A handful of quick-lime, some prefer to cure sour sap. The best run of sap occurs when a frosty night is followed by a warm sunny day. If cold weather set in after the trees have been tapped, it is sometimes necessary to tap them a second time.

After the sap has been boiled down to thin molasses, it is then brought in to be sugared off. The syrup must be carefully strained through a woollen strainer ; eggs are then beaten up, with the shells, and poured into the cold syrup, which is now ready for boiling into thick syrup, or ic ugaring off.

Where the su/ bush is far from the house, some persons prefer having a small shanty put up, of logs, and thatched with bark ; it may be built so as to enclose a large stump, to which may be affixed a wooden crane, by means of a socket in which, the upright part of the crane can be made to move ; to the cross beam of the crane the pots can be hung, and a fire, with a few large stones or a great log at the back, fixed, lighted beneath. The advantage of the crane is this : that if the syrup boil too fast to be kept down; by aid of a wooden hooked stick, or a bit of chain affixed to the upper limb, it can be moved forward in an instant from the fire.

Care must be taken to watch the syrup, ladle in hand, till the scum is seen to rise in a thick mass, which it does just a minute or two before boiling commences ; this scum is then to be taken off with a skimmer or ladle, and if this part of the business be well done, the sugar will be good and bright, and clear-looking. It is the want of care in clarifying the sugar, that gives it the dark look and bitter taste that many persons object to in maple sugar. Keep removing the scum, as it rises from time to time ; if it has been well scummed the syrup will look as clear as the finest Madeira wine. Rub the edge of the kettle with clean lard or butter when you first set it over the fire, but do not depend on this preventative for boiling over, as when near sugaring, the liquid is very thick, and rises rapidly. It is prudent always to keep a little cool stuff by you to throw in, should it rise too fast. Towards the close of the boiling, the greatest care and watchfulness is required. When the syrup boils in thick yellow foam, and the whole pot seems nothing but bubbles, the sugar is nearly come ; it then drops ropy from the ladle, and experienced sugar makers can tell by blowing it off the edge of the ladle, if it be done; it then draws into long, bright threads that easily stiffen when cool. Others drop a little into a pail of cold water, when, if it hardens, they say it is ready to pour out into pails or pans, or any convenient vessel. Most persons grease the pans or moulds before they pour the syrup into them, that it may turn out easily.

Much maple sugar is spoiled in its quality by being over-boiled. It is true it hardens more readily, but loses in excellence of grain and colour.

In the course of two or three days the sugar will be formed into a solid cake, and may be turned out ; but if you wish to have a good fine grained sugar, after turning it out of the moulds, pierce the bottoms of the cakes, and set them across sticks, over a clean vessel ; a sugar trough will do, and the wet molasses will drain out, which will improve the look of your sugar, render it easier to break up for use, and removes any coarse taste, so that you may put it as a sweetener into cakes, puddings, tea, or coffee, and it will be as nice as the best muscovado.

The larger coarse-grained maple-sugar, which looks like sugar candy, is made by not over-boiling the syrup, pouring it into shallow pans, and letting it dry slowly in the sun, or a warm room. This I like better than the cake sugar, but it is not so convenient to store. To those who have few utensils or places to put things in, as a sweetmeat for eating, the dark heavy-looking sugar is liked the best, but I prefer the sparkling good grained sugar, myself, for all purposes.

The Indian sugar, which looks dry and yellow, and is not sold in cakes, but in birch boxes, or mowkowks, as they call them, I have been told, owes its peculiar taste to the birch bark vessels that the sap is gathered in, and its grain to being kept constantly stirred while cooling. I have been told that a small bit of lime put into the syrup whitens the sugar. Milk is used to clarify, when eggs are not to be had, but I only made use of eggs. Four eggs I found enough for one boiling of sugar.

As I know of no better authority for the process of making sugar than that of my brother, Major Strickland, I shall avail myself of his directions, and abridge from his last volume, 18th chapter, such passages as may add to the settler's knowledge, what I have already collected from my own experience, and other sources.

He says, "The settler having selected his sugar-bush, should underbrush, and clean the surface of the ground, by removing all rotten logs, and fallen trees. It should be surrounded by a fence, to hinder the cattle from drinking the sap, and upsetting the sap-troughs, which they are very apt to do to the great loss and annoyance of the sugar-boiler. The boiling site should be as near to the centre of the bush as possible, from which roads wide enough to admit of the movements of a sleigh and oxen, should be cut in every direction."

"Settlers commonly suspend the boilers over the fire, from a thick pole, by means of iron chains; but this is liable to accidents. The best plan is to build the sugar kettles into an arch,* either in the open air, or in a small shanty built for the purpose of sugaring off."

"A store trough should be made from the trunk of a large white pine, capable of holding from fifty to one hundred pails of sap. This should be placed near the boilers, and any empty casks or barrels may also be mustered in case of a good run."

"In a good season from eight to twelve hundred pounds of sugar and molasses can be made with five hundred sap troughs. Let the troughs be made of pine, black ash, cherry, or butternut, capable of holding three or four gallons each."

"No sap wood should be left in making the troughs as it is sure to rot them. As soon as the season is over, let the boys collect all the troughs, and set them upon end, against the North side of the tree, which preserves them from cracking with the sun."

---

*This no doubt is a good plan when sugaring is carried on with good help, and on a large scale; but where women and boys do the work, it would hardly, I fear, be carried into effect.—Ed.

"If the farmer desires, as of course he will, to preserve his sugar bush, the best way is to tap the tree on the South, or sunny side, with an inch and quarter augur, and use hollow spills. Care must be taken to set the trough directly under the drop, and as level as possible. Many use the axe only, in tapping, but this soon kills the tree.

"The sap runs best after a frosty night, followed by a warm sunny day, and brisk westerly wind. The tap should be made in the early part of the season, on the South, and when it requires removing later, on the North.

"The most expeditious way of gathering the sap is to drive through the roads with the ox sled, on which a puncheon or barrel is securely fixed; in the bunghole of this receptacle, a wooden tun dish should be inserted, large enough to hold a pail of sap; in the hollow of this a bit of tin or iron punched full of holes is inserted to act as a strainer."

"As soon as a sufficiency of sap has been stored, and the kettles filled, the fires are lighted, and boiling begins, and should now be kept up night and day, till a sufficiency for a batch of sugar has been boiled down into thin molasses. It is then allowed to cool, and settle, and should be poured into the sugaring vessel, free of the sediment. Eggs are then beaten up—six will clarify fifty pounds of sugar. The beaten eggs are stirred into the cool liquor, the pot slung on the crane, and *as it rises to the boil*, the thick black scum, must be instantly removed. If properly scummed, the liquor will be bright and clear as white wine."

"Great attention must now be paid by the sugar-boiler; he must not leave his station, unless his post be taken by a careful hand. The liquid, as it thickens, is continually rising to the surface, and unless watched with care, would boil over; it is well to keep a little always cooling at hand to dash in in case of a sudden rise."

"To the uninitiated, the greatest difficulty is to know when the liquid has attained a sugaring point. When it boils in one continued yellow froth, throwing up jets and puffs of steam, it is not far from being ready; but to try this, take a thin bit of wood, in this make a narrow hole an inch long, and an eighth of an inch wide, if this is dipped into the molasses, a fine thin film will fill the hole, which, if blown, will throws out a long-shaped bubble, if the sugar is sufficiently boiled. Some can tell by blowing a thread of it from the edge of a ladle, or by dropping it on the snow, when, if hard, it is done, and the sugar may be poured out into pans to granulate."

"Sugar-making," adds the writer of the above, "is one of the most laborious occupations, while it lasts, yet a vast quantity of maple sugar is yearly made in the back woods by the joint operations of the settlers' wives, and their children; and though it takes place at the most changeable and unpleasant season of the year, when the frosts and thaws are alternate, and the work is done in the wet snow, it is very rarely that you hear of ague attacking the sugar-makers. March and April are not the seasons for ague ; it is in the hotter months this disease prevails."

NOTE.—I have given this useful extract from Mr. Strickland's work, "Twenty-seven year's experience in Canada West," because it embraces some valuable points of advice on the subject, very clearly expressed, and as the price of his book places it beyond the reach of a large proportion of the emigrants and poorer settlers, I considered it was conferring a benefit upon my readers.

MAPLE SYRUP.

This beautiful addition to the table is simply a portion of the syrup, taken out when it begins to thicken to the consistency of virgin honey. It sells at nine pence or ten pence a-quart readily ; if for use in your own family, boil it rather longer, and cork it tight, setting it by in a cool cellar to keep it from fermentation. It is used as sauce for pancakes, puddings, and to eat with bread. Those persons who do not think it worth their while to make sugar, will often make a gallon or two of molasses. Some call it maple honey, and indeed it comes nearer to honey in taste, and consistency, than to treacle.

MAPLE SUGAR SWEETIES.

When sugaring off, take a little of the thickest syrup into a saucer, stir in a very little fine flour, and a small bit of butter, and flavor with essence of lemon, peppermint, or ginger, as you like best; when cold, cut into little bricks about an inch in length. This makes a cheap treat for the little ones. By melting down a piece of maple sugar, and adding a bit of butter, and flavouring, you can always give them sweeties, if you think proper to allow them indulgencies of this sort.

MAPLE VINEGAR.

Those persons who make maple sugar generally make a keg of vinegar, which, indeed, is highly advisable ; no house should be without it; it is valuable, both s an article of diet, and medicine; and as it is easily made, and costs nothing but the labour, I shall give directions how to make it.

At the close of the sugar-making season, in the month of April, the sap loses much of its sweetness, and when boiled down, will not make sugar, but it will make good vinegar:—for this purpose it will only be necessary to reduce five pails of sap to one by boiling; twenty-five gallons of sap, boiled down to five, will fill your little five gallon keg; but it is better to boil rather more, as you will need some after the fermentation is over to fill up the vessel. This is the common proportion, five pails reduced to one; but I do not think that six to one would be too much to allow in boiling down. While blood-warm, strain the liquor into the vessel, and pour in half a tea-cupful of rising; set the cask in the chimney corner, or at the back of the stove, and let it work as long as it will, then lay a bit of glass over the bunghole to keep out dust, and let it stand where it will keep moderately warm for some weeks. It will be fit for use by the summer; if it is too weak put a little more sugar to it.

In the hot weather a nice cooling drink can be made with a quart of hot water, a large spoonful of maple syrup, and as much vinegar as will sharpen it; when quite cold, grate a little nutmeg on it, or drop a little essence of lemon, to flavour it. This is very refreshing in harvest weather.

MAPLE BEER.

This is made with sap, boiled down as for vinegar, to which a large handful of hops boiled, and the liquor strained in, is added, with barm to ferment it; some add sprigs of spruce, others bruised ginger.

MAPLE WINE.

Boil down six pails of sap to one, in proportion to the quantity you wish to make. Set it to ferment with a little yeast, and stop it soon; let it stand in a cool cellar after it is bunged. It may be drunk in a few weeks, as it has not much body, and would soon sour. A finer wine may be made with sap, boiled down, adding a quarter of a pound of raisins split.

This wine should be made when the sap is at its best; it is not prudent to defer it till the end of the season. Birch wine can be made in the same way, only it requires sugar, as there is much less sweetness in the sap of the birch, than in that of the sugar maple. From the soft, or swamp-maple, no sugar can be made, but a strong black ink is made from boiling the bark, and setting the color with copperas; a little sugar is necessary, or a small quantity of gum-arabic to give it gloss, and consistency; many settlers use no ink, but that which they manufacture themselves.

CURING OF MEAT.

The cutting up and salting of meat is attended to in most farmhouses by the men, but sometimes it falls to the lot of the settlers' wives, and it is necessary that they should possess some knowledge of the process, as circumstances may oblige them to take an active part in the business, or give directions to their servants, as the case may be.

The meat should be hung in a cool place till it is stiff: it may then be cut up for salting. The usual way of dividing the hog is to take off the head; cut out the hams, and fore legs, ham shape; and divide the rest of the carcass in pieces, which are cut clean through, chine fashion. These are rubbed and packed in clean salt, as tight as the barrel can be packed, and the barrel is then filled up with strong brine. A barrel of pork, containing nothing but the side pieces, should contain two cwt. of *pork*. This sells at the highest market price, and goes by the name of "MESS PORK." "Prime mess" contains the hams and shoulders, as well as sides, and sells for less. And "PRIME," which is the whole hog cut up indiscriminately, is the lowest in market value; but a barrel of either must weigh two cwt. of meat. Hams are sometimes sold separately at 6d. or 7d. per ℔., dried or smoked. Pigs are often sent to market, or to the stores in a frozen state, and sold by the cwt. In purchasing a barrel of pork, it is necessary to ascertain the sort of meat you are buying, and not to pay for "Prime" or "Prime Mess" the same as for "Mess." As the emigrant, on first commencing housekeeping, is obliged to provide stores of this sort, it is well that he should be on his guard against imposition. And when the storekeeper sees that his customer is not ignorant of these matters, he will be less disposed to take unfair advantage of him. Always endeavour to make your dealings with persons of respectability of character. And now to return to the curing of the meat for household use.

PICKLE FOR HAMS, CHEEKS, AND SHOULDERS.

* Fourteen pounds of good salt, half a pound of saltpetre, two quarts of molasses or four pounds of coarse brown sugar, with water enough to dissolve the salt, and a pint of good beer or of vinegar, if you can command either. Bring this liquor to a boil, and scum off all the impurities that may rise to the surface. When cold, pour this

---

* This quantity will be sufficient for two cwt. of meat. In salting down meat, it is better to have one to rub the meat, and another strong hand to pack into the barrel. Some prefer meat dry-salted to pickling it.

over your hams, which should be cold, but not frozen. The addition of pepper, allspice, and cloves is made by some who like a high flavour to the hams. The hams should remain in this pickle six or eight weeks; being turned and basted every two or three days, and then hung in the smoke-house. The best woods for smoking are: sugar-maple chips, hickory, birch, corn-cobs, white ash, and beech. When removed from the smoke-house, sew each ham in any old linen or cotton cloth, and if you give this covering a coating of whitewash, with a whitewash brush, it will preserve it from the flies. There is a small dusky beetle, with two dull red or orange bars across its body, which injures meat more than the flies: it deposits its eggs in the skin and joints. These eggs turn to a hairy worm, which destroy the meat; and unless some precautions are taken, will render it unfit for use. If you find by examining the hams, that the enemy has been at work, I would recommend a large boiler or kettle of water to be put on the fire, and when it boils, immerse each ham in it for five or even ten minutes. Take them out, and when dry, rub them over with bran or saw dust, and pack them in a bag of wood ashes, or of oats, as the Yorkshire farmers do: you will have no trouble with the weevil again. To preserve pork free from taint, or to restore it if it be injured, pack charcoal in the barrels. The use of charcoal as a preserver of meat is very great: I have restored meat that was much injured, by first putting off the bad brine—scraping the meat—and washing it in cold water—burning some cedar-bark in the barrel, and repacking the meat, laying lumps of charcoal between the layers of meat, a strong brine being again poured on to cover it.

A pint of the drippings from the stove-pipe joints added to the brine will also restore meat, and give it the flavour of smoke,— or a small quantity of pyroligneous acid. Where the brine has been allowed to stand in barrels too long, the burning of cedar-bark in them will purify them for use. A bad cellar may be purified by the same means, care being taken to secure the building from danger of fire. Where roots have been kept in a cellar for any time, such purification is very essential in the spring of the year.

PRIZE HAM.

Rub your ham, which should be of fine-grained, well-fed pork, when quite cold, with fine salt, to which add a little red pepper, and half a pint of molasses. Let it remain in the pickle, basting and turning it for six weeks. Then hang it up, and smoke for six weeks. About the first week in April take it down; wash it in cold water, and rub it over with unleached ashes. If you have any number of hams, let them lie for a week, heaped together; then hang them in a cool room, having sewed them in canvass or old cotton covers. (Hamilton prize ham.)

TO BOIL HAM.

Soak it over night in soft water ; wrap a lock of sweet hay about it, and boil in plenty of water, three, or if very large, four hours : let the ham remain in the water to cool gradually. Next day remove the skin, and trim all unsightly parts away : the ham will retain its flavour and juice much better than if skinned hot : this of course can only be adopted when you do not require to serve the joint up hot to table : in that case skin it ; grate crumbs of bread over the surface, and let it stand a few minutes in the oven to crisp the bread crumbs.

BACON—TO PREPARE FOR SMOKING OR DRYING.

Having taken off the hams from a side of pork, chop the rib-bones close to the back, so as to remove the back-bone the entire length of the side. With a sharp knife, raise all the small long bones from the meat, and trim all rugged portions carefully away. Then mix a pound of coarse sugar to 2 oz. of saltpetre, and 4 lb. of salt. Rub this well over the meat on all sides : two sides of bacon will not be too much for the above quantity. Cut them in two pieces, and lay each piece above the other, the rind downward, and strew the remainder of the salt mixture over the last piece. A shallow wooden-trough or tray, with a hole and peg at the bottom, is the best to salt your bacon in : it should be placed a little sloping forward. Every second day, draw off the liquor that runs from the meat, into a vessel, and carefully pour it over the meat again, having first shifted the bottom pieces to the top. In six weeks time, take them out ; rub with bran, and lay on the rack to dry, or smoke them : this process makes excellent meat.

Much of the goodness of pork, ham, and bacon depends upon the meat itself—the breed of hogs—and their treatment in fattening.

A great deal of the barrels of pork sold in the stores, is coarse, loose, flabby pork—distillery-fed, or else nut-fed ; the swine having nearly fattened themselves in the woods on beech-mast, acorns, and such food. This pork is known by its soft, oily fat ; the meat running away to oil, in the act of frying. Of course, meat like this is not profitable to the buyer. Such meat is better dried or smoked, than eaten fresh from the pickle. It is better to purchase your meat fresh of some respectable farmer, or salt it yourself, or buy well-dried meat, though you must, of course, give a higher price for it. By referring to the market-table, you may ascertain the prices of meat, both salt and fresh.

Here is an excellent recipe, furnished by a gentleman, who considers it the best in use : I have eaten excellent meat at his table thus treated.

PICKLE FOR BEEF OR PORK.

To three gallons of pickle, strong enough to float an egg, add ¼℔. of alum, 1qt. of treacle, 1oz. of potash ; mix them well together ; pack the beef or pork, and pour the pickle on it ; cover it close : in about three weeks it will be fit for use. *The meat must not be salted,* but packed as it comes from the butcher, and the pickle poured over it.

LARD.

This is made from the inner or kidney-fat of the hog. It should be cut up in small portions, and boiled down on a slow fire. Let the fat boil till all the oil is extracted ; but be careful not to let it burn. When it has ceased to make a noise, be on the watch : it is ready to strain off into clean, dry jars. The best, are the stone-jars, with covers to them : these can be bought in any of the stores : they are made in this country, or in the States. The coarse red pottery is very cheap. It is manufactured in large quantites, in many parts of the Province ; and is used in dairies, and for all kinds of household purposes.

Lard sells at 6d. and 7d. per ℔. in the market at Toronto : it used formerly to be much cheaper. It is now used as a substitue for oil, in parlour lamps.

VENISON.

They who live in the backwoods, often have venison brought in, either by their own people or by the Indian hunters, who gladly exchange it for salt-pork, flour, or vegetables. A few hints as to the best method of dressing this meat may not be quite unacceptable to the Canadian settler's wife.

TO ROAST VENISON.

The best joints to roast are the haunch and the loins, which last should be cut saddle fashion, viz., both loins together.

If the deer be fat and in good season, the meat will need no other basting than the fat which runs from it ; but as it is often lean, it will be necessary to use lard, butter, or slices of fat bacon to assist the roasting. Venison should be cooked with a brisk fire—basted often

—and a little salt thrown over it: it is better not overdone. Being a meat very open in the grain and tender, it readily parts with its juices, and takes less time to roast than any other meat.

BROWN FRICASSEE OF VENISON.

Fry your steaks quite brown, in hot dripping; put them in a stew-pan with a very little water, a bunch of sweet herbs, a small onion, a clove or two, and pepper and salt. When it has boiled for a few minutes, roll a bit of butter in flour, with a table-spoonful of catsup or tomato-sauce, and a tea-spoonful of vinegar; stir this into the fricassee, and dish it quite hot.

FRIED VENISON.

Cut your meat in suitable pieces: dust them with flour, and season with pepper and salt; fry in boiling lard, or with some nice thin slices of ham or fat bacon. A little seasoning of onion in the gravy may be added, if not disagreeable. A little dust of flour in the pan, with a table-spoonful of boiling water, and a little tomato-catsup will make the gravy.

VENISON-PIE.

Season your pieces of venison with pepper and salt, a little allspice, and three or four cloves; flour each steak as you lay it in the dish; pour in a tea-cupful of water, and cover the dish with a nice short crust. If the meat be very lean, a few slices of ham or bacon will improve the pie.—Small balls made with crumbs of bread, chopped ham, parsley shred fine, seasoned with pepper, and made up with an egg improves the pie.

VENSION-SOUP.

The leanest and worst pieces of the deer. will make an excellent soup, if boiled down long enough. A handful of Indian rice may be put in when first set on the fire, but should be soaked in water for an hour or two, and drained and picked clean before adding it to the soup. Season the soup with onions and sweet herbs, pepper and salt.

The meat after long cooking will be of little worth, as all the good and nourishing qualities have been parted with in the soup.

CORNED VENISON.

When you have more fresh meat of this kind than you think will keep good, rub it with salt, and hang it in the root-house or dairy.

VENISON-HAM.

Make a mixture of sugar, salt, and a very little saltpetre; rub the haunch well with this every day, for three weeks; hang it to smoke for three more. It is very good grated, or if dried, cut in thin shavings, as a relish with bread and butter for tea or breakfast, with salad.

Jerked venison is the flesh cut in strips, and dried in the open air.

BEEF.

Beef needs to be well packed in the barrel, and a good deal of salt strewn at the bottom. Strew a handful of salt between each layer of meat, and then make a brine that will float a middle-sized potato. To this add a quarter of a pound of saltpetre, which always improves the colour of pickled meat, and four pounds of coarse sugar. Boil your brine; scum it, and when cold, pour over your beef: it should be quite covered, and a lid put on the barrel. Unless you need beef for immediate use, say a week or ten days, no salt need be rubbed on. If you want dried beef, remove a joint—the half leg is best—from the pickle, after a month's time, and hang it up to dry,—or season a leg with the same pickle as you use for hams, adding 2oz. of allspice, ½oz. of cloves, and 2oz. of black pepper to your pickle. Let it be turned and basted daily for six weeks, then hang it to dry and smoke. This is usually shaved, and eaten with no other cooking than what the drying process gives.

As this is not a regular cookery-book; but is confined to the preparing of food, as practised in this country, it will be unnecessary to give all the various methods of cooking beef or other meats, as commonly practised, and which can be taught by any cookery-book.— It is my aim, in this work, to supply the female settler with information to meet her daily wants; and to put her in the best way of acquiring the knowledge she needs in making use of what material she has at her command, and turning them to the best advantage, with the least expenditure of money and trouble.

CANADIAN PARTRIDGES.

These birds, which are of two different varieties,—the spruce partridge, and the ruffed grouse, are more like the pheasant than the English partridge—the meat being white instead of brown; but they have not the high gamy flavour of either the partridge or pheasant. They are, when in season, very good eating; but about the end of the winter, the flesh becomes dry and bitter. This arises from the nature of their food, which, in the thick woods, consists chiefly of the resinous buds of the spruce, the bark and buds of the birch, and some berries, which they find beneath the snow ; with various mosses and lichens, which give an astringent taste to the flesh. At all other seasons they are very good and fleshy, and are excellent roasted and stuffed with fine bread crumbs, pepper, salt, a little butter, and sweet herbs. They require much basting, as they have no fat in themselves. Half an hour, with a good fire, will cook a partridge. To stew them, cut them up, dust with a little flour, pepper, salt, and stew gently with a small quantity of water ; thicken with a little cream, flour, and a little nutmeg, grated ; serve with toasted bread cut as sippets, at the edge of the dish.

PIGEONS.

During the spring and summer months, numbers of pigeons linger to breed in the Canadian woods, or pass over in straggling flocks, when they are shot in numbers by the settlers. These birds are good any way you cook them : roasted or in pies.

ROAST PIGEONS.

Pluck and draw your birds ; mix bread crumbs with a little parsley chopped fine, some butter, pepper and salt ; put a little into the body of each bird ; lard and roast them : twenty minutes, with a good fire, is long enough. The basting will serve for gravy,—or add a little butter, and a very little boiling water after you have taken up the birds, and heat it in the pan your pigeons were roasted in.

PIGEONS IN CRUST.

Stuff your birds as above, and cover each one with a thin crust, of short pastry ; bake half an hour.

PIGEON-PIE.

Season your pigeons well with pepper and salt ; as many as will lie in your pie-dish ; dust a little flour on, thin ; add a cup of hot water ; cover your pie, and bake an hour.

POT-PIE.

Pigeons stuffed, larded, and cooked in a bake-kettle, are very nice ; and are tenderer, and more savoury than when baked in the stove. To make a pot-pie of them, line the bake-kettle with a good pie-crust ; lay in your birds, with a little butter put on the breast of each, and a little pepper shaken over them, and pour in a tea-cupful of water—do not fill your pan too full ; lay in a crust, about half an inch thick ;

cover your lid with hot embers, and put a few below. Keep your bake-kettle turned carefully, adding more hot coals on the top, till the crust is cooked. This makes a very savoury dish for a family.

Pigeons are best for table just after wheat harvest: the young birds are then very fat.

BLACK SQUIRRELS.

These little animals are often found in great numbers, in the beech and oak-woods in Canada, and are considered very delicate food; being free from any strong flavour. They are roasted like rabbits, or cut in pieces and fried, fricasseed, or made into stews or pies. Some people object to them, simply because they have not been accustomed to see them brought to table, or even to hear of their being used as an article of food, and others consider them as insipid. This last objection is, perhaps, the most weighty; but by seasoning them well, it may be overcome. Nothing can be more cleanly than the habits of these little creatures; their food consisting entirely of grain, or fruits, or vegetables. When fresh meat is scarce, as it often is in the woods, the black and even the red squirrel may be eaten, as a wholesome change of diet. The lumberers and hunters will use the musk-rat, porcupine, and beaver for food, and even the wood-chuck or groundhog, which is a species of marmot. But though its food is vegetable, it is very fat and oily; and does not make pleasant meat. The bear is also made meat of by the backwoodsman. The meat when cooked, either roasted or boiled, is like coarse beef, and would pass for such, if a person was not told to the contrary. The bear is certainly a more cleanly feeder than the hog. The hams, when well cured, are considered very excellent.

CANADIAN HARE.

This is another of the native wild animals. It is not so well-flavoured as the English hare, or so large; being in size and colour more like a white rabbit. The colour in spring and summer is brown, but it grows white at the approach of the cold weather. They are taken by snares set among the bushes, in their run-ways, which are easily detected in the snow. They frequent cedar-swamps, and also abound on the Plains-lands. The meat is dark coloured, like the common hare. They are inferior to that animal; but make a pleasant variety to the salt meat; and may be cooked either roasted like rabbits, stewed, fried, or made into pies. The fur of the Canadian hare is very worthless: it is loose, comes off at a touch.

The snipe and woodcock are cooked the same as in other countries; and the quail, which abounds in some districts, may be dressed like the partridge.

WILD DUCKS.

Wild fowl of this kind abounds on the shores of lakes and rivers, or any open, marshy spots. Some of these birds are excellent; others fishy. The best are: the canvass-back, the red-headed duck, the swamp or blue-billed duck; the ring-necked, the mallard, the winter duck, wood-duck, and blue-winged teal, are among the best; but there are many others that can be eaten. The usual mode of cooking, and the best is, to roast them.

The feathers and down of these water birds are valuable, and should not be thrown away; as they sell well, and are of great value in a household, for beds and pillows. It is best to put them in paper bags, and hang them in a dry place, till you have collected enough for putting into cases.

WILD GEESE.

Sometimes the flesh of the wild goose is fishy and oily, and it is best to parboil them for a few minutes, to extract the superfluous oil. They may then be stuffed with bread-crumbs, sage, onion, and a good deal of pepper and salt, and roasted. The fat is sufficient for roasting them, without any addition of lard or butter. The liver, head, pinions, and gizzard should be well parboiled; the water put off, and fresh added; and gravy made by boiling them a long time, with a few rings of onion, a crust of browned bread, and pepper and salt; pour into the dish when the goose is served up.

Most excellent pies may be made of the blackbirds of Canada, which come in great flocks upon the fields of ripe grain, in the summer, and commit great ravages on those farms in the vicinity of fresh lakes and rivers, where they assemble to breed, and bring up their young. They are of good size, fat, and tender, and are delicious eating at the harvest season; and make a dainty dish, either roasted or baked in a pie. They fly in large flocks, and are often mixed with the rice-bunting, redwing, and others of the same family. I have often seen these birds dressed for sick persons—who could bear no rich meats—who found them lighter, and more nourishing even than chickens. The Canada robin is also eaten. These birds are the size of a blackbird or starling.

ESSENCE OF BEEF.

This excellent form of nourishment, for sick persons, is procured by cutting up some lean beef in small pieces, and putting it into a covered jar, which is then set into a pot of boiling water, and suffered to remain for some time, till the juices of the meat are quite extracted. A single tea-spoonful of this extract, given from time to time, contains more actual strengthening matter than a pint of beef-tea or broth, made with water in the usual way. For sick infants, who have been reduced to great debility by ague or dysentery, a few drops from time to time, have restored them more rapidly than any other sort of food would have done. The juices of any meat may be obtained in the same way, and a little seasoning added if required. In cases of great debility, when the stomach is too weak to bear the weight of ordinary food, this essence of beef is of great value, and is so easily manufactured, that it is within the reach of the most common cook to obtain it, however unskilful in the culinary art she may be.

All seasoning herbs, as savory, thyme, marjoram, and the like, should be gathered green, dried for a few minutes in the oven, and preserved in bottles for winter use. Horse-radish scraped down into vinegar and bottled, is very useful.

FISH.

To those who live near the shores of lakes or rivers, fish forms an important article of diet, in Canada. So plentifully supplied are the waters of this fine country with fish of the finest quality, and largest size, that they can be procured with little trouble by the most inexpert angler. In the months of April and May, the lakes and rivers swarm with myriads of perch, of all sizes, from an ounce to two or three pounds weight; sun-fish, a small flat fish, of splendid colours—gold, and blue, and red; pink-roach, a very delicate, silver-scaled fish—not very large, but very delicate; with rock-bass and black bass. These last are very fine fish—are taken near the shores with a hook and line, while the larger sorts, such as masquinonge, which varies from a few to thirty pounds in weight, are either speared by torchlight, or caught with a trolling line. As soon as the ice breaks up on the lakes, the dark nights are illumined by the lights used by the fishers, to aid them in spearing these noble fish, which furnish a delicious meal when fresh, either fried or boiled, and may be salted, dried, and smoked for future use; while those to whom money is an object of importance, sell the surplus, for which, if they live near a town or village, there is always a ready market. There is one thing more to mention. This is, that there are no laws restricting the poor man from casting his line into the waters, or launching his night-canoe or skiff upon the lake, to supply his family with the blessings which God has bestowed upon all, alike, in this free and happy land of plenty. But now having told you how easily your husbands and sons can obtain this most excellent article of diet, it is necessary for me to give you a little instruction in the best modes of dressing it for the table.

MASQUINONGE.

Scale and clean your fish, if possible before the skin becomes dry and hard; but should it not come to your hands for some time after being taken out of the water, lay it on some clean stones, in a cool place, and throw over it a bowl or two of cold salt and water: this will render the scales less difficult to remove. With a sharp knife remove the gills and the inside. Few people cook the head of the masquinonge unless the fish is to be boiled, or baked whole, when the head and tail are tied and skewered so as to form a circle. Be careful, in cleaning this fish, not to wound your flesh with his sharp teeth or fins, as the cut is difficult to heal. Take out the roe, and throw it into salt and water. It should be floured, peppered, and salted, and fried as a garnish to the dish, but requires to be thoroughly done through: if it be soft and jelly-like, it is not sufficiently cooked.

If you design to fry the fish, it must be cut in pieces, quite through the thickness of the fish, about three inches in width; dry on a board; flour the pieces, and sprinkle with salt and pepper; or, beat up an egg, dip the pieces in the egg, and strew crumbs of bread, and lay them in the boiling lard : this is the best way. But sometimes the Canadian housewive may be obliged to resort to a more homely method, that of frying some slices of fat pork to obtain the dripping in which to cook her fish; and if well attended to, even thus, her fish will be no despicable dish for a hungry family.

TO BOIL MASQUINONGE.

Having cleaned your fish, strew a handful of salt within side, and let it lie all night. Tie the tail and head together, and place your fish in a shallow pan—a fish-kettle if you have one, of course, is best; cover it with cold water—the water should just cover it and no more; let it come to a boil, and be careful to remove all scum. If your fish be any size, let it boil slowly for five or ten minutes; but when the fish has boiled five minutes, pass a clean knife in the thick part, near the back-bone, and if it parts from the bone, and looks white and flaky, it is cooked enough; but if soft, and has a pinky look, and adheres to the bone, let it simmer longer, but not long enough to break the fish : a little salt thrown in, when boiling, helps to preserve the firmness, and improves the flavour. A very thick, heavy fish will require a longer time to cook; but by trying it as I have directed, you can ascertain the time it will take. There is nothing more unwholesome than under-done fish. Melted butter, and any fish-sauce may be served with masquinonge; but where persons are unprovided with such luxuries, vinegar and mustard may be eaten with it. To the poor man, no sauce seasons his dish so well as a good appetite, which makes every dish savoury.

FISH-SOUP.

In the month of May, the lakes and rivers abound with perch, sunfish, and many other kinds, which are caught by children with the simplest of all tackle—a stout thread and a small perch hook, tied to a wand cut from some green sapling on the lake-shore. Any bait will be seized : a bit of meat, a worm, a fish cut up in small pieces, will give your little angler as many fish as you can cook at two or three meals.

When you have abundance of the smaller sorts of fish, there is no better way of cooking, than making them into soup. To do this, lay aside the larger ones, and boil down the small fish till they are broken to pieces; strain them through a colander, and put on the liquor, with a crust of bread, into your stew-pan; season with pepper, salt, parsley, savory or thyme, and a few green chives cut up, or a young onion. Have ready about a dozen, or two dozen of the largest sized fish, ready cleaned and scaled ; put these into your soup ; mix a teaspoonful of fine flour, a slice of butter, and a table-spoonful of tomato-catsup, if you have it by you, and mix with a cup of thin cream or milk. When the soup boils up, stir this mixture in, and remove the pot from the fire. Your dish is now ready, and requires nothing more than a little toasted bread and a good appetite, to be found an excellent meal, at a very small expense, and far more wholesome than salted pork or beef.

The roes of the fish should be boiled in the soup to thicken it, or fried by themselves.

A few slices of fat bacon will serve to fry any of the small fresh fish, when lard or butter are not plentiful.

In frying fish, the fat should be quite hot, and the fish or pieces of fish, dry, when put into the pan. As sauces are not so easily procured in country places, and by those who are too poor, or too prudent to expend money upon luxuries, it is common to season fried fish with pepper and salt whilst frying them, and many serve them with gravy made with a little butter rolled in flour, half a tea-cupful of water, a table-spoonful of vinegar, and pepper and salt, heated in the pan, and poured into the dish with the fish.

For boiled fish, melted butter with mustard, vinegar, and an egg boiled hard and chopped fine, may be used. Tomato-sauce is served with fish, as mushrooms are not as common in the newly-cleared lands as on old farms, or as they are in the old country. The morel, which is often found in old beech-woods that have been partly cleared, is a very good substitute and quite wholesome, but not so high flavoured as a good mushroom. They are conical in shape, of a pale brown colour, and covered with hollow cavities like a honey-comb, on the outside. They are good, fried in butter with pepper and salt, and may be manufactured into catsup.

FISH-PIE.

Boil fresh bass, masquinonge, or white fish, till it will readily part from the back-bones, which must be carefully removed ; pound the fish fine, adding as you do so a pint of cream, a small bit of butter rolled in flour, a table-spoonful of walnut, mushroom, or tomato-catsup, a table-spoonful of vinegar, a little parsley scalded and chopped fine, and the yolks of two eggs bruised fine ; smooth in a pie-dish, and bake half an hour.

A large masquinonge, trussed, with the head and tail tied or skewered together, and stuffed with bread-crumbs, butter, pepper, salt, and sweet herbs, and moistened with a couple of beaten eggs, with butter sufficient to baste the fish, if put into the oven or before the fire and baked, is a most excellent dish. To try if it be cooked, pass a knife in near the back-bone; if it parts directly, and the flesh looks white, it is ready; but if it adheres, and is soft and clear, it requires longer cooking.

POTTED FISH.

Boil any sort of fish—not too much; remove the bones from the back and fins;—this can be done by running a knife along the edge of the back and laying back the meat, first on one side and then the other, breaking it as little as you can help. You can easily separate the fins; any other bones are not of much consequence, unless your fish be of the larger sorts. As you cut your fish, lay the pieces in a deep dish or pot, and sprinkle between each layer, pepper, salt, a little cayenne, a few cloves, and whole allspice. When your dish is full, pour on good vinegar, as much as will just cover the fish, and set it in a slow oven all night, or for some hours, covering the dish close with a plate or a coarse crust of dough, just to keep in the steam. This potted fish should stand for several days: it may then be used as a breakfast or supper dish, with bread.

SALT HERRINGS POTTED.

Steep them for twenty-four hours; cut off the heads, tails, and back-bones; skin them and lay them, packed close, in a pan; pour boiling vinegar over them, in which you have boiled whole pepper, allspice, and ginger; let the pan be covered close, and stand in the oven for an hour; when not very hot, set aside, and use as required: it will keep for some weeks or months.

EELS.

The eels caught in the Canadian waters are of a very large size, and very rich, but coarse. The best way of cooking them is, first, to parboil them, then open, and carefully remove the oily fat which lines the back-bone; cut out the bone the whole length, and also the tail and head; wash the fish clean, and spread it open; strew over the whole inner surface plenty of chopped parsley and thyme, or summer savory, pepper and salt, with a little allspice; then, beginning at the tail end, roll the fish tight into a bolster, and bind it well with tape or strips of calico; over this fold a piece of clean cloth, and tie it at each end; put it into boiling salt and water; (a handful of salt will be enough;) boil slowly for four or five hours, if your fish be large and the roll thick: do not remove the binders till the fish is quite cold; pour over it half a pint of vinegar, and when served, cut it in slices; garnish with parsley.

TO DRY MASQUINONGE OR SALMON.

Split the fish down and remove the back-bone; having gutted and scaled it, wipe it dry, but do not wash it; lay it on a board, and strew salt on the inner side ; let it lie for two days, turning it each day ; then wash the inside from the salt, string on a willow-wand, and hang up in the sun and wind to dry for several days ; smoke it, but not to much.

The Indians use but little salt in drying their fish, and smoke them with the wood or bark of red cedar ; but this fragrant wood is not common, and other wood will answer. Some merely dry them in the sun, without smoking. Corn-cobs burnt give a fine flavour either to meat or fish, and should be laid aside for such purposes.

When required for the table, soak for a few hours in warm water, and boil or fry.

WHITE FISH.

This is, by most people, considered as the richest and finest of all our fresh water fish, and abounds in the lake Ontario. Vast quantities are caught every year, and salted for sale ; when they may be bought by the barrel. A few years ago, a barrel of white fish could be bought for three dollars ; but now the price is much increased.

The fresh white fish are so rich, that they require no other fat than that which they contain to fry them.

Before dressing the salted white fish they must be steeped many hours, and the water twice changed. Most persons parboil them before frying them, and season them with pepper :—slightly salted, dried and smoked, they are very fine, and are esteemed a great dainty.

BLACK BASS.

There are two kinds of bass—the rock-bass and the black bass—the latter are the largest ; but both are good. The black bass may be taken with a hook and line, in deep water ; the rock-bass, nearer to the shore. They vary from half a pound to three, four, and even five or six pounds weight. The flesh is firm and sweet :—by many people the bass is preferred to the masquinonge. The usual way of cooking these fish is frying ; but they are excellent broiled or boiled.

The best fish that are bred in our Canadian waters are the salmon-trout, the masquinonge, white fish, and black bass.

One of the most nutritious of all dishes is fish-soup ; but this mode of cooking is very rarely adopted. Any fish may be dressed according to the recipe given for the small fish, and will be found excellent.

SOAP MAKING.

Soap is made from a union of the lie of wood ashes, and any sort of grease, the refuse of the kitchen ; even bones are boiled down in strong lie, and reduced. The lime of the bones are, by many soap-makers, thought to improve the quality of the soap. The careful Canadian housewives procure a large portion of their soap-grease from the inside, and entrails of the hogs, and other beasts that are killed on the farm. Nothing in this country is allowed to go to waste, that can be turned to any good account. Before I give you directions respecting the manufacturing soap, it will be as well to say a few words about the ashes, and setting of the leech barrel.

THE LEECH.

The ashes made use of for soap-making, should be from hardwood : such as oak, maple, beech, hickory, and the like; the ashes of *none* of the pine tribe, nor any other soft woods, are to be made use of, such as pine, hemlock, spruce, larch, or soft maple; swamp maple, bass-wood, and some others are also not good. Too much care can hardly be taken with respect to storing ashes. An old iron or tin vessel, pot or pan is the safest thing to remove the hot ashes in from the hearth, as live coals are often taken up with them, which might burn any wooden utensil, and if left on a verandah or floor, endanger the safety of the house. Most persons put up a small covered hut, made shanty form, in which the ashes are stored. This building should be apart from any of the house offices.

The careful soap-maker never allows sweepings of the house to be mixed with the ashes for soap making.

The ash barrel is usually any old flour barrel, or a hollow log that has been burnt out, leaving only a shell ; this is sawn into the proper length, and set upon a sloping board, raised from the ground high enough to admit of a trough or pail standing beneath it, to receive the lie ; at the bottom of the leech, sticks of split lathing or twigs, are placed across each other ; a handful of dry straw is next laid over the twigs, and about a pint of unslacked lime scattered upon that. Two quarts or more of good lime are allowed to each barrel of ashes. The lime has the effect of neutralizing some of the salts, which are prejudicial to the good qualities of the soap.

If a barrel is used for the leech, it will be necessary to bore three or four holes with a half inch augur at the edge of the bottom of the barrel, in the direction of that part which will be sloped towards the front of the stand. You may support this stand with logs or stones; or put legs of wood into holes bored, the two front legs being shorter than the hinder ones, to give a proper inclination for the lie to run off into the trough below. If you can manage to have two barrels set up, so as to collect a larger quantity of lie, it is better, especially if you have much grease to boil down. Do not be afraid of your lie being too strong : the stronger the better for consuming the grease. More soap is spoiled by weak lie, than any thing else ; neither let the dark colour of the lie deceive you : the colour is not strength.

The ashes should be put into the leech barrel, and pounded down with a long beetle. You may distribute the lime as you fill it up, or dissolve the lime in a pail of boiling water, and pour on after the barrel is filled up, and you commence running the lie.

Make a hollow in the top of the ashes, and pour in your water ; as it soaks in, keep adding more; it will not begin to drop into the trough or tub for many hours; sometimes, if the ashes are packed down tight, for two or three days; but you must keep the hollow on the top of the barrel always supplied with water—soft water is best, if you are near a creek, or have a rain water tank (which is a great convenience to a house), and the water you run your leech with should be hot at first.

Remember that you should be careful to keep any wet from getting to your ashes, while collecting them, previous to making the lie, as that weakens and destroys its effect.

I have been told that twelve pounds of grease will make a barrel of soft soap, but I do not vouch for it. Some say three pounds of grease to a pail of strong lie is the proportion; but experience is the best teacher. Of one thing you may be sure : that the strongest lie will take up the most grease: and after boiling several hours, if there be a thick scum still upon the soap, you may know that the lie has taken up all it is capable of boiling in ; or if it should happen that your lie is not strong enough to consume the grease, add more strong lie. This is the advantage of having two barrels of ashes; as it affords you the chance of increasing the strength of the lie, if required ; but if the soap, after long boiling, does not thicken, and no scum is on the top, of any account, add more grease.

To try if the soap is too strong, for it will not thicken sufficiently if it be so, take, with an iron spoon, a small quantity, say two spoonfuls into a saucer, add one of water, and beat it—if it wants water, it will thicken the soap ; add more water as long as it makes it thicker ; if it thickens well with one spoonful of soap to one of water, then your soap, when poured out into the soap barrel, may have as many pails of water added, as you have pails full of soap; if very good lie has been used, a double quantity of water may be added; but it is better not to thin it too much.

To try the lie, float an egg or a potato; it should be buoyed half up. You can always lessen the strength after the soap is made, by adding water. A pint of pure turpentine, such as runs from saw-logs, or from a gash cut in a large pine, may be boiled in with your soap; or some resin; but the turpentine is best.

So much depends on the size of your pot, and quantity of grease, that it would be difficult to tell you how much to put in with your lie, when about to boil off; but as the lie will only boil in so much grease, according to its strength, you need not mind having a good deal of grease, as it can be scummed off, after the soap is done boiling, and is all the better for boiling down when you have a fresh supply of lie.

No tin vessel should be used in soap-making, as the lie eats off the tinning: iron to boil the soap in, and wood to keep it in, answers best.

There is another method which requires no boiling at all; this is known as

COLD SOAP.

This is less trouble—the sun doing the work of the fire. The same process of running the lie must be gone through, and the grease to make good clean soap, should be boiled down in weak lie, and strained into the barrel, into which fresh run lie may be poured, and the barrel set in a warm sunny place, keeping it stirred from time to time, to mix the grease and the lie. This is all that is done in making cold soap. If it does not thicken after a week or ten days, add more grease, or more lie if there be too much grease; the lie should be poured hot on the grease. Some persons treat the grease in the following way: they have a barrel or tub in the cellar, or any convenient place, into which they put hot strong lie, and throw in all the grease, as it is collected, from time to time. When they have as much as they need, this half-made soap is boiled up for some hours, and strained off into a vessel, and if more grease floats than can be taken up, it is either boiled with more lie, or hot lie is thrown in to consume it, and set out in the sun for some time, and stirred, as above.

HARD SOAP.

This is made from good soft soap. I have not made it myself, but I give the directions of an experienced house-keeper on the subject.

If the soft soap be good, there is little difficulty in making it into hard soap. When you find the soap of a good thickness, take two or three good handfuls of salt, and stir into your pot or kettle: if it be a large kettle, you may put in six or seven handfuls: let it boil till you see the soap separating; boil it about ten minutes longer, and set it by till the next day, when the soap will have formed a thick cake on the top of the vessel, and the lie have separated and remain below, a dark reddish-brown fluid. Remove this cake of soap, and put it into a pot on the fire, adding to it a pint of turpentine or resin. When the soap begins to boil up, add more salt; if the soap cuts like soft putty when you put it into the pot, several handfuls of salt will be required; but if it cuts firm, one or two will be enough—but experience must be your guide, or, seeing the process, which is better than learning from books.

When the soap is boiled a few minutes after the salt has been stirred in, pour it into a flat wooden box, or mould, about three or four inches deep; it may be cut into bars, or square pieces, when perfectly cold, and set up on a shelf, in some dry place, to harden.

To remove paint, pitch, cart-grease, or the resin from cedar or pine, which will stick to the hands and clothes, if touched, nothing more is required, than to rub the cloth, cotton, or flesh, with clean lard, butter, or grease, then wash it well with hot soap-suds; but it is useless if you wet the part with water first. A weak solution of pot-ash, or pearl-ash, will also remove stains of this sort, or grease spots from cloth, or silk. Spirits of sal volatile, or hartshorn, will remove acid stains from silks, and restore the lost colour.

SCOURING MIXTURE FOR BOARDS, OR TO BE USED AS THE WASHING MIXTURE.

Take about two pounds of quick lime: pour over it one-and-a-half gallon of boiling water; when cold, clear off one gallon: cut two pounds yellow soap into a gallon of water, and boil until melted. Into the gallon of lime water, put one pound of sal-soda,* and boil together for half an hour, covered close: then half an hour uncovered; pour it into an earthen pan, and when cold, cut it up in squares for use; it does not harden much.

This quantity will make fifteen or twenty pounds. You may use it as for the Washing Mixtures *(which see.)* It is excellent for scouring boards.

POTASH SOAP.

I have no experience of the following compound, but I give it in case any one should feel disposed to make the experiment.

Six pounds of potash, which would be equal to as many pails of good lie, four pounds of lard, or fat, boiled down, and cleansed, one quarter-of-a-pound of rosin, pounded; mix these ingredients, and set aside, in

---

*This is sold in most stores, by the name of washing soda. It costs 5d. per pound.

a vessel, for five days; put the mixture into ten gallons of hot water, stir it twice a day, and you will have one hundred pounds of good soft soap. The cost, if you buy the fat, and other materials, is stated to be about seven shillings and six pence. I should think that a much larger proportion of grease would be required to make the quantity of soft-soap here mentioned; however, it can be tried first with four pounds, and more grease added, if it does not thicken into soap.

I will now give an excellent receipt, called

LABOUR-SAVING SOAP.

Take fourteen pounds of bar-soap, or five gallons of good common soft soap, three pounds of sal-soda, sold by the name of washing soda, one quarter-of-a-pound of rosin, pounded, two ounces spirits of turpentine, eight ounces salt; boil together in five gallons of soft water, till the ingredients are all melted, and well mixed. Let it cool, and cut out for use.

When required for use, melt a piece in a pint of soft water, and stir it into as much warm soft water as will be sufficient to soak the clothes, which may be done over night—the white clothes by themselves: pound them a little, and wring out; lay on a clean board, and put them into your boiler with a piece of soap dissolved; let them boil for half an hour: take them out into a clean Indian basket, set across two bars, over your tub; while the liquor drains off, wring the clothes into another tub of clean water; then wring again in blue water.

ANOTHER WASHING MIXTURE.

Soak the clothes in soft water, the night before washing; take half a-pound of sal-soda, four ounces of quick lime, and dissolve each separately, in a quart of soft water; boil twenty minutes, and set by to settle. On the washing morning, pour off your lime-water clear, and add to the soda; boil in a saucepan together for a few minutes; cut a pound of soap into ten gallons of water, in your boiler, and add the soda mixture and lime to it; when the soap is melted put in your clothes, having wrung them out, and rubbed a little soap on the collars, and wrists of the shirts; let them boil half an hour; drain, and wring, and rinse as above.

It is sometimes necessary to rub the sleeves and collars of shirts, but this method is a very great saving of soap and of labour, a matter of great moment to such as have been unused to the hard work attending washing for a large family.

A washing board is always used in Canada. There are several kinds. Wooden rollers, set in a frame, are the most common, but those made of zinc are best. These last do not cost more than the wooden ones, wear longer, and being very smooth, injure the fabric of the clothes less. In Canada no servant will wash without a washing-board.

CANDLE MAKING.

There is no mystery and not much skill required in making candles; any girl of ten or twelve years of age, that is careful, can make candles.

Good candles require clean well strained tallow, and strong smooth wick. When suet, or fat of any kind, mutton, beef, or lamb, is to be tried down for tallow, let the vessel it is put into be clean, and a tablespoonful or two of water be put in with the fat; this keeps the fat from burning to the bottom, and goes off in steam, during the trying down. Cut the fat into small pieces, and throw into the pot; a stick should be put in, which enables you to stir it from time to time; the handle of a metal spoon or ladle is apt to get too hot. Let the suet boil on a slow fire till the whole fat is well rendered. Be careful not to let it burn; remember when it ceases to make a noise, and becomes quite still, it is then *really* boiling hot, and is more apt to burn. You had better now remove it, and with a ladle pour it all clean off into a pot or tin dish, through a sieve or colander, over which you have tied a flannel strainer. The last drop of fat, as long as it is not discolored, may be drained out of the scraps, and the refuse may be placed in the receptacle for soap grease—no refuse fat of any kind being allowed, in a Canadian farm-house, to go to waste.

When quite cold, the cake of tallow may be turned out of the dish and set by, ready for candle-making.

You have now the tallow—at any of the tinsmiths in the towns, you can buy a stand of moulds, or get them made to order, from a stand of four to two dozen; but six or eight are best, and easier cleaned and handled. Every house-keeper requires candle moulds, and it is a bad way to depend upon borrowing of a neighbor. In careless hands these things are easily injured. The wick is sold in the dry-goods stores in balls, from $3\frac{1}{2}$d to $7\frac{1}{2}$d a ball; the whitest and most thready looking is better than the soft yellow looking wick: this last is fitter for lamps.

When about to make your candles, measure a double length of the wick, allowing a bit for tying; you must have some slender sticks, a bit of pine wood cut like a skewer, will do; slip the double wick through the holes in the bottom of the mould, leaving the loop end uppermost, the stick having to go through the loops to support the wick and keep it straight, and also to draw out the candles from the mould, when cold, by. Having run all your wicks, slip your sticks through the loops at the top and put them even, then turn up the mould, and tie the ends tight at the bottom ; and be careful that all your wicks are set evenly : if the sticks are slanting in any way, your wick will not be in the middle of your candle ; and this not only causes the candle to look ill, but affects its burning. You are now ready for the tallow : let this be melted, but not made *too* hot, and poured into the moulds. It is best to keep an iron or tin saucepan, holding from a pint to a quart, for melting your grease in ; use it for no other purpose ; also a small pitcher with a spout, a common delf cream pot will do, for pouring the fat into the moulds. A tin mug with a spout is still better. Set your moulds aside, to cool ; when nearly cold, fill up each mould again, for, as the fat cools, it shrinks, and a vacancy is made at the top of each candle, to the depth of half an inch ; this would make a difference in the time of the candles burning. When thoroughly cold, there is little difficulty in drawing your candles, if your tallow be good ; but if it is of inferior quality, it will not harden so well, and requires other means than simply cutting off the knot at the bottom, and drawing them out by means of the stick which you passed through the wick. Hold your moulds over a pan, or your sink, and pour boiling water from a jug over the outsides of your moulds, and draw the candles as quickly as you can. Good housewives never make candles just as they want them. Things done in haste are seldom well done. When a large quantity of tallow has been rendered down, after the killing of beef or mutton, it is better to make it up into candles as soon as possible, packing them, as they cool, into a box, till all are made. This is the most economical method as well as the most satisfactory. Candles burn much longer and better that have been made some time ; and you are spared the mortification of findding yourself out of this necessary article, perhaps, when it would be highly inconvenient for you to make more.

If you have lard, as well as tallow, a mixture of one part of lard, to three of beef or mutton suet is an improvement ; lard alone will not make candles : it is too soft. It is cheaper to buy tallow and make your own candles than to buy them ready made.

The farmer's wife gets six-pence or seven-pence a pound for clean hard mutton or beef tallow at the stores, but if she buys a pound of candles, she gives ten-pence, and in country stores one shilling per pound. Some time ago candles were eight-pence or nine-pence, varying in quality from very bad to good ; but you pay for the ready-made article just as much for the bad as the good. It is much better to make your material up in your own house, and make it well.

In the backwoods where the poor emigrant has not yet cattle enough to afford to kill his own beef, the careful housewife burns no candle ; a tin cup, or a simple tin lamp, holds any clean fat she can get from the pot where meat has been boiled, and a bit of twisted rag serves her for wick ; but even this light is often dispensed with, and the girls knit or sew by the red light of the blazing log-fire, or the pine knots which yield a great deal of resin, and burn with a vivid light. These pine knots are gathered up about the fallow, by the children, where large dead trees have fallen and mouldered away upon the earth. The substance called "Fat pine," which is picked up in the forest, is also sought for and burned. The old upturned roots of pine trees will burn with a strong light, for they also are saturated with the resinous substance. These things are the poor emigrant's candles. Candles should be kept in a dry cool place, and carefully covered from the mice.

The cleanings of the chamber candlesticks, should be put into any old crock, and melted down and strained, or else put to your soap grease.

I have been told that steeping the wicks of the candles, previous to making them up, in a strong solution of saltpetre, improved the brightness of the flame, and tended to destroy the strong smell which newly made candles, especially if not made of pure tallow, are apt to emit. I have not tried this plan; I merely suggest it.

Very handsome globe lamps are now much used, in which melted lard is burned instead of oil, at half the expense of oil.

Much care, however, is required in cleaning and lighting these sort of lamps. The destruction of the glass makes the saving between lard and candles somewhat doubtful. A portable tin lamp, for burning of fine lard in the kitchen, is considered a great saving, by careful housekeepers; and one of these can be bought for one shilling and six-pence at the tinsmiths.

If the fat that rises from boiling beef, be carefully clarified by boiling it down in clean water, letting it stand to be cold, and then boiling the cake of fat again, on the top of the stove, till all the watery part has gone off in steam, very good candles can be made. It must be strained before it is used, as all fat should be, to make good candles.

MANAGEMENT OF WOOL.

The usual time of shearing the sheep in Canada is about the latter end of May, if the weather is warm and dry. The sheep having been washed, are left in open dry pastures for a day or two, that the fleece may be well dried before shearing: the wool being removed, is generally left for some little time, and then carefully picked and sorted by the women and children: all dirty wool is thrown aside, and those who are very careful will sort the coarse from the fine in separate parcels. The wool when picked is then greased with lard, oil or refuse butter, which is first melted and then poured over the wool, and rubbed and stirred about with the hands till it is all greased: about three pounds of grease is allowed to seven or eight pounds of wool, it is then fit for the carding mill: very few persons card at home now, but when first I came to the colony there were very many farmers wives who carded their own wool, but now the greasing as well as the carding is done at the mills. The usual charge is two-pence per ℔ if the wool be greased and picked at home, and three-pence if it be done at the mill: this includes the carding.

Those that sell the wool do not pick it, but sell it in the fleece, just as it comes from the hands of the shearer. Some years ago wool was as low as nine-pence and one shilling per ℔, but now it is more than double that price: one shilling and six-pence cash, per ℔, was given last year, and one shilling and nine-pence, if you took the payment in cloth or yarn. Sheep are decidedly the most profitable stock that can be fed on a Canadian farm: the flock in favourable seasons usually doubles itself. The expense of feeding is not great: peastraw, a little hay and roots, with salt occasionally, and a warm winter yard being the chief requisites. The lambs should not come before the middle or latter end of April, as the cold March winds are very trying to the tender flock. Wool sells at a good price, and mutton and lamb always meet with a market. Sometimes neighbours kill sheep or lambs in the summer, and exchange meat, weight for weight; this is a great accommodation, as in hot weather the meat will not keep more than two or three days good. If however you must kill a sheep to yourself, rub salt on the legs, and hang them in a cool root-house or cellar, and they will be good at a week's end: turn back or remove the flap or skinny part between the loin and the leg. The skin of a sheep or lamb with the wool on it will sell from two to four shillings, according to its size and goodness. The pedlars that travel the country with tins are always willing to trade for skins of sheep or calves: they give you no ready money, but sell tinware, and also buy rags, old iron, bottles and many other things. These pedlars penetrate into the country in every direction: many of them are respectable men and fair dealers ; the housewife often supplies herself with tin milk pans, pails, strainers, mugs and many other conveniences, by selling such things as would otherwise be lost.

Many people think that there is little saving in manufacturing your own wool into cloth, and that it is as well to sell the raw material and buy the ready made cloth. But where there is a large family of girls who can spin on the large wheel (and any one can learn this useful art in a few lessons,) I should say that making home spun cloth and flannel was a decided advantage. The price of weaving flannel is five-pence per yard: it may be six-pence; as all labour has risen in price since the rise in breadstuffs; and full cloth seven-pence or eight-pence per yard. The cloth thus manufactured is generally much more durable than any that is bought at the factory or in the stores, for which you must pay from four shillings to six and three-pence per yard, narrow width. Flannels from two shillings and three-pence to two shillings and nine-pence per yard, yard wide. The home-spun flannel is a long-enduring article, either with cotton-warp or all wool. The usual dresses for home wear both for women and children, among the small farmers, is the country flannel. This is dyed in different colours in the yarn, or made plain grey with a mixture of black wool, in the proportion of one black fleece to three white ones : this is mixed for you at the carding mill, and carded together so as to make the proper colour called sheep's grey. In a subsequent article you will find some notice of dying. The thrifty industrious farmers' wives usually spin yarn for making into flannel sheets, which are very fine and soft and warm for winter wear, and last a very long time: home spun blankets too are made, sometimes on shares with the weaver. These are often checked with a blue or red cross bar, but sometimes are made plain, with only a broad red or blue border. Those families who know nothing of spinning can hire a spinning girl by the week, and this is frequently done and is a very good plan: these spinning girls are usually the daughters of farmers, and generally are respectable and honest.

DYING.

Those who spin their own wool should also know something about dying it. The industrious economical Canadian farmers' wives generally possess some little knowledge of this kind, which enables them to have many varieties in the colours of their home spun garments. The common grey flannel and fulled cloth worn by the men is made by mixing the wool of the black sheep with the wool of the white : one part of black wool to three parts of white, makes a light grey ; but the shade can be increased by adding a little more of the black ; or a dark brown may be produced by adding one fleece of white to three of black. The chief objection made to the black wool by itself, is that it is not so strong as white wool dyed, and is apt to fade in wearing. It is very useful as a grey cloth, for common home-wear, and also as a mixture for socks. This colour is commonly known as "sheep's-grey."

If you have black wool of your own, you can get it mixed at the carding-mill, light or dark, as you wish it ; and even if you have no black wool of your own, they will generally change with you, if you desire it. By paying so much per pound, you can also get different colours dyed for you, if you name them, by your weaver ; but most women prefer preparing their own yarn for weaving.

There are many vegetable dyes that are made use of here, such as the butternut, which dyes a rich, strong, coffee-brown, by steeping the inner bark in cold water for several days, and soaking the yarn in the strained liquor. The flowers of the golden-rod, a plant which grows abundantly in Canada, and blooms in the latter end of summer and fall, boiled down, gives a fine yellow ; and yarn steeped first in this, and then in indigo, turns to a bright full green. The lie of wood-ashes, in which a bit of copperas has been dissolved, gives a nankeen-color or orange, if the strength of the lie be sufficient to deepen it ; but it is hurtful from its corrosive qualities, if too strong. Logwood steeped for some days in house-lee, strained from the chips, and boiled with copperas, gives a permanent black. The yarn should be boiled in it half an hour, and then thrown into cold spring-water, and rinsed up and down many times : two or three waters may be used, and then the hanks hung upon a stick, in a shady place, to dry out of the sun.

The yarn before dying must be well and thoroughly washed, to remove the oil which is made use of in the carding-mill; and well rinsed, to take out the soap used in washing it ; as the soap would interfere with the colours used in the dying process.

Horse-radish leaves boiled, give a good yellow; and the outer skins of onions, a beautiful fawn or pale brown.

To cloud your yarn of a light and dark blue, for mitts, socks or stockings, braid three skeins of yarn together, before you put them into the indigo-vat, and when dry and wound off, the yarn will be prettily clouded with different shades, from dark to very pale blue.

The same effect can be produced in dying with any other colours, if you braid or twist the yarn before you put it into your dye-stuff.

Yarns must be well scoured with hot soap-suds, and rinsed in soft water, before putting them into the dying liquor ; and also wetted in soft water, before you proceed to dye them, or the colours will not be equal: most dark colours are prepared in iron vessels, but light and delicate tints in brass or tin. The dyers use a composition for bright blues, called "Chemists' Blue," a few drops of which will give a beautiful colour to silks, deepening the shade by adding more of the compound. Greens are easily dyed, by first steeping the articles in yellow dye, and then in the blue. The common yellow dye used by the settlers, is either a decoction of the Golden-rod; of a weed known as Smart-weed, (a wild persicaria it is;) or horse-radish leaves; and some others, which any of your neighbours that are used to dying, will describe to you. Fustic, which is sold in the drug-stores, dyes yellow. White-maple bark, boiled, and set with alum, gives a brown grey; but it must not be boiled in an iron vessel.

Logwood, boiled in cider or vinegar, with a small bit of copperas, gives a black dye: it should be boiled in iron.

These are only a very few of the dies made use of: there are many others to be learned.

LOGWOOD DECOCTION

is made by boiling half a pound of logwood chips in two quarts of soft water, and dissolving in it a small bit of pearl-ash. The weed Purslain, boiled down, and the liquor mixed with the logwood, gives a bright blue: set with alum.

To brighten faded purples or lilacs, in cotton prints, rinse in water in which you have dissolved some pearl-ash. If you wish to restore reds or pinks, use vinegar, or a few drops of diluted acid of vitriol, in the rinsing water.

A SLATE-DYE FOR COTTONS.

Having washed the goods to be dyed, clean, in soap-suds, rinse them well in warm water. Put a pound of sumach-bark in a sieve; pour boiling water over it, and let it drain into a pan; put in your goods, and let them steep for two hours, lifting them up and down, from time to time, that it may take the colour evenly. Then take it out, and steep it in a pan of warm water, in which half an ounce of green-copperas has been dissolved for five or six minutes. It will then be a full leaden-grey. But to turn it to a blue-slate colour, run the article through a weak decoction of log-wood, made by boiling an ounce of logwood in a quart of water, with a small lump of pearl-ash; then throw it into warm-water, and handle it, for some minutes. Dry in the shade. For lavender, add a little Brazil-wood.

RAG-CARPETS.

Rag-carpets are among the many expedients adopted by the Canadian-settlers' wives, for procuring comforts at a small cost, and working up materials that would, by the thrifty housewives of England, only be deemed fit for the rag-merchant. Let us see now how a careful settler's wife will contrive, out of worn-out garments, mere shreds and patches, to make a warm, durable and very respectable covering for the floor of her log-parlour, staircase and bed-room.

I asked the wife of the resident-minister of P., what she was going to do with a basket of faded, ragged clothes, old red-flannel shirts, and pieces of all sorts and sizes; some old, some new, some linen and cotton, others woollen. "I am going to tear and cut them up, for making a rag-carpet," she replied; "they are not good enough to give away to any one."

I fancied she was going to sew the pieces like patch-work, and thought it would make a poor carpet, and last no time.

"I will shew you," she said, "what I am going to do with these things." She then took a piece, and with the scissors began cutting it into long narrow strips, about a quarter of an inch wide, not wider; and indeed the narrower the strip, the better. She did not cut quite through, when she came to the end, but left just as much as would serve to hold it together with the next strip, turning the piece in her hand, and making another cut; and so she went on cutting or tearing, till that piece was disposed of: she then proceeded to a second, having first wound up the long strip: if a break occurred, she joined it with a needle and thread, by tacking it with a stitch or two. Sometimes she got a bit that would tear easily, and then she went on very quickly with her work. Instead of selecting her rags all of one shade, for the ball, she would join all kinds of colours and materials. "The more lively the contrast, the better the carpet would look," she said. Some persons, however, wind all the different colours separately, in large balls, and then the carpet will be striped. A white and red ball, wound together, makes a pretty chain pattern, through dark stripes.

My friend continued to cut and tear, join the strips and wind up, till she had a ball as big as a baby's head; and I continued to watch her, still puzzling my brains to think how these big balls could be turned into a carpet; till she lightened my darkness, by telling me that these balls, when there was a sufficient weight of them, were sent to the weavers, with so much cotton-warp, which should be doubled and twisted on the spinning-wheel. If you double and twist the warp, yourself, the weaver will charge 6d. a yard for the weaving; but if he doubles and twists, he charges 8d. A pound and a half of rags will make one yard of carpet, with the warp. Many persons dye the warp themselves: lie of wood-ashes, with a little copperas, makes a deep yellow: logwood and copperas makes a black, and indigo and lee from the house, gives a full blue. Made up with the coloured warp, the carpet looks better, and does not dirty so soon.

The white cotton rags are better washed clean, and then dyed with any of these dyes. Those who do not care to take this trouble, use them as they are, but they soil soon.

The best sort of rag-carpet is made by intermitting the colours as much as possible, cutting the strips through, instead of turning the corners: you have more work in joining, but the effect is better; and there are no unsightly ends on the surface of the carpet. Bits of bright red flannel, of blue, green or pink mousselin-de-laine, or stuffs of any bright colour, old shawls and handkerchiefs, and green baize, will give you a good, long-enduring fabric, that will last for eight or ten years, with care. Children can be taught to cut the rags, and join and wind into balls, ready for the weaving.

To the more wealthy class this humble manufacture may seem a very contemptible affair; but it is not for the gay and luxurious that such things are suitable; though I have seen them in the houses of some of our best settlers, who were wise enough, like the wife of the rector, to value whatever was comfortable, and save buying. When well assorted, I assure you these rag-carpets make by no means a despicable appearance, on the rough floors of a Canadian farmer's house

I would recommend the settler's wife to keep a basket or box, into which all scraps of woollen and cotton, and any worn-out clothes, can be put. A rainy day may be chosen for the cutting and winding.— Another box may be appropriated for the reception of the balls when wound up. The thinnest cottons, and even muslins, can be used for the purpose; only that the latter articles may be cut half an inch wide.

To wash a rag-carpet let it be ripped into breadths, and taken to a creek or river, and flounced up and down, and then laid out to dry: no rinsing is required: the edges should be well bound with a broad strip of cloth. Thirty pounds of rags will make about twenty yards of carpetting; and when you consider that you can buy no sort of carpet worth making up, under 4s. a yard, in any of the country stores, this simple substitute, made out of refuse materials, is not to be despised.

WOOLLEN HOME-SPUN CARPETS.

Those farmers who keep a good many sheep, and whose wives and daughters are well skilled in the homely but valuable art of spinning on the big-wheel, often turn the coarser wool to good account by spinning a stout yarn, dying it of various gay colours, and sending it to the weavers to be woven into carpetting. The warp and woof are of wool, and if well done, make a handsome appearance: a dark green ground, with checkers of red, yellow or blue, look well; or sheep's-grey and checked with red, like a drugget, looks neat and unpretending on the floor of a log-house.

Among the emigrants into whose hands this little book may go, there may be some who have followed weaving as a trade: to them no instruction is requisite on the simple art of weaving druggets; and let me tell such an one, that many a poor settler has become rich by setting up his loom in the backwoods of Canada, in their own house, or in the small villages. Blankets, shawls, plaids, cloaking, the country flannel, both white and grey, and carpets such as I have described, will give plenty of employment to the industrious man, while his sons carry on the labours of the farm.

Women often weave, and make a good living; and I have heard a very respectable farmer's daughter say, that she could weave from ten to twelve yards of plain flannel a day. Sometimes she wove the wool on shares.

Carding is not so often done in the settlers' houses as it used to be, so many carding-machines now being in operation, and mills in all the towns for fulling and carding; but many years back this work was chiefly done by hand.

Neither flax nor hemp are much grown in Canada at present; consequently there is little home manufacture of that kind. The big wheel is generally substituted for the small spinning-wheel, as being more suitable to wool; though for fine yarn, perhaps, the latter is as good.

KNITTING.

If you do not understand this useful art, I strongly advise you to turn your attention to it as soon as possible: children cannot learn to knit too soon. Those who are not already able to knit a sock or a mitt, will find some kind neighbour ready and willing to teach them; it will be nice work on the voyage out: a few pounds of coloured or white yarn is no ill store, for your boys and husband will need plenty of woollen socks and mitts in Canada.

There is no country where there is so much knitting-work done as in Canada, for when the household of the settler is supplied with socks, stockings, mitts, and gauntlets (these are long, thick mitts, that come halfway up the arm, and are used in driving), the surplus yarn meets with ready sale at the stores when manufactured into socks, &c. Men's socks sell at one shilling and six pence to two shillings and three pence, according to their goodness: the best article in Canada, as elsewhere, fetches the best price. The second or even third-rate wool, knitted up, can be made more profitable than the best wool sold in the fleece; and children and women will earn many a dollar if they are industrious, in the evening, between twilight and candle-light.

I knew a settler's daughter who knitted seventy-five pairs of socks one year, to provide clothes for her marriage,—and a complete wardrobe she made up, without any cost to her parents; for she had been given a ewe-lamb, and this in due time produced an increase, so that she had a little flock of her own, and clothed herself from the wool, which she could card, dye, spin, and knit herself.

It would be useless for me to describe all the different patterns that the skilful knitter can devise, for mitts and children's socks, or the colours chosen for that purpose; but I have seen striped mitts, flowered, spotted and plain, ribbed and unribbed. A young lady in my neighbourhood, has gained many a prize at the County and Provincial Agricultural Shows, by her socks and gauntlets: the same chance is open to every one who has skill and taste in this useful art.

Every young woman is prized in this country according to her usefulness; and a thriving young settler will rather marry a never, industrious girl, who has the reputation for being a good spinner and knitter, than one who has nothing but a pretty face to recommend her. This is as it should be; and I would bid the young daughters of the emigrant to bear the fact in mind, if they wish to become the wives of steady young men, and wish to prosper in the world. Nor do I confine my advice, on this head, to the daughters of the poorer class of emigrants. In the new country to which they are going, knowledge of the simple art of knitting must form one of the occupations of the females of the higher or more educated class, who reside in the agricultural portion of the colony.

A family who are too proud or indolent to work in Canada, will sink into absolute poverty :—they had better never have crossed the Atlantic. To the mind of the well-regulated female, there is no disgrace in so feminine an occupation : she is kept in countenance by ladies of her own rank ; and indeed would be considered as a very useless and foolish person, if she despised that which every one here practises. Here, as in Germany and Holland, young ladies take their knitting-bag out with them, and carry it to the house of a friend when they go out : it is certainly a very sociable employment. The earlier children learn to knit, the better ; those who learn late in life, seldom acquire the same quickness, as those who learn in childhood. I have myself experienced the disadvantage of not learning this sort of work till I was old, and my finger joints had lost their flexibility, consequently I am a slow and unskilful knitter : I can hardly shape a sock or a stocking.

Many persons knit cradle-quilts, and large coverlets for beds, of coloured yarns, and among the town-bred young ladies, curtains, tidies for sofas, and toilet covers, of all sorts and patterns are manufactured with the knitting-needles, and cottons of suitable qualities.

Because store goods are now lower than they used to be formerly, and socks can be bought cheap, let not the farmer's daughter despise the useful art of knitting and spinning : they belong to her station in life, in this country, and few grow rich who abandon this homely occupation.

THE DAIRY.

The following remarks, on the management of the dairy, were published last year, under the title of an "Essay on Butter-Making;" and for which a prize was awarded to the authoress by the members of the "Hamilton Agricultural Association, and Farmers' Club." It was copied by several Agricultural periodicals, and weekly papers, which induced me to give it in an abridged form for the benefit of the female emigrant; its usefulness having received the sanction of many practical Canadian settlers.

The want of succulent food, during the long winter, is one of the causes of a deficiency in the butter-producing qualities of the milk. Where roots, such as good sound turnips, cannot be had, the deficiency might be supplied by boiling oats, in a good quantity of water; a quart of oats thus given, morning and night, will keep a cow in good order, with her ordinary food, and greatly increase the quantity of her milk; or bran mashes made thin, with boiling water, left to cool down twice a-day, with a handful of salt once a week, will tell well. Some of the careful small farmers, will take the trouble of boiling a lock or two of hay with water, sufficient for a good drink; but I should think the boiled oats, or the bran, or a handful or two of indian meal, boiled in water would be preferable, affording nourishment, as well as milk. Having thus far spoken in behalf of the treatment of the animals, as respects their food, and general comfort, I would next observe, that regularity in the time of milking, is of great importance. In the morning, as early as possible, the milking hour should be established, that the cow may go forth to feed *while the dew yet lies fresh upon the herbage.* This is of great consequence in the hot dry summer weather: it is soon after sunrise, in the early spring time of the day, while the grass is wet with the clear refreshing dew of night, that the beasts of the field shake off their slumbers, and rise to feed; they then can afford time to lie down during the noon-day heat, to ruminate and digest their food. The wise man will consider this, and will derive advantage from studying the natural habits of the animals under his care. Those persons whose occupation is too small, to admit of keeping their cows in constant pasture, would find it an advantage to make an enclosure, even if the ground be but scantily provided with grass, as a night yard. The early milking will enable them to be let out to feed. I allude to such cows as roam at large in the woods and wastes, and on the plain land. A little occasional fodder, given to encourage them to return to the usual milking place, will generally ensure their coming home, and they should not be kept waiting, but be attended to at once. I recommend this plan because I have known much loss of time, caused by the looking up the cow, loss of milk and butter, and what may sound strangely to some persons, *loss of life*. How many of the children that have, at different times, been lost in this Province, have been sent out in the forest to seek for the cows, and straying from the beaten path, or bewildered by converging ones, have returned no more to their home, but have perished miserably.

Cows can be taught to come home at the sound of a horn: if food be given them at such times—the habit will be easily established. I have known this practised in Canada, and I have heard that it is common in the pastoral countries on the continent of Europe, for the herd boy to collect his cattle in that way. No doubt the shepherd's pipe was used for this purpose, as well as for the shepherd's own amusement. I have heard of cows coming home in towns regularly, at the sound of a factory bell, which they learned to regard as a signal for the milking hour. The advantage of establishing regular hours needs hardly to be further insisted on. We shall now proceed to make a few remarks on the next most important matter, which is the dairy.

The coolness in summer, and warmth in winter of the dairy, are two most essential points to be considered in the making of good butter. The dairy-maid may be skilful and orderly, and yet if the place in which the milk is stored, be not perfectly cool and airy, her labour will do her little credit; with her superior knowledge, she may make a *better* article than some of her neighbors, but not the best. In this country, the dairy women often work under the greatest disadvantages. Frequently she has nothing better to keep her milk in, than a close damp cellar or root-house, where to preserve thorough ventilation is impossible: without proper utensils, and conveniencies for carrying on the process, complete success can hardly be expected. Instead of being surprised that there is so little really fine butter sent to market, the wonder should be, that under such disadvantages, there is so much. Let the men look to the providing of a suitable place where the work of the dairy can be carried on, and the result would speedily repay the cost and labour bestowed upon it. The space allotted to the dairy is generally too limited: it should be large enough to admit of thorough ventilation, and room for carrying on the necessary work of churning, cheese-making, &c. A sunk floor, well paved with brick, or stone, and a covered drain, and grating, are advisable, to carry off any moisture. The floor can then be kept cool in hot weather, by throwing a few pails of water down, which is a constant practice in the dairies in the home country. I have seen dairies built with good stone foundations, and the walls of squared cedars, placed upright, forming a solid compact building, the windows latticed, and each window supplied with a wooden shutter, which could be lowered at pleasure, to exclude the sun, wind, or rain ; by this simple arrangement, the sun's rays need never have access to the dairy. A porch, with shelves, and a bench, on which the empty pans, trays, pails, &c., can be set up to dry after scouring, are great conveniencies.

Pans of thick glass are much used in home dairies; also pans lined with zinc, and a species of enamel, such as the iron-stone pan, and preserving pans, are coated with ; trays of wood about four inches in depth, with peg holes for letting off the milk, used to be much the fashion, but I think wooden ware is liable to crack and warp, during hot weather, and is less easily cleansed from the sour particles of the milk.

With respect to the churn, a small volume might be written on the kinds : in my opinion the simpler the machinery the better. The old-fashioned upright churn, worked with the staff and cross-dash, may be as effective in the end, but it imposes a greater amount of labour, than such as are wrought with a winch. The simplest churn, and one that I have heard much praised by every good dairy-women, is a box churn, the sides of which are sloped, so as to leave no acute angles and corners, always difficult to keep clean ; the sides are provided with dashers, and a dasher also is affixed to the beam of the handle, which passes through the churn : this can be unscrewed, and the buttermilk is drawn off by means of a plug-hole, near the bottom of the churn. This churn may be bought at a cooper's for 12s 6d. I have also seen a churn with an iron wheel, turned with a winch, which is very easy to work. There is the old barrel-churn, which is also simple and effective, the advantage of this last being, that the butter can be washed before being removed from the churn, ready for salting. Earthenware pots, or good stoneware jars, are best for storing the cream in. With each jar there should be a clean, smooth, wooden staff, for stirring the cream ; this is a matter that dairy-maids pay little attention to here, and yet it is of some importance, in thoroughly mixing the cream together, so as to prevent any sour milk, or whey from settling below, thus giving a disagreeable taste to the whole mass of butter. In cool weather, scalding the cream, just before churning, greatly facilitates the churning, and obviates the necessity of putting hot water into the cream, a practice in very common use, but which I believe is very injurious to the richness and good colour of the butter, giving it a white, greasy, poor appearance. In the winter season, the cream jars should be brought into a warm room over night, which will thicken the cream, and bring it to the required temperature for churning. Frozen cream will make frothy butter, or no butter will be obtained, after much labour. In hot weather the churn should be allowed to stand some time with clear cold water in it, and if the weather be very hot, immerse the churn in water; if a plunge churn be used, it can be place in a tub of cold water, during the churning. Many excellent dairy women are in favour of churning cream and the strippings, while others prefer the cream only; I think myself that the richest butter is produced from the cream alone, but possibly a larger return may be obtained from the former practice.

Where cows are fed on turnips, a small quantity of saltpetre, dissolved in a little warm water, and mixed with the cream before churning, is said to remove the flavour of the turnips from the butter. I knew a farmer's wife who always practised it in the winter season. This same person, who was celebrated in the part of the country where she lived, for good butter, used, during the hot weather, to put half a pint of cold spring water into each of the milk pans or trays, to raise the cream, and in winter she put the same quantity of boiling water to raise the temperature, for the same purpose.

Many approve of the Devonshire and Cornish plan of scalding the milk, but careless servants are apt to let the milk get over-heated, which decidedly injures the flavour of the butter; but very good butter is no doubt made by heating the milk, and the largest amount of cream is thus raised. The milk should stand some hours before it is heated. It has another advantage, that of keeping the skimmed milk sweet for the use of the family.

In a North-Lancashire paper, I saw the following advice to dairy-women, which, as it is easily tried, I will insert. "Heat two pans of the same size with boiling water, let them stand a few minutes, then pour off the water, and pour in the new milk; cover the pan that has the milk in it, with the empty heated pan; this will raise the cream in less time, and in larger quantity than if put into cold pans. Try it?" Some persons never wash their butter, but absorb the buttermilk in the following way: They place a lump of butter in a coarse linen cloth, and beat against the sides of the churn, wringing the cloth from time to time in cold salt and water, repeating the beating process until the milky particles are completely removed. The famous Epping butter is thus treated; this butter has the character in London, of being the finest in England; very little salt is used for seasoning it; but as the sale of it is so rapid, probably the keeping properties have hardly been tested.

The thorough extracting of the milky particles, and the working of the salt well through the mass cannot be too much insisted on. Attention to cleanliness, coolness in summer, and a moderate temperature in winter, are the three most important matters for securing good marketable butter.

The following recipe was given me by an old country farmer's wife, who was celebrated for the excellent quality of her butter, both for flavour and keeping :—

To thirty-two pounds of well-washed butter, she allowed the following mixture: two and a-half pounds of finely-rolled salt, six ounces of saltpetre, and half a pound of fine, rolled, lump sugar; these materials were well ground together, and worked into the mass of butter, which was then packed into a stone jar; over the top of the butter, she poured a strong clear brine, sufficient to cover the whole surface two inches in depth; a white cloth was then laid over the jar, and above this the stone lid pressed tightly down. This butter, she said, would be as good at the end of the second year as the first.

Those cows that get their living all spring and summer, roaming at large through the forest, often feed upon the wild leeks, which spring up in the rich leafy soil of the woods; the flavour imparted to the milk by this sort of food is very odious. The milk is almost useless, excepting for the feeding and fattening of calves; but while this circumstance annoys the settler not a little, there is one advantage that makes amends, in some measure, for the leek diet; which is, that the cattle that are poor and weak, and often in a diseased condition from poor feed, during the long winters, are restored to health and good condition very speedily, by feeding upon the green leeks.

A small piece of saltpetre dissolved in the cream, I have been told, will remedy the ill flavour, but of this I cannot speak from experience. There are other plants also, on which cows feed in the woods, that give a rank, weedy taste to the milk. These evils are confined to those who, having settled on the new land, cannot command pastures for the cattle to feed in.

During the chopping season, the cattle browse a great deal upon the shoots of the felled trees, particularly upon the sugar maple, the bass, elm, beech and other hardwood trees. It used formerly to be the practice to let the calves run with the cows, but this is a very unwise one; and now it is more usual to take the calf from the mother before it has sucked at all, and feed it by finger; in a few days it may be taught to drink out of the pail, and is then put into some small enclosure where it can pick a little grass. A month's new milk is all that is allowed; then a sufficiency of skimmed milk all the summer. Many calves are killed by being given sour milk in hot weather. A little very thin flour gruel, with a little milk in it, is sometimes given, when there is a scarcity of its proper nourishment.

Salt is necessary for cattle and sheep in Canada, to keep them in health; it also induces them to return home.

In winter, wood ashes, and clay are left near the feeding places for the use of the sheep and cows.

Warm yards are of as much use as good feeding, and this is a point often miserably neglected by the small holders. The Irishman, however miserable his own dwelling may be, will generally take care that the cow and the pig are warmly housed. I actually once saw a patchwork quilt, pegged up in front of the shed where the cows were stabled, though from the appearance of the dwelling house, I should have supposed it could ill have been spared from the children's beds, but the cow must be sheltered whoever else suffered from the cold wind and snow.

A want of attention to the comfort of the cows also imposes much discomfort upon the females who have to milk them, exposed to the biting blast of cold and frost, and drifting snow. Men should bear this in mind, and provide as well as they can, against such evils; it is bad policy, as well as cruelty. A dairy-woman cannot execute her task perfectly with hands benumbed by cold. The excuse for the want of attention to these things is: "we have so much to do clearing land, and fencing, and building, cropping and harvesting, that we have no time to make sheds, and fence in cattle yards." The same thing is said about making gardens. "We really have no time for these things." But a wise man would rather clear an acre or two less land, and take the time for adding to the comfort and health of the family. I notice this error as a friendly hint to husbands, and masters of families, which I hope they will act upon.

CHEESE.

It is only of late years, that much of the attention of the Canadian settler has been turned to the subject of cheese-making. The reason of the neglect of this valuable portion of dairy produce, is evident. During the process of clearing wild land, the want of a sufficiency of pasture for the cows, obliges the prudent farmer to limit this branch of his stock, according to his supply of fresh grass or dry provender for their support; consequently, for some years, he is unable to keep cows enough for the profitable manufacturing of cheese as well as butter; but now that the country is opening out on every side, and there are many fine cleared farms of long standing, and under good cultivation, dairies are increasing everywhere, and the farmer's wife is beginning to see the great advantage of making good cheese, for which an excellent market can always be obtained.

Good rich cheese will sell at 7½d per ℔; inferior fetches 5d. Now this is of course encouraging, and it is well worth taking pains to make a superior article, when it meets with a remunerative price.

I will condense, as much plain instruction on the subject of cheese-making, as will afford a general knowledge of the subject, for the benefit of such of my female readers, who may be strangers to the process of making cheese; with a few hints on various subjects, which may prove useful to the bush settler's wife, whose operations are confined to making cheese upon a very limited scale ; and, first, let me give directions as to the common method of preparing the rennet.

THE RENNET

is prepared from the first stomach or maw of the sucking calf. Any milk-consuming animal will, I believe, answer the same purpose for curdling milk ; such as the lamb, kid, and even the sucking pig; but the calf's maw alone, is used in the dairy work of cheese-making.

The calf's maw being emptied of the curd and slime, is carefully turned, and well and thoroughly washed with clean water, then thrown into a brine of cold salt and water for about twelve hours; it is then rub well with salt, and stretched upon a flexible stick, by bending it, and holding both ends in one hand : over this, the bag is drawn, and tied at the open end, near the ends of the stick; it may then be hung up to dry, in the house, or in the sun, on the house-wall in the open air, till quite hard ; then take out the stick, and put the rennet bag into a paper bag, and hang up in a cool place : it is better for keeping a year, I have been told ; but it may be used in a few weeks or months. Some persons, after washing, picking, and salting the bag, put it into a strong brine, in an earthen vessel, and tie it close down ; others fill the bag quite full of salt, tie, and hang it up. In the second plan, a spoonful or two of the brine only is used, but if the rennet is dried, as in the first and last instance, a small piece is cut off, and steeped in warm water for some hours before putting it to the milk. Whether cheese is made, or not, in a family, the rennet should be preserved, as it is convenient to have a little sweet curd and whey, as an addition to the dinner or supper table, especially with a little ripe fruit ; it makes a nice dish for the children. If the rennet brine be good, a dessert spoonful will set a good dish of milk ; the milk should be as warm as when first drawn from the cow ; if too hot, the curd will be tough; if cold, not firm enough to separate from the whey.

TO MAKE GOOD ONE-MEAL CHEESE.

This cheese is made entirely of the morning's new milk, strained into a well-cleaned cheese-tub. If the milk be too much cooled in its transit from the milking yard to the dairy, a portion of it must be heated, but not boiled, in a clean vessel, on the fire or stove, and returned to the tub, pouring in as much as will make the whole quantity the same heat as new milk just drawn from the cow ; some add a small portion of hot water for bringing the milk to a right temperature, and say that the water comes off in the whey, without impoverishing the curd; it is certainly less trouble. The Wiltshire cheese, I have been told, is done so, and even has scalding water thrown upon the curd.

The rennet is then stirred in: if good, half a teacupful should curdle a good-sized cheese. In about twenty minutes, or half an hour, the curd will be formed, and with a saucer, a small wooden dish, or a wooden cheese-knife, the curd may be cut across in several directions, till the whey rise clear between the gashes you have made on the curd. It may then be broken lightly, and left for a few minutes longer. Have ready a cheese basket; this is a loose square, or round basket without a handle. Set it across your tub on a wooden frame, called a cheese-ladder, which is a simple contrivance: two long sticks, and two or three short bits, nailed across to support the basket or vat: a thin cloth being laid in, the basket being large enough to admit of the edges hanging over the sides: the curd is laded out of the tub, and to aid in the draining off the whey, from time to time bring the ends and sides of the cloth together gently, so as to give an increase of pressure; when the curd is well drained, bring your vat beside the basket; have a fresh cloth laid in it; remove the curd into the vat, breaking it up, as you put it in; mingle in it a little salt, not very much, and continue to fill till the vat is full; fold over the sides of the cloth, and turn it in the vat with care; tuck the sides and ends neatly in a little way, and set your cheese in the press, not putting on the full power of weight, at first: slow pressure is best, till you again cloth your cheese. Some break the curd up fine the second removal, and increase the pressure.

At the end of sixteen or eighteen hours, the cheese may be removed to a shallow tray: a little fine salt is sprinkled over the upper surface. Some make a brine, in which they lay the cheese, and turn it, after eight or ten hours time, washing the sides with the brine, before removing it to the shelf. If very rich, a linen binder, the full depth of the cheese, may be fastened round to prevent the cheese from cracking and bulging. Care is required in turning these rich cheeses at first, but in a few days the rind begins to harden, and it can be be moved with less difficulty.

A RICH CHEESE.

This is made by adding the nights' milk with the cream, warmed to the heat of new milk, to the morning's milk, instead of making it of new milk alone. This cheese is generally considered richer than the new milk cheese, and is, I believe, the mode used in Cheshire.

The larger the quantity of milk, the better will be the quality of the cheese made. To make the fine, blue moulded cheeses, so much admired by some cheese-fanciers, sprinkle a little fine flour in between the layers of curd, when putting it into the vat. This was a secret told me by a dairy-woman, famous for the manufacture of the blue cheeses.

A BUSH CHEESE.

If the settler's wife desires to make a few cheeses during the hot weather, and yet has not a sufficient quantity of milk for the purpose, the following plan is often adopted. We will suppose that the dairy consists of only three cows, the milk of which would be insufficient to make a cheese of any size. Set out the night's milk, reserving only a bowl for the use of the family ; add this to the morning's milk, warming it a little, to bring the whole to the proper heat; mix in a good spoonful of rennet, and set as usual; drain the curd, leave it in the cheese-basket, covering it over with several folds of clean cloth to prevent its getting dry and hard, and set it aside in a cool corner of the dairy, cellar, or root-house, or wherever you keep your milk. The following morning, do the same; add the night and morning's milk, and curdle as before; add this day's curd to that in the basket, and if you have enough curd with the two gatherings, braid and mix all with your hands; throw in a very little salt, and put into your vat, and press as before. Sometimes three of these double meals are required for making one good-sized cheese. A simple press is made by the bush farmers, with a long lever, and a big stone or two; but this can be seen at any of your neighbor's, and would be understood far better by sight than description. I used to press my bush cheese with heavy stones on a board, put on the top of the vat; but it is not so regularly pressed this way. A far easier and readier way of preparing cheese was told me by a Sussex farmer's wife; the same as that practised in Stilton ; which I recommend to be adopted by Canadian farmer's wives.

SELF-PRESSING CHEESE MOULD.

This consists of a tin cylinder, about a foot in depth, and eight inches in diameter ; this is perforated with holes, at intervals of about two inches from each other, all over its surface. At each end is a moveable lid, that fits on like the lid of a common tin canister. The curd is put into this mould, when it has been fully set, and drained from the whey ; the whey that still remains with the curd, flowing freely out from the holes without any other pressure; all that is necessary being to turn the mould about every hour or so, bottom upwards, for a couple of days, or till it is firm enough to turn out, and put in the salting tray. Some persons have a broad wooden hoop, that they slip over the cheese, and suffer to remain round it till it is time to remove it to the shelf for drying. I have seen cheese brushed over with whitewash to preserve it from flies, and linen binders, passed round to keep it in shape.

A GOOD HOUSEHOLD CHEESE

Is made by skimming the night's milk, and adding the milk without the cream, to the new morning's milk. This is called by some, two-meal cheese, and is very good for household use; and eaten before it becomes very dry, is a pleasant cheese, equal to the single Gloucester. It has this advantage, that it enables you to make a little butter for the table, while you are making cheese. A small pinch of saffron, steeped in warm water, may be mixed in with the milk to give a richer colour to the cheese; but a really good rich cheese needs no colouring.

CREAM CHEESE.

Take one quart of rich cream, when well soured; put it in a linen cloth, and tie it as close as you can, as you would a batter-pudding; hang it upon a hook, with a pan below it, to drain for two days; then turn it into another clean cloth, and let it drain for another two days, till it becomes solid; then lay it on a clean fine cloth, spread on a plate; fold the cloth neatly over on each side, and turn it over in the cloth on the plate; lay another smaller plate over it, turning every six hours; sprinkle a little fine pounded salt, and lay vine leaves over and under to ripen; it is fit to eat in a few days, when slightly coated.

POTATO CHEESE.

This cheese is made with mashed potatoes, salted slightly, and mixed with cheese curd, taking care to braid it well together, and press as other cheese.

POULTRY.

In these days, when all the world is running after Cochin China and Shanghai, Bantams and Dorkings, Dutch, Spanish, and Poland fowls, the omission of a chapter on the poultry-yard would, I fear, be regarded as a grave neglect in a work that is chiefly devoted to instruction on points of rural economy.

Of the management of the rarer breeds of poultry, I have had no experience myself at present, but I have been assured by those who have been most successful in their rearing of Shanghai and Cochin China fowls, that they have had no more trouble with them than with the common barn-door fowls. The want of having good fowls and plenty of eggs, seems simply to consist in attention to their being well-supplied with good food, clean water, ashes, lime, rubbish and charcoal; a clean, airy pen in summer, and a warm, sheltered roost in winter. A supply of animal food seems greatly to promote vigor in fowls. Where fewer dogs are kept, the fowls come in for much valuable food, which tells well upon the richness and increase of their flesh and eggs. Those persons who succeed best with poultry, are careful to cater well for them, and will boil up all sorts of refuse vegetables, especially potatoes, carrots, parsnips, and other roots to mix with their grain. Boiled Indian corn, or crushed corn steeped, makes very satisfying food for fowls.

In this country, fowls in general, are left very much to take care for themselves. They have the run of the barn-yard, and are even allowed by some of the improvident, small growers, who are seldom the most economical managers, to have the run of the barn itself. That such a plan is a very wasteful one it hardly needs any one to declare. Not only is there a vast and unnecessary expenditure of valuable grain, but a considerable deal that is injured and made unsaleable. By a little care of the dross and refuse corn, the fowls would be equally well fed without that woful waste which the want of a proper system of management produces. I have known this plan pursued even among farmers who were careful in other matters, but whose wives were so short sighted, as to persuade them into the belief that, because they were able to sell a few dozen of eggs at tenpence or a shilling a dozen, in the early part of the season, that this was all clear gain—quite forgetful of the loss and injury to the valuable grain.

Fowls fed with scalded bran, or the coarse part of the flour, generally known here as sharps or canaille, mixed with potatoes or other vegetables, any scraps of meat and refuse grain, and curdled milk scalded so as to harden the curd, with access to ashes and gravelly substances, will ensure plenty of eggs without giving them access to the barn or granary.

Besides the eggs consumed in the family, since the commencement of the laying season, my children have sent to market upwards of one hundred dozen eggs, which have been sold at prices varying from one shilling to seven pence halfpenny per dozen. The fowls have received little grain, and not much attention—in number they were about thirty-five. They were shut out from the barn, and had no access to the seed in the fields. With more attention we might have had a still larger return, but this is sufficient to prove that fowls are well worthy of the attention of the Canadian housewife.

During the grain-sowing season, and if there be any wheat fields near the farm yard, it will be advisable to confine the fowls within an enclosure—a green yard, with a high picket fence round is the best sort of fowl-yard. A coarse thread, of common Dutch twine, tied from post to post, will effectually prevent any fowl from attempting to fly over the fence. A shelter at one end of this inclosure for roost and laying place; plenty of dust and ashes in a heap for them to roll in, with a trough for water, will be all-sufficient; a tree makes a good summer roost, and a few bushes for shelter from the great heat of the sun is also advisable for the comfort of this fowl-yard. The confinement need not last long at either season, and it is well worth the trouble of having such a covenience made to prevent loss and vexation of spirit. When once made it lasts for years, and would soon repay the farmer for the outlay of a few days labour, and a few nails for fastening up the pickets.

The young chickens are seldom cooped for more than a few days, if the weather be fine and warm: they will thrive as well abroad, or in the enclosed yard.

For the rearing of geese and ducks with profit, they should have access to a creek or pond of water, mill-dam or lake. On the rice-beds geese fatten finely, and do well; but as the goslings are hatched in the spring, a season which is usually very changeable, more care is required for keeping the tender goslings from the cold and wet, than is usually bestowed upon the chickens, which come later and are more hardy. The goose is usually cooped in a large coop, and this is surrounded with a fence, enclosing several square yards of green turf. A flat pan with some stones in it is given for the goslings to wash in: the stones enable them to stand and keep themselves dry while drinking, as too much wet is bad for them during the first week or ten days. Scalded bran, curds, and crumbs, or soaked and crushed Indian corn may be given them, which, with the grass in their yard, will be all-sufficient. At a fortnight's end, if the weather be dry, they may be let out.

Geese are often found great depredators in the young wheat fields. The old gander and brood geese are treated with a yoke or neck-ring: this is simply an oblong piece of shingle, shaped into an oval form, with a hole in the centre. This is drawn over the head of the goose, and effectually keeps it from breaking into the fields through the rail-fences:—a goose is never at the trouble of climbing, so the remedy is always effectual.

I have known geese sold as low as one shilling and three pence a-piece; but now they are double that price.

To make geese profitable, the farmer's wife plucks them twice and sometimes thrice in the season; but the quills are not touched, so that the animal suffers but little from the operation. The head of the goose or gander is put into a bag; (an old sock is sometimes used;) this is tied about the neck—the darkness keeps the creature quiet—and the feathers are plucked into a basket: a still day and a warm one is chosen; and in the moulting season the feathers fall easily, and perhaps the loss of them may be a relief from the heat of such a thick covering.

Turnips chopped small; raw and boiled potatoes, with the run of the barn-yard, is the goose's fare in the winter. A low log-shed, with a door to shut them in at night, is necessary. They also, as all fowls do, require lime and ashes in their house in winter. The goose begins to lay in March or April; but if the season be at all mild, in the latter part of March. The egg should be brought in as soon as laid, as the frost chills it very quikly; placed in a box of bran or saw-dust, till the goose is ready to sit, and the goose must be given water, or let out to wash and feed once a day—she sits thirty days. It is better to remove the early-hatched goslings, when strong enough, to a basket, but I would not feed them; return them at night to the mother, and you will most likely have the rest of the family by the following noon. Late-hatched goslings are often allowed to go abroad under the care of the old ones without any shelter, and in some dry seasons they will succeed as well as those that have had a great fuss made with them; but in cold wet springs care and shelter are requisite to ensure the lives of the little family. If the cock be remarkable for his tender care of his wives, the gander is no less admirable as a father in protecting and cherishing his young ones. There is much that is interesting and admirable to be learned in the poultry-yard by the careful observer; and many a pleasant, cheerful hour may be passed in the care of the domestic birds about the farmer's yard: children learn lessons of care and kindness, and many a moral lesson the wise mother may inculcate, even from so homely a creature as the common hen.

In suitable localities the duck is easily managed; but they need a constant supply of water, and will not thrive unless they have free access to a stream or pond. The little ducklings require to be cooped with the mother, and fed with curds, bran, or some soft food for a few weeks. They are very useful in freeing a garden from insects; and thrive well in dry weather, while very young. Near lakes and mill-ponds they get their own living on the weeds and shell-fish; but where no water is, they require a great deal of feeding.

The turkey breeds well in Canada; but the young ones are great ramblers, and do much hurt to the young grain; and for this reason the farmer is shy of breeding them. Some manage to confine them by tethering the hen to a stake, when the young will not ramble far from her.

The Guinea fowl are hardy enough to be kept; and even the tender pea-fowl prosper and breed well in Canada; roosting within the barn in the winter; and it is not often they die from cold if well fed. I know many farmer's wives who rear the young to sell, which they do at various prices, from seven shillings and six pence to three dollars a head.

Of late years poultry have been more attended to as a matter of profit, as well as of amusement, and no doubt will well repay the care bestowed upon them.

FIRE.

Among the casualties that bring danger and alarm into a Canadian settler's homestead, there is none more frequent than fire—none more terrible ; but, one, where a little presence of mind, and knowing what best to do on the spur of the moment, may save both life and property. As a timely care will often do more by preventing the danger, than much exertion after it has occurred, I will warn those whose houses are heated by stoves, to have the pipes taken down, especially where there are elbows or turns in them, twice during the long winter months ; have a sheet of tin or iron nailed down on the floor below the stove :—this is less troublesome than a box, as in old times was the custom, filled with sand. The kitchen stoves are, from their construction, less liable to take fire than any other : the dampers being pushed in will stop the draught from ascending into the pipe. If it is a chimney that is on fire, after throwing water on the logs, hang up a cloth, rug, blanket, or anything you can get hold of, made wet, in front of the chimney, and keep the doors shut ; a wisp of wet straw, or old woollen rags tied on a long staff, and put up the chimney, may extinguish the fire. All houses should have a ladder at hand ; there are usually ledges left on the roof, near the chimney, to facilitate cleaning them ; a bunch of pine-boughs, or a bundle of straw fastened to a rope, and drawn up and down by two persons, is the common chimney-sweep of a Canadian house. A quantity of salt thrown on the fire will damp flame. A mass of fire may be put out or kept down by covering it and pressing it down ; and many a child has been saved by being wrapped tightly up, so as to exclude the access of air. Even a cotton garment, if pressed closely and the air excluded, has been safely used to smother fire ; but linen or woollen is best of anything for this purpose. A table-cover, carpet, rug, any large thing should be caught up, unhesitatingly, to extinguish fire.

One of the great causes of destruction of houses by fire, in Canada, may be traced to the want of care in removing ashes, among which some live embers will often be hidden. No wooden vessel, pail, or box should be used to take ashes away in, and no ash-barrel should stand on the verandah, or near a wall. A proper ash-shed, away from the house, should be made, and an earthen or stone floor should be below the ash-barrels.

Sometimes people are exposed to considerable peril in new clearings, from the running of fire in the woods, or new fallows. In such case, where there is any danger of the fire getting to the homestead or standing crops, and there is no near supply of water, much can be effected by beating out the advancing flames, and still more by opening the earth with hoes, spades, or better still, by men yolking up the cattle and ploughing a few furrows, so as to interpose the new earth between the advancing fire and the combustible matter. Women, yes, weak women and children have battled against a wall of advancing fire, and with hoes and other instruments have kept it back till help could be obtained. This subject may seem out of place to dwell upon, but I have seen many instances where, if women had not roused themselves to exertion, *all* would have been lost.

The summer of 1845 was one of almost tropical heat. From the first week In July to the end of August the heat exceeded that of any season within the memory of the oldest settler.

For days together the temperature varied from ninety to ninety-six, and sometimes ninety-eight degrees in the shade. We began to think any degree of heat below ninety moderate. The earth became dust; the grass, stubble; the small creeks, and most of the springs were dried up. No rain fell for many weeks. The clouds when they rose were watched with longing eyes, and every one speculated, and hoped they were charged with rain. A thunder-storm was really looked forward to as a blessing; but none came to cool the glowing atmosphere, and cool the parched earth. The cattle wandered far for water—it was a bad summer for the dairy.

A new source of anxiety arose from the fires which, as usual, had been kindled on the newly-chopped fallows.

Encouraged by the dryness of the wood, and absence of moisture from the ground and herbage, it spread with fearful rapidity— driven onwards by a strong wind.

We were surrounded by fires on all sides of the clearing. At one time the log-barn was in imminent danger of being destroyed: the fire was burning among the roots, and had got to a log-fence near the barn. This had to be removed with all speed, or the building would have been destroyed. The fire ran among the standing grass, and old rotten stumps. At night the scene was very striking:—an old log-house, used as a hay-barn, was burnt down—it was full of new hay. The hay was saved; the horses stood patiently with the fires within a few yards of them while it was removed. A quarter of an hour afterwards the building was on fire, and a fine spectacle it made. Day after day the stumps and roots continued to burn. Sometimes the fences were on fire, and all hands were obliged to assist in subduing the destructive element. The springs were dry:—we had every day to open new holes to get water to put out the fires, and the supply was so small that, if it had been our only resource, we must have been burned out ; but upon the hoe, the spade, and the plough was our main reliance placed.

Help from our neighbours we could not obtain. When we sent a messenger for one, he and all his family were battling with the fire on their own clearing ; to a second, his fences were on fire—all hands were employed in saving the crops ; a third, the barn was in danger ; and so we were forced to rouse every energy that we could to overcome the danger. Ourselves, women, and little children—all had to help ; and this continued day after day. At night we got rest ; for as soon as the breeze went down, and the dews fell, the fires ceased to run. The air then became oppressive to a degree of suffocation, being loaded with the smell of the rank weeds, and burning roots and stumps of decayed trees. Each night the sun went down in a red haze ; no rain fell, and still the fires burned on. The wind carried the sparks into a thick cedar-swamp, not far from the house, a few acres intervening, and there it blazed and leaped from tree to tree. The children were never tired of looking at it. I trembled lest the wind should change and bring it back upon us. Often we would wonder in such case how we should save our furniture, for the fires were around us on all sides. At last, in the month of September, rain fell, and the earth smoked and reeked as it came down. The Autumn rains finally extinguished the fires all over the country, and the dread of their ravages was at an end for that year ; but it was neither the first time nor the last that I have seen the fire within a hundred feet of the dwelling-house, and been obliged to give my own feeble help to assist in subduing it.

In cases of emergency, it is folly to fold one's hands and sit down to bewail in abject terror : it is better to be up and doing.

A FEW WORDS ABOUT AGUE.

Every one considers Canada a healthy country : it is so, generally speaking ; but there are diseases, such as ague and rheumatism, which are more common here than in Britain. Dysentery in children prevails during the hot months, especially among very young infants ; and erysipelas, among persons exposed to the great heat of the sun in summer, having the perspiration suddenly checked by cold bathing, drinking very cold water, or being suddenly chilled by change of atmosphere. These, however, are chances which only happen to the few. The same causes would produce similar effects in any country.

Many years ago it was a rare thing to hear of colds, coughs, or influenzas,—now it is very common, and I believe, with many medical men, that the stoves have to answer for these disorders. People heat their rooms like ovens, and go out into the sharp, frosty air ; they return again from the keen frosty air into heated rooms ; their tender organs of respiration are not fitted to stand such reverses, and pulmonary disease and colds in the head are the result, which not unfrequently end in consumption. Formerly open fireplaces were seen in every house, and the inmates of them were healthy ;—now they have stoves in every part of the dwelling, even in the bed-rooms, and the result is sickness and loss of complexion. The largest log-fires, in an open fireplace, will not produce the same general heat ; but it will be far more conducive to health. A Canadian house may be kept very comfortable, without being over heated, by means of a good hall-stove and fireplaces in the sitting rooms—a porch, enclosing the outer doors, also helps to keep the house warm in winter. The inhabitants of the Lower Province, where the cold is more intense, and the winters of longer duration, understand the art of warming their houses better, and constructing them so as to keep out the cold better than we do in Upper Canada. The commonest log-house should have a verandah—no matter how homely the construction ;—if only made with unbarked poles of cedar, and shingled, it will add not a little to the comfort of the family. It makes the house cooler in summer and warmer in winter ; it saves much work, as the house is kept cleaner ; it serves for a summer eating-room ; its pillars, wreathed with hops, give a pleasant, rustic look to the otherwise unsightly log-house, and keeps off the glare of the sun through the long summer's day. At the kitchen-end of the house, the stoop serves for a summer kitchen, and it is there that the housewife keeps her pails, and pots, and pans—her washing tubs and barrels. The want of this convenience is often sorely felt by the females ; and I would advise every settler who builds, by no means to omit this addition, if he has any regard for the comfort and tidiness of his house. And here I must observe, that it is the total inattention to the comfort and convenience of women, that often makes them unhappy and discontented in their new homes. Like the captives of Israel, they are often expected to make bricks without straw.—Let the men do all they can to make the house as convenient as circumstances will admit of their doing, and the females must, on their part, put up with those wants that are the result of this new order of things. Let each comfort and cheer the other, and bear the privations and trials that befal them as cheerfully and as hopefully as they can, and thus the burden will fall lighter upon all.

The constitutional grumbler will, of course, find many causes of complaint in Canada ; but so she would do in Australia or any other colony, and so she would in her own country. To such unhappy tempers, all climes, all countries, and all situations are alike—for her there is no happy land ; for she bears within her breast the seeds of misery, which will cast its baneful shadow across the threshold of her home, to embitter all its domestic joys. In her path, thorns and thistles spring up, and choke life's fairest flowers.

Ague is the disease most dreaded by new settlers, and to many persons it has proved a great drawback, especially to such as go into the uncleared lands. They who live in the long-settled parts of Canada, seldom have ague : it arises from the exhalations of the vegetable soil, when opened out to the action of the sun and air. As long as the soil is unbroken, and the woods uncleared, no such effect is felt. I have heard some of the hardy, old trappers say, that they never had ague in the woods ; but on the newly-cleared land, or by lakes and swamps, where the sun had access, there they would have ague. Some people never have ague ; others, only the first or second year after coming to the country ; but some seldom pass a year without an attack of it. A singular error prevails among some of the old settlers, that those who put a stop to the disease, when it first attacks them, will be subject to it for life :—believe it not ; but use vigorous means to check it as soon as, or before, it is confirmed. Remedies for the ague are as plentiful as blackberries ; but the following mode of treatment, I believe, to be the best of any : I have experienced its efficiency in my own family, and as it was the prescription of a skilful physician, well acquainted with the diseases of this country, I do not hesitate to give it :—

AGUE.

For an adult female, divide six grains of calomel into three doses ; take one of these doses every two hours ; at the end of the sixth hour take a large tea-spoonful of Epsom salts. On the following day take a wine-glassful of the following tonic mixture : dissolve twenty grains of quinine in a pint of water, to which add four drachms of diluted sulphuric acid : if too acid, add more water to reduce it. Take the dose at seven in the morning—at eleven—and again at four, as long as the bottle lasts. When you have finished it, take a dose of senna and salts ; and in most cases the ague will cease ; but it generally returns at the end of twenty-one days. As it is sure to give you notice of its approach, have recourse to the same doses of calomel and salts, as before, followed by the quinine and sulphuric acid ; or you may take three grains of calomel the second time, divided into two doses : it seldom fails of curing. Should the disorder shew any symptoms of returning the third time, do not wait for a confirmed fit, but take a few doses of the tonic mixture, diminishing the quantity from two doses to one, till you leave it off altogether.

Rest is essential for ague patients : total rest from labour, if possible, and good nourishing diet, that is not hard to digest, and change of air if the patient can leave home. Poor diet is one of the causes of ague : those who can afford to live well, seldom suffer from ague, unless in low, marshy situations.

There is an Indian remedy sold in all drug stores, in Canada ; it is called Indian Cologue ; it is very nauseous ; but I have been told it is very effectual as a cure.

The inner bark of the wild, black cherry, steeped in whiskey, is also taken as a tonic for ague ; but I have more reliance on the treatment of the disorder, as I have given above.

For a man, the dose of calomel is seven grains, in three doses ; and for a child, three grains, at intervals of two hours between each grain, and a dessert spoonful of castor oil at the end of the third dose ; a tea-spoonful of the tonic mixture, diluted with water, thrice a day. I have found the fit much relieved in a young child, by putting it into a warm bath and wrapping it in warm blankets, and giving it a few drops of antimonial wine, in warm drink, to promote perspiration. An emetic is often administered previous to taking any other medicine.

DYSENTERY IN CHILDREN.

This disease is often fatal to young children—frequently baffling the skill of the most experienced physician.

I lost two infants who were under the care of the most careful medical men ; but saved another by the use of a wild herb, that was given me by a Yankee settler's wife. A plant called spikenard, (or spignet, as she called it,) that grows in the forest, with a long spindle root, scraped, and a small quantity boiled in milk, thickens it, as if flour had been put in : it has a sweet, astringent taste, slightly bitter. A tea-spoonful, thrice given in one day, cured the child, who was wasting fast under the disease. This spikenard belongs to the same family of plants, as the sarsaparilla : it bears black berries, not unlike the elderberry in size and taste. There are many of the old settlers who know the plant. No one should use the wild herbs without the experience of a careful person, to whom their sanatory or hurtful qualities are well known. The old Canadian settlers are often well skilled in the use of the native plants—they may, possibly, have learned the value of them from the Indians, or from long experience, taught by necessity, in a country where, formerly, educated doctors were far from being as commonly met with, even in the towns, as they now are. Possibly, in those days, there were fewer diseases to cure, and the simple medicines that the forest afforded were sufficient for all curative diseases. In lonely places, where the aid of a medical man is difficult to be obtained, even severe wounds are healed, and simple fractures are reduced by the inhabitants themselves. Some one among them who has more nerve, or more judgment than the rest, is consulted upon such occasions, and faith goes a great way with many patients in effecting a cure.

When emigrants first arrive in this country, they are apt to fall ill : the change of diet, of air, and many other causes, possibly the want of comfort on board the vessel, may operate upon them to induce disease. A little care, and some doses of simple medicine, will often save themselves and children from fevers or other serious complaints. Timely attention to health on landing is very advisable, and it would save many from much suffering if they went at once to a skilful medical man, and procured medicine and advice, which is often supplied to the poorer class of emigrants free of all cost.

BEES.

Of late years the long established settlers have begun to turn their attention to the cultivation of bees. In the Eastern, or Lower part of Canada, honey has long been a source of commercial profit to the farmer.

As an article of luxury, it stands unrivalled at our tables. As a medicine it is invaluable in its soothing, purifying, healing qualities—nay, even moral lessons have long been associated in the mind of the young child with the labours of the "Busy Bee."

It is a pity that the cultivation and profitable management of the bee is so little attended to in a country where nature has strewn the wilderness with flowers for their sustenance.

If the Lower Canadians are able, with a little care, to cultivate the hive to advantage, there can be no doubt but that the inhabitants of the Western Province might derive a considerable profit from the proceeds of this stock.

Why should we import either honey or wax if by our own labours we could raise these valuable articles on our own farms.

The British peasantry generally contrive to keep bees, and understand the management of the hives—I mean the practical part, that of housing the young swarms and abstracting the honey from them at the close of the season. They would require to pay some attention to the difference of seasons. The extreme cold of the long Canadian winter, must, of course, be taken into consideration when removing the comb. The shortness of the flowering season must also be taken into account, and proper shelter provided for the hives during the cold weather. Those cultivators from whom the stock is bought will not refuse to impart their experience, which has the great value of having been acquired after many losses and vexatious failures; they will be your best guides and advisers in the management to be adopted. I know at present of no simple practical work that has been written by the bee-keeper in Canada, for the instruction of the public: unfortunately I have no experience of my own to offer on the subject.

The Canadian emigrants will naturally desire to know something of the natural productions and general features of the country to which they are about to direct their steps. To enter minutely into details of the natural history of so large a portion of country, which from its geographical extent includes many varieties of climate and productions, would far exceed the limits to which this small book must necessarily be confined. A few general remarks as to climate and the vegetables and animals indigenous to the Upper or Western portion of Canada may not be uninteresting to my readers. I shall convey these in the form of a notice of the months; at the same time observing that in the parts of Canada between the shores of Lakes Ontario, Erie and Huron, a difference exists in the coming on of the winter and the approaches of early spring, which are considerably in favour of that part of the Province; many kinds of fruit coming to perfection west of Toronto, which are cultivated only with great care and difficulty on the banks of the St. Lawrence and in the counties eastward and northward of it. Vegetation is thus a fortnight or three weeks earlier in the western part of the Province than in the eastern. Some forest trees grow there which are not found with us, such as the button-wood, the black-walnut, the sweet-chestnut, the sassafras and many others.

JANUARY.

This month, though we date our new year from its commencement, as in the old country, is not really the first month of our Canadian winter, which often commences as early as the first week in November; some years however it is later, and I have seen fine mild open weather far into December; yet you must not be surprised at snow showers and severe frosts in those two months, and winter clothing should all be prepared before the chances of a November cold setting in. The month of January forms, as it were, a break in the winter's cold. I have known many new year's days when there was not snow enough on the ground to make sleighing practicable: this present January for instance, when the earth was brown and bare, and wheeled vehicles alone were seen on the road.

The first new year's day, viz., 1833, that I passed in Canada there was no snow to be seen, and the air was so warm that we sat with the outer door open, the heat of the stoves being too oppressive for comfort. We had had snow showers as early as November the 3rd, but no intense degree of cold till after the 27th of January; after that time we had heavy snow storms and intense cold all through the month of February and up to the 17th of March, when a warm rapid thaw set in and cleared the snow off by the middle of April, even in the woods.

In the year 1846 the new year's day was warm and we walked on the dead leaves in the woods. This year 1855, there was snow about the middle of November which lay till the 22nd, then the weather was mild again. We had intense cold the week before Christmas, but a thaw commenced on the 23rd and the snow disappeared, the ground being bare till the 13th of January, when a scattering of about an inch fell, but it was not till the last week in that month that any quantity of snow fell, greatly to the discomfiture of the farmer, who reckons on the sleighing season for the easier transport of his grain to market, and as a season of recreation for his family.

There is always a January thaw in the early part of the month, when the December snows melt off. The frost then relaxes its iron bands, and a moist atmosphere takes the place of the keen frosts of early winter : rain frequently falls and high winds blow. A change is sure to take place again on or about the twelfth of January : snow again covers the ground. After heavy snow storms a cold north-west wind begins to blow ; the new fallen snow is sent in clouds like smoke over the open fields, drifting in high banks on the road sides, filling up the corners of the rail fences, and blocking the narrow lanes : the cutting wind plays fantastic tricks on the edges of these snow drifts, sweeping them out in hollows and caves, sculpturing their spotless surfaces in curved lines of the most graceful forms, so that you would imagine some cunning hand had chiselled them with infinite care and pains. But while these changes are going on with the snow-falls in the open country, in the great forest it is very different. There undisturbed by the war of winds, the snow flakes fall in ceaseless silent showers till the whole dark unsightly mass of fallen trees and broken boughs are covered with the spotless deposit. The thick branches of the evergreens receive the load that falls from the lofty pines and naked hardwood trees, as moved by the wind they shake off the feathery burden. Go into the forest the morning after a heavy snow storm and you will behold one of the purest, one of the loveliest scenes that nature can offer you. The young saplings bent down with the weight of snow, unable to lift their heads, are bent into the most graceful arches and hang like bowers of crystal above your path ; the keen frost has frozen the light branches and holds them down to the hardening surface, so that these bent trees remain in this way till the breath of spring sets them once more free, but often they retain the bent form and never recover the upright shape entirely. The cedar swamp which is so crowded with trees, of all ages and sizes, from the tiny seedling, rooted on the decayed trunks of the old fallen trees, to the vigorous sapling striving to make its way upwards, and the hoary trunks, over the bleached and mossy heads of which centuries have passed, now presents a curious aspect, filled with masses of new fallen snow, which forms huge caverns and curtains lying in deep banks on the prostrate trunks, or adorning the extended fanlike branches with mimic flowers of purest white.

January parties, balls, pic-nics and sleigh rides are frequent in the towns and long settled parts of the country ; so that though the cold is often intense, this season is not without its pleasures. The backwoodsman is protected in his drives by the ancient forest, which excludes the wind and is equal to a second great coat in travelling.

No vegetation is to be seen going on in this month : silence and stillness prevail. The bear, the raccoon, the porcupine, the groundhog, the flying squirrel and little striped chitmunk or ground squirrel, with many other smaller animals lie soundly sleeping in their nests or burrows. The woods are deserted by most of the feathered tribes, a solitary tree creeper, the little spotted woodpecker, with some of the hardy little birds called Chickadee-dee by the natives, are alone seen on sunny days in the thick shelter of the pines and hemlocks ; while around the houses of the settlers the snow birds in lively flocks whirl hither and thither in the very wildest of the snow drifts, or a solitary whiskey jack (Canada Jay) ventures to gather up the crumbs which have been swept outside the door. Sometimes the graceful form of a black squirrel may be seen running along the outstretched branch of a tree, his deep sable fur contrasting very remarkably with the glittering silver snow, over which he gambols as gaily as if in the warmth of a July sun.

FEBRUARY.

This is indeed the coldest of the Canadian winter months, and though the lengthening of the days gives you more sunshine it seems to add little to your warmth. Cold and clear the sun shines out in a blue and often cloudless sky, but the thermometer often indicates a very low temperature, 10, 12, 18, nay, sometimes as low as 28 and even 30 degrees below zero. Warm wrappings are now indispensably necessary to the traveller. In event of any person finding their ears, hands or faces frozen, which accident can be seen as well as felt, the part becoming of a livid whiteness, and feeling hard and stiff, the remedy is at hand, and must be applied immediately to the frozen part, viz., snow rubbed on hard till the flesh resumes its former healthy appearance : some apply spirits of turpentine or brandy, or spirits of any kind, after the snow has been rubbed on well.

The care of the cattle and sheep, drawing in firewood, splitting of rails for fencing, and preparing sap troughs, are the usual operations in the settlements during this month.

MARCH.

The early part of March often resembles February, with this difference, the longer days cause a relaxation of the severe cold during the sunshining hours; the very surface of the snow thaws, patches of bare earth begin to appear towards the middle of the month; the weak but pleasant note of the little song sparrow and the neat snow sparrow in its quaker-like plumage may be heard and seen as they flit to and fro, picking the seeds of the rough green amaranth and tall woolly-stalked mullien which stand faded and dry in the garden patch or on the road side. The equinox is often attended with rough gales and snow storms: these past, the sun begins to melt off the snow, and a feeling of coming spring is experienced in the soft airs, and a look of life in the bark and birds. The rising of the sap is felt in the forest trees; frosty nights and sunny days call forth the activity of the settlers in the woods; sugar making is now at hand, and all is bustle and life in the shanty.

I have largely entered into the details of this busy season in the earlier part of my book. We will now proceed to April.

APRIL.

April in Canada is not the same month in its general features, as the lovely, showery, capricious April, that month of smiles and tears, of storms and sunshine, in dear old England. It is often cold, stern and harsh, yet with many hopeful changes that come to cheat us into the belief that winter is gone, and the season of buds and flowers is at hand, and some years it is so; but only once in five or ten years does the Canadian April prove a pleasant genial month.

Some warm, lovely, even sultry days, misty like Indian summer, are experienced, and the snow melts rapidly and a few flies creep out and sport awhile in the warm beams of the young sun, but " by-and-bye a cloud takes all away." The wind blows chilly, snow showers fall, and all is cold, cheerless winter again.

In fine Aprils a few blossoms peep out from under the thick carpet of dead leaves, and then you see the pretty snow-flower or Hepatica lifting its starry head and waving in the spring breezes on the way sides, on upturned roots and in the shelter of the underwood where the forest is a little thinned out so as to admit of the warm beams of the sun; pale pink, blue of two shades, and snowy white are the varieties of this cheerful little flower. Violets, the small white, and a few pale blue ones, are next seen. The rich rank soil at the edges of your clearing produces the sanguinaria or blood-root—the modest white flower shrouded at its first breaking the soil in a vine-shaped leaf, veined with orange. The root of this plant affords a bright red dye to the Indians, with which they stain the bark of their mats and baskets. You may know the blood-root, on breaking the leaf or the root, by its red juice.

In low, open, moist ground the mottled leaf of the dog's-tooth violet (erythronium) comes up, and late in April the yellow bells, striped on the outside of the petal with purplish brown, come up in abundance. Spring-beauty, too, is an April flower, a delicate little flower with pale pink striped bells—Claytonia is its botanical name—but we love to call these wild flowers by some simple name, which simple folks may easily remember.

As the snow melts off in the woods, the leaves of various evergreen plants appear still fresh and green. Among these are the pyrolas or sweet-wintergreens, a numerous and lovely family of Canadian plants; several varieties of the club-moss, one of which is known as the festoon pine, and is used to make wreaths for ornamenting the settlers' houses with. The wild garlic, too, shows its bright green spear-shaped leaves early in this month. This plant so eagerly sought for by the cattle to which it is a very healing medicine, is dreaded by the dairy-maid, as it destroys the flavour of the milk and spoils the butter.

If the month of April should prove cold, many of the above named flowers put off their blossoming time, appearing in the ensuing month of May.

April unlocks the ice-bound lakes, and streams; and it is during this month, that the winter snows are dissolved: the warmth which in sunnier climes brings to perfection the bulbs, and gives odour to the violet and blue bell, the pale primrose, and the narcissus, here must be expended in loosing the frost-bound earth from its icy fetters, and the waters from their frozen chains. Let us therefore not despise our Canadian April, though she be not as winning and fair as her namesake at home.

MAY.

Clear skies, cold and bright, often mark this month: such weather is useful in drying up the moist earth, saturated by the snow which April has melted away, and hardening the soft earth which is to be made ready for the spring crops.

This is a busy month, the busiest in all the year, for the work of two must be crowded into it.

Ploughing, sowing, planting, goes on incessantly : no time now for the gardener or the husbandman to be idle. Every thing is full of life and activity, from the little squirrel and tiny titmouse running up and down the trees, gathering its moss and grey lichens to build its curious oven-shaped nest.

What crowds of birds now visit us. The green frogs are piping in the creeks and marshes. The ground is now yielding us flowers of all hue. Yellow, blue, and white violets ; butter cups, anenomes, or wind-flowers, the wood daffodil, or bell flower. The snow-white trillium, moose flower some call it, wild vetches, blue and white.

Vegetables of all kinds are sown during the month of May; and the grain, such as spring wheat, barley, oats, and peas, with early potatoes, and, later in the month, Indian corn, must be put in all through May.

The bright skies and sunshine, the singing of the birds, the bursting out of the leaves and buds of all kinds make May a charming month. There is far less rain in the Canadian Spring than in the same season in Britain. There is less need for it, as the earth has received so large a share of moisture in the form of snow, during the winter months. May is usually a dry month here—sometimes cold drying winds prevail, and frosty nights are not uncommon, which often check vegetation. The new growth of the pine takes place in May.

JUNE.

This month perfects the leafage of the late deciduous trees, such as the oak, butternut, ash, and some others. It is in this month that the forest trees are seen in their greatest beauty, so intensely green, so varied that the eye is never tired with wandering over their living verdure. Later in the summer these charming tints seem to lose their youthful freshness, and assume one uniform color of sober green. There are frequent thunder storms and often heavy rains early in June, and sultry heat: the musquitoes and black flies, in situations favourable to them now appear ; but it is in July the musquitoes are the most troublesome, especially in the close pine woods, and near lakes and streams. On open old cleared parts of the country these pests are less known and less heeded. Flies always attack the new comers with more virulence than old settlers, who scarcely feel the annoyance.

Some of our most beautiful flowers—I mean the wild flowers— blossom during this month, such as the yellow mocassin, (and later the white and purple,) the large orange lily lilies of many kinds, the blue lupin, the splended euchroma or painted cup, which may be known by the brilliant scarlet colour that tips the leaves and involucrum of the flowers ; this beautiful plant is found chiefly on dry sandy soil, or on the open plain lands: it continues from June till September. The sweet scented round leafed winter green, called lily of the valley, (it should be lily of the woods), with several of the same lovely family, bloom all through June and July.

The evening air at dewfall is now filled with the perfume of the single red-rose, a dwarf rose with crimson stems and greyish thorns, which grows in vast profusion on the plains. The sweet scented shrub Ceanothers or New Jersey tea, with white feathery flowers, also adds its perfume along with the sweet scented Monarda or mountain sweet.: but these are only a few and a very few of the blossoms that you will find springing in the open fields, the deep forest or the roadside wastes.

The wild strawberry which is sure to spring up in old clearings, and new meadows, now begins to ripen from the tenth to the end of the month; you will find them red and ripe and far finer in size and flavour, than any that are to be found in the woods in the old country.

Potatoes are often planted in the early part of this month, and hoeing both of corn and potatoes, is continued, with other work on the farm.

JULY.

July is the hottest month of the Canadian year: there is often a succession of heavy thunderstorms and showers, which give a sultry heat, which is less bearable than the clear dry atmosphere that marks the harvest month of August. The raspberry and huckleberry ripen during the month of July, the rice comes in flower with many other aquatic plants. On the still flowing lakes, now may be seen vast beds of that most beautiful flower, the large white nymphæa or double white water lily, looking down through the clear water : these flowers may be discovered in every stage of progression, from the soft young bud closely folded up in its oily olive coloured calyx, to the half opened blossom, showing its ivory petal, and the nearly full-blown flower still shielding the lemon-tinted anthers, which are seen only fully developed in the perfect blossom which sits as a crown upon the waters, giving out its exquisite odour to the soft breeze that gently stirs the limpid bosom of the lake. The deep golden cup of the yellow nymphæa may also be seen, seldom far removed from the white blossomed ; and the arrow-shaped leaves of the blue spiked pondwort and rosy flowers of the persicaria, form a beautiful sight on hot sunny days.

The meadows are now mowed, and the hay harvest is in full operation ; and if the weather have proved sufficiently warm, the earliest sown fall wheat will be now cradled, i. e. mown with the cradle scythe; an instrument which has quite set aside the old reaping hook and sickle. A good cradler will cut three acres of heavy wheat in a summer's day : one or more following in his steps to bind and stock up the sheaves.

The cherry, currant and garden raspberry, are now ripe—peas and some other vegetables—but early potatoes are still rare unless care has been taken to plant early kidneys, which should be put in early in May to ensure their being fit for table in the middle of July.

Many splendidly coloured butterflies are seen during the hot months of July and August, some of a superior size to any seen in England. The large brimstone swallow tail, the great scarlet and black ; admirals of several sorts, with a variety of small gay winged species, and some very fine moths, one of a delicate green with coloured eyes in its wings, red feet, and a thick body covered with white feathery down ; besides sphinges and tiger moths, with an endless list of dragon flies, and beetles of various hues appear.

The humming birds may now be seen, making frequent visits to the flower garden, hovering over the open blossoms of the larkspurs, morning-glories, scarlet bean, and any other honey yielding flowers. In the forest you may chance to see the gay glancing wings of that shy but splendid bird, the scarlet tanager or summer red-bird ; while in the orchard and gardens, the blue-bird and the wild canary, or American gold-finch, dart to and fro in the sunshine ; and at night, the rapid voice of the whip-poor-will is heard from eve till dawn, especially where there are groves of trees, near the house : you will know the oriole by its orange and black plumage ; the cat-bird by its long tail, dark dove coloured coat, and squalling note, much like that of a cat calling her kittens. The saucy blue or crested jay, calls " Thate, Thate," and the " Phœbe," repeats its own name in a variety of tones. It is pleasant to know even a bird or a flower by name, and though some of my readers may care for none of these things, there may be others, and perhaps not a few, who may be glad of the information I have given them about the wild flowers and wild creatures of the strange land they may be destined to sojourn in for many years. It may enable them to teach their children the names of the natural productions, and create an interest in their young minds in the new country, which will not be without its beneficial effects upon their minds. Little children love simple knowledge, and ask for it eagerly. To acquire the name of any object that strikes its fancy, is the first step on the young child's ladder to learning.

AUGUST.

Harvest, if not begun in the last-named month, commences the first week in this. The grain now ripens as fast as it can be cut and carried. The weather is generally hot, dry, and clear all through this month, with splendid sunsets; but the nights are often cool—almost chilly. It is during the hot season that agues and other intermittents usually prevail, more than in the moister months of the spring. The heavy dews should be avoided as much as possible. Towards the latter part of August, it is not very unusual to experience slight frosts at night. I have seen a change on some of the forest-leaves before this month was out. Some of the earlier sorts of apples may be used now—the early Harvest-Yellow, Harvest and Early Joe, with some others.

Sunflowers of many kinds are now in bloom, with many sorts of fruit. The mandrake or May-apple may now be gathered: the berries of many wild plants are ripe. The flower-garden is in all its glory. Melons ripe, and all kinds of vegetables. Nature is perfecting her great work. Not only is man busy with the harvest, but the wild animals are also garnering up their winter stores. The squirrels are busy from morning till night, gleaning the ripe grain, and laying it up on the rail fences and stumps to dry in the sun before they venture to carry it off to their granaries and burrows: they are a lively, busy race; ever at work or at play. They seem to me the happiest of all God's creatures, and the prettiest.

The flowers that are most commonly seen now are of the starry or syngenesian class—sunflowers, asters of many kinds, golden-rod, lion's-foot, liatris or gay-feather, with many others.

SEPTEMBER.

This is one of the most delightful months in the year. The heat is sometimes very great in the first week; but after that is past, a genial warmth, with a clear air, is felt. The warm rich tints steal by degrees over the trees, especially those that grow at the outer edges of the clearings, and the soft maples and dogwood bushes that skirt the water; but it is not till the rains of the equinox, and its subsequent frosts, that the glory of the autumnal foliage is seen in all its splendor.

The harvest is now over; and the fall ploughing has begun with great zeal: by the second week in this month, most of the wheat will have been sown, unless where sickness or other causes have delayed the work. September, like May, is a busy month in Canada. The

Indian-rice is now ripe, and the squaw goes forth in her light bark canoe, to gather in her harvest—one which, like the birds of the air, she gathers, without having scattered the seed, or toiled for its increase.

OCTOBER.

There is generally a season of rain during the last week of September, lasting until the tenth or twelfth of October. This may be looked for almost as a certainty. The weather generally clears about that time, and frosty nights and mild days ensue. Indian-summer, for the most part, succeeds close upon the rainy season. Warm, sultry, hazy days. The autumn foliage is fast covering the earth with a thick carpet of variegated leaves, returning to her bosom that which was derived from her, to be again resumed in due season, to form fresh leaves and buds, and woody fibre. How much wisdom may be imparted to us even by the fall and decay of the leaves of the trees; and to man alone has been given the privilege of looking upon these things with the eye of faith and reason, that by the small and weak things of earth, his soul may be lifted up to Heaven, to adore God the Creator in all his works.

The last flowers that linger yet are the Gentians. These belong to the months of September and October, exclusively, and are among the most beautiful of the Canadian wild-flowers. The large, bright-blue, fringed gentian, may be seen lifting its azure blue and white-fringed bell, by shady banks and open woods, in size varying from the plant of two or four inches in height, to the tall branching one of two and three feet high, with flowers proportionably large. The pitcher-shaped gentian, of deep cerulean blue, closed at the lips, is found in damp spots; not in the close swamps of the forest, however, but in open places, a little marshy, and among small thickets. The pale lilac whorled Gentian grows more frequently in half-cultivated fields, and waste lands; while the full, deep-coloured purple of the large bell-flowered gentian, the Calathian violet, is found on dry sandy and gravelly soil. This is one of the most beautiful of all our wild-flowers, and is worthy of a place in any garden. I have seen it in conservatories at home, tenderly nursed and guarded with care, while here it braves the first chilling frosts, and may be said to lay its head almost on the lap of winter snows.

The lovely asters, the late everlasting, the golden-rod, and a few more hardy plants, linger on in bloom through the Indian-summer; and then wither with the first hard frosts.

It is during the Fall months that the Northern-lights are so frequently seen illumining the horizon—a novelty which will attract the attention of the emigrant, and fill him with pleasing admiration. It is seen at times all through the year, but in September, October and November more frequently, especially before the setting in of the Indian-summer.

Early in this month, the root-crops are stored, and such trees planted out, as you desire, in the orchard.

NOVEMBER.

Our year is fast drawing to a close : all Nature seems preparing for the change. The squirrel and wood-chuck have laid by their stores of nuts and grain and seeds. The musk-rats and beavers have built their houses, and the latter have repaired their dams. The summer birds have left us : the discordant cry of the blue jay is heard only at intervals. Only a few of our old feathered friends abide with us, and they seek the warm shelter of the woods, and doze away the long cold winter in silence and gloom.

November is very unlike the foggy, cheerless, dark, soul-depressing month, bearing that name in Britain : it often, it is true, wears the garb of winter, but this is by no means a certain characteristic of the season. There are often delightful days of sunshine and clear frost ; and, in some years, Indian-summer falls into this month, and gives an aspect of warmth and loveliness to the very borders of Winter's frozen garments.

The plough is now busy preparing the fallows for the ensuing Spring crops, that the soil may be mellowed by the Winter frost and snow. This work continues as long as the ground is open. The only plants now of any interest are the wintergreens. The red berries of the cranberries, and the purple clusters of the frost grapes, give liveliness and beauty to the scenery.

DECEMBER.

Sometimes this month is open and fair during the first week or so ; but it varies from moderate to intense cold. We must not be surprised at finding the streams ice-bound, the earth hardened into stone, or deep snow covering the earth ; but this is according to our climate; and to those who look for its approach, and are in any way prepared for its severity, the Canadian winter is a cheerful season.

I have brought my year to its close. Some will think my sketch too fair a one, because they will experience many changes and discomforts; and seasons are brightened or darkened by our individual feelings and domestic circumstances. To the sad and sorrowful all seasons are alike gloomy.

"To feverish pulse each gale blows chill."

I have chosen a medium year from among those of which I have kept a faithful diary, and I consider it a fair average of the Canadian climate, or of that portion of Canada lying between Toronto and Kingston. Above, it is milder; below, colder, but less variable.

Some decided changes I have marked in my time. The year 1834 the Spring came on very early: the snow was all gone in March, and earlier in the sun-exposed clearings: leaves were out in the first week in May; but a severe frost and snow took place on the 14th and 15th of May, and cut off vegetation for a time; nevertheless, we had a long, dry, hot Summer, and fine Fall.

We then had three successive wet harvests; which, with a visitation of cholera, checked emigration for several years: this, joined to the rebellion, proved a great drawback to the prosperity of the colony. Good, however, sprung out of evil, and many ills and abuses were remedied, which might have remained to this day, but for the attention of the rulers of the people being turned towards them.

We have had winters of comparative mildness, with plenty of snow, but no very intense cold. The Spring of 1839 was very early, but the Summer was hot and moist; and that year we had a long Indian-summer; while some years we have had scarcely any weather corresponding to that uncertain season.

Spring is the most uncertain of our seasons. The Fall is the wettest, but often the most delightful of them; but to such as are of a contented spirit, there is good at all seasons, and in everything: for as the old poet says—

> "Not always fall of leaf, nor ever Spring;
> Not endless night, nor yet eternal day;
> The saddest birds a season find to sing,
> The roughest storms a calm may soon allay:
> Thus with succeeding turns God tempers all,
> That man may hope to rise, yet fear to fall."

---

* These lines form a portion of an admirable little poem called "Times go by turns," written by Father Robert Southwell, who was the victim of religious persecution during the reign of Queen Elizabeth.

I now subjoin a few valuable extracts, selected from some well-written letters, which were published in 1853 as a supplementary sheet to a newspaper issued in Toronto, entitled the "Old Countryman."

These "Letters from Canada" are deserving of a wide circulation, as I think the selections I have made for my readers will prove. The limits of this work forbid my introducing a larger portion of the valuable matter contained in the original publication.

EXTRACTS FROM "LETTERS FROM CANADA."

" All the favourable impressions of Canada, which I named to you before, have been fully confirmed upon a more accurate enquiry into her *wonderful* resources and capabilities ; if there be any country which deserves to be known at home, that country is Canada. We seem never to have realized what Canada really is, and have always thought of her as a desolate and chilly place, the abode of anthropophagi and musquitoes, from whence we got ice and pine timber ; instead of which, it is a country about four times the size of the British Possessions in Europe, producing almost everything which can minister to the comforts and luxuries of life, and where, within the space of less than fifty years, millions of acres of land have been converted from forest and swamps into fruitful and well-cultivated farms, supplying not only the wants of its own rapidly-increasing population, but enabling us to export produce to the States and England to the value of some millions sterling every year. This, however, it is desirable to prove by something more than mere assertion. Canada has a fruitful soil and a fine climate—she has before her a glorious prospect, and her sons and daughters a lofty mission—she is a land of kindling energies, and of untold and undeveloped resources, which will give her soon a place and a name among the nations of the earth: she entertains a warm and affectionate regard for the " old house at home," and a deep feeling of loyalty towards her Sovereign, and it would have delighted that distinguished Personage could she have seen the way in which her last Birth-day was celebrated on this side of the Atlantic.

"It is truly cheering to see how fondly "home" is spoken of here, for it is by that endearing word that England is known here, and when I say England, I mean of course the United Kingdom. It makes my old heart stir within me to hear our far-off home thus spoken of in the Provincial Parliament and in the shanty of the settler. There is indeed a mighty and enduring force in old and early

associations, which time and distance cannot obliterate or diminish.—
There is a magic in the word when uttered here which I cannot describe. It is a word that conjures up memories of the past on which
the heart loves to linger—the memory of prayers uttered on bended
knees at the feet of departed parents—who blessed our early and guided
our advancing years—when the passions of youth were unsubdued and
the principles of manhood unconfirmed. It recals the abode of distant,
most loved, and loving friends, and brings back scenes on which the
eye has not rested for many a year of anxious struggle and final
success. I must tell you a little anecdote on this point which moved
me exceedingly. I called, one day, while in the Bush, at the house of
a venerable old man of eighty—a soldier and a gentleman—who had
been here forty years, and seldom got any tidings from home. I happened
to have in my pocket-book a primrose, which dearest —— sent me in a
letter, and I placed it on the old man's knee and said, "Did you ever
see a flower like that?" The old man took it up and when he recognised it he kissed the pale flower over and over again, and bending his
aged head he wept like a child, so long and so violently that I was
alarmed. Who can tell what thoughts this little flower awakened
in the old man's mind? The thoughts of some shady lane, perchance,
near the unforgotten home of his childhood—

"The first love-beat of his youthful heart,"

a mother's gentle look, a father's word of approbation or sign of
reproof ; a sister's gentle love, a brother's fond regard, handsful of
flowers plucked in green and quiet meadows—birds' nests admired, but
not touched—the Sabbath call to prayer and praise. It was too
sacred a sight for a stranger's eye. I don't *think* he could have
spoken, I am *sure* I could not. So I wrote in pencil a few words
promising to see him again, and, if we should be both spared, that he
should next spring, have a pale memorial of spring and home from
the same green lane as the one which had, much to his honour, elicited,
"A Soldier's Tear."

In order that you, and other friends at home, may known how this
Province is divided, I send you a small diagram.

4th.

The dark lines, running North and South are road allowances, and
called Concession lines, the others are side lines, the smaller lines are

the division of each block into 200 acre lots, which are all numbered; and, on asking, you would be told that "the Old Countryman lived on Lot 3, on the 4th," meaning the 4th Concession.

Another thing has surprised me, and I want much to have it explained, viz., why a Medical School, conducted here by very eminent members of the profession, was done away with. Canada is a very healthy country, no doubt, but accidents and diseases must happen; and nothing can be more important to a community than that we should have well informed, well instructed and cultivated medical men, to whom to entrust our lives and limbs. If any one will send me a temperate history of this matter you shall it; but there must be no personalities beyond those which are necessary to elucidate the matter. There are some cases of personal hardship connected with the matter I *know* of, where medical men having given up their private practice to become professors in the medical school, have little left them but hearty sympathy, blighted hopes, ruined prospects, and severe, though silent, suffering.

The consumption of timber here is most wonderful, and I shall write to you more at length on this subject.

There are scarcely any hedgerows here, and the long dreary miles of roads and fences, made of what are called snake fences, give a cold look to the country. There is also a sad want of clumps of trees for shade, and shelter also, about the homesteads. With the early settlers every tree was a weed of gigantic growth. "Down with it" was the universal motto. Many persons have wasted and burnt timber to the value of the fee simple of their estates.

The side lines are singularly long and dreary roads, and have not the advantage of the "long perspective view, with a church at the end of it"—the definition of a College Fellowship. I submit the following sketch very respectfully to the path-masters, and fence-viewers of Canada, and I leave them to consider which side of the road looks best.

A CANADIAN SIDE LINE.

AS IT IS.   AS IT MIGHT BE.

There is glorious fishing and shooting in this country. Fish abound everywhere. ―――― has caught them by the hundred weight on those lovely lakes, Simcoe and Couchiching. This is a beautiful and an interesting spot, and if there were hotels affording good accommodation at Atherley and Orillia, lots of people would go there. We shall soon be within three hours of it by the Northern Railroad, and a Steamer in connection with it. The interests of the public and the railroads are identical, and we are looking forward to increased and cheap facilities for locomotion by the issue of season, day, and return tickets ; and a reduction, by means of the railroad, in the price of cord-wood, which is now five dollars a cord here, and only one dollar on the lake shores of Simcoe and Couchiching. We shall soon see houses on the line of railroad, as we have at home; and writing of this, there are two classes of houses wanted here, some of about £25 per annum, for the gentry, and some of much less rental, for mechanics. If the former could be had, many families would resort here to educate their children. They should be brick or stone houses, wooden houses should be discouraged, and, in some places, strictly *forbidden!*

At Mara and Rama we saw many Indians, of whom I will tell you more hereafter. Poor Indians ! the White Man has brought them disease, and taught them drunkenness, and they are dying out fast. Small Pox is very fatal to them. I do hope that the Indian Presents may not be discontinued, at least suddenly. Even now the subject is forming matter of discussion at their Council, and they talk, poor simple-minded harmless, creatures, of sending a deputation to their Great Mother ! Canada ! thou art prosperous and prospering, set not your heart too much on riches ! The Lords of the Soil have lost their hunting grounds and even the birch bark for their frail canoes is getting scarce. There will soon be no place for the Red Man's foot or the free bird's wing. You have asked for their broad lands and they have given them. What have you given *them ?* Disease, and Whiskey and Death ! I saw the bereaved parents of a young Indian, who was drowned when drunk, bending meekly in a Christian Church at Orillia, with a devotion that might be imitated by many a white Christian. The mourners were an Indian Chief and his wife. On my pointing the next day to the crape on his hat, he said with a tone of grief and resignation I shall never forget :—" Mine first-born ! Whiskey too much ! Drowned !" Let them be weaned by kindness and persuasion from this horrid vice. Give the poor things their presents yet for a few years. Earth is *their* school as well as *ours.* Heaven their Home as much as ours ! Fit them for both !

England and Canada should never forget the time when the Red Man was their Ally, and fought and bled in the fore front of many a stricken field ; and now when they are comparatively a " feeble folk," heir good services should not be forgotton for the sake of a few thousands a year. When National Faith has once been pledged or implied to any contract, it should *never be broken*, and the value of the pledge will be measured and estimated by the magnitude and character of the nation giving it. I will conclude this letter with an interesting anecdote on this subject.

St. George's day was this year celebrated in a very gratifying way, at New York, by Americans and English. In replying to a Toast, Major Sprague, of the U. S. army, said :—" Some years ago I was engaged in removing some Indians beyond the Mississippi, and one day when encamped I saw a party approaching me. I took my glass and found they were Indians. I sent out an Indian with the *Stars and Stripes* on a flag, and the leader of the Indians immediately displayed the RED CROSS OF ST. GEORGE ! I wanted him to exchange flags, but the Savage would not, for said he—' I dwell near the Hudson's Bay Company, and they gave me this flag, and they told me that it came from my Great Mother across the great waters, and would protect me and my wife and children, wherever we might go. I have found it as the White Man said, and *I will never part with it !*'" "I could not," added the gallant officer emphatically, "but admire the feeling of confidence and the sentiment."

I hope these letters wont tire you, but Canada is an exhaustless theme, and well deserves to be examined throughout and known. She presents a vast opening to the agriculturist, a most interesting field of study for the botanist, the naturalist, the geologist, and an interesting and much needed mission for the Divine.

You must bear in mind that when I name the price of any Canadian produce, the sum named is in *currency*, unless I distinctly call it sterling value ; the simple way to bring which into sterling money is to deduct one fifth."

I have now brought my labours to an end, and will close my book with some lines, which, though copied from a translation of a Chinese poem, appear to be well suited to the flourishing state of the Canadian colony :—

> Where spades grow bright, and idle swords grow dull,
> Where jails are empty, and where barns are full ;
> Where churchyards are with frequent feet outworn,
> Law courts are weedy, silent and forlorn.
> Where doctors foot it, and where farmers ride,
> Where age abounds, and youth is multiplied,
> Where these signs be, they clearly indicate,
> A happy people and well governed state !

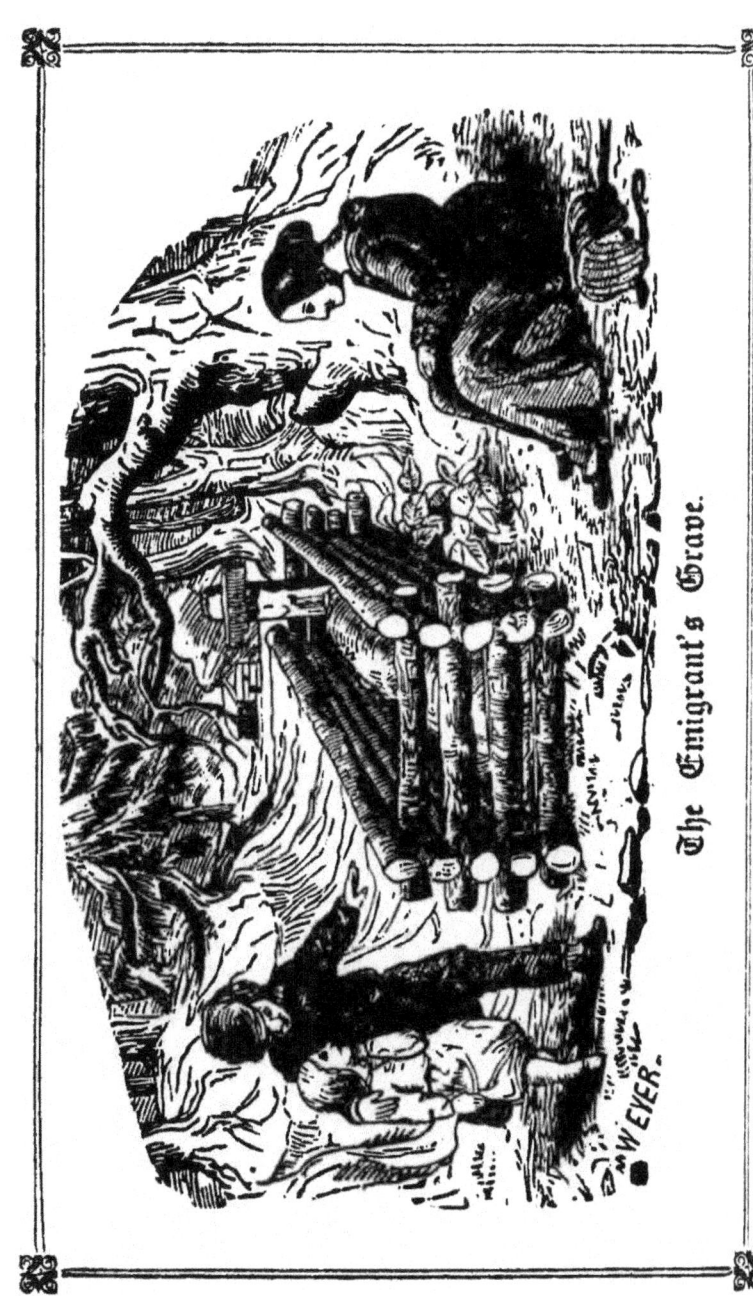

The Emigrant's Grave.

THE GRAVES OF THE EMIGRANTS.

They sleep not where their fathers sleep,
   In the village churchyard's bound;
They rest not 'neath the ivied wall,
   That shades that holy ground.

Not where the solemn organ's peal,
   Pours music on the breeze,
Through the dim aisle at even hour,
   And swells amid the trees.

Not where the turf is ever green,
   And spring-flowers blossom fair,
Upon the graves of the ancient men,
   Whose children sleep not there.

Where do they rest, those hardy men,
   Who left their native shore?
To earn their bread in distant lands,
   Beyond the Atlantic's roar?

They sleep on many a lonely spot,
   Where the mighty forest grew,
Where the giant pine, and stately oak,
   A darkling shadow threw.

The wild bird pours her early song,
   Above their grassy graves;
And far away through the stilly night,
   Is heard the voice of waves.

And the breeze is softly sighing,
   The forest boughs among,
With mournful cadence dying,
   Like harps by angels strung.

And lilies nursed by weeping dew,
   Shed here their blossoms pale;
And spotless snow-flowers lightly bend,
   Low to the passing gale.

The fire-fly lights her sparkling lamp,
   In that deep forest-gloom;
Like Hope's blest light that breaks the night
   And darkness of the tomb.

The mossy stone, or simple cross,
   Its silent record keeps,
Where mouldering in the forest-shade,
   The lonely exile sleeps.

(From the Old Countryman.)

A SONG FOR CHRISTMAS.

THE OLD HOLLY-TREE.

Oh! the old holly-tree is a beautiful sight,
With its dark, glossy leaves, and its berries so bright;
It is gay in the winter, and green in the spring,
And the old holly-tree is a beautiful thing.

It gladdens the cottage, it brightens the hall,
For the gay holly-tree is beloved by us all:
It shadows the altar, it hallows the hearth—
An emblem of sacred and innocent mirth!

Spring blossoms are lovely, and summer flowers gay;
But the chill winds will wither and chase them away;
But the rude blasts of Autumn and Winter may rave
In vain round the holly, the holly so brave!

Though the "fine old English gentleman" no longer now is seen;
And customs old have passed away, as things that ne'er have been;
Though wassail shout is heard no more, nor missletoe we see;
Yet they've left us yet the holly-green, the bonny holly-tree!

                                            C. P. T.

Oaklands, Rice Lake.

MEMORIES OF CHRISTMAS DAY IN THE BACKWOODS.

When first I came to Canada, I was much surprised at the cold indifference which most people showed in their observance of Christmas day—with the exception of the then few residing English families, the church was scantily attended. For in those days there was no dressing of the houses or churches with evergreens as is now so generally the custom, (long may it continue); and I missed the heartfelt cordiality that seems on that sacred day of Christian gladness to overflow all hearts, and break out into smiles of loving kindness to the poorest and least cared for of our fellow creatures. There be many—who with a scoffing eye look upon the decoration of our hearths and altars on that day, and loudly condemn it as a rag of Romanism. But are we really better Christians for casting aside all those old customs, that tended to hold us in the bond of unity and Christian love? I cannot but think that this old custom had its origin in the palm branches, that were strewed in the way of our Lord when the multitudes cut down branches from the trees, and strewed them in the way, crying "Hosannah to the son of David." Did Christ reprove the people for this simple sacrifice in honour of him?—Why then should our observance of this old custom draw down upon us the rebuke of our neighbours?

I remember the first Christmas day I passed in Canada—being laughed at because I wandered out on to the plains near Peterboro', and brought in a wreath of the boxleaved trailing wintergreen (which with its scarlet berries reminded me of the varnished holly with which we were wont to garnish the old house at home), and hanging it over the mantel piece, and above the pictures of my host's parlor, in honor of the day. It seemed to me these green branches might be held as emblems to remind us that we should keep faith bright and green within our hearts.

But while the *nativity* of our Lord was little regarded, all its honor and glory was conferred on the New Year's day. This is with the Canadians the day of days. The world claims that, which used to be given to Christ.

The increase of British settlers however has done something towards restoring a Christian feeling among us, and now our churches are duly dressed with evergreens, our hymns and anthems sung, and our friends and families meet together as of old.

I remember one Christmas day in the Bush. It was the year after the memorable rebellion in Canada: my brother-in-law had been appointed to a company in the Provincial Battalion then stationed in Toronto ; my sister who had remained behind with her infant family was alone, and we were anxious that she should spend this day with us, and that it might look more like an English Christmas day, I despatched Martin, the boy, and old Malachi, the hired man, to bring a sleigh load of evergreens, from the swamp to dress the house with, but when all our green garlands were put up, we missed the bright varnished holly and its gay joy-inspiring red berries, and my English maid Hannah, who was greatly interested in all our decorations, remembered that there were high-bush cranberries, at the lake shore, and winter greens in the swamp, but these last were deep beneath a covering of two or three feet of snow. With the red transparent berries of the cranberry we were obliged therefore to content ourselves, and little Katie brought her string of coral beads and bade me twist it among the green hemlock boughs, clapping her hands for joy when she saw it twined into the Christmas wreath.

Then we sent off the ox sleigh for my sister, and her little ones, for be it known to you, my reader, that our settlement in those days was almost the Ultima Thule of civilization, and our roads were no roads, only wide openings chopped through the heart of the forest, along which no better vehicle than an ox sleigh could make any progress without the continual chance of an overturn. We bush-settlers were brave folks then, and thankfully enjoyed every pleasure we could meet with, even though we had to seek it through means so humble as a ride in a rude vehicle like an ox sleigh, through the wild woods, with the snow above, and the snow below, and in good truth many a pleasant ride have we enjoyed travelling through that dim forest, through bowers of snow-laden hemlocks and dark spruce, which shut us out from the cold wind, like a good fur-lined cloak.

Reposing on a bed of hay covered with buffalo or bear skins, or good wool coverlets, and wrapped in plaids, with well wadded hoods, we were not a whit less happy than if we had been rolling along in a gay carriage, drawn by splendid horses, instead of the rudest of all vehicles, and the most awkward and clumsy of all steeds. At night our lamps, the pale stars and the moon, walking in brightness in the frosty sky, casting quaint shadows of gigantic form across the snowy path, or wading through misty wrack or silver-edged cloud.

A glorious goose fattened on the rice bed in our lake, was killed for the occasion: turkeys were only to be met with on old cleared farms in those days, and beef was rarely seen in the back woods,—excepting when some old ox that was considered as superannuated was slaughtered to save it from dying a natural death. Remember this was sixteen years ago, and great changes have taken place since that time in the condition of all ranks of people in the Province; now there are luxuries, where before necessaries were scarce. However there was no lack of Christmas cheer in the shape of a large plum pudding, to which our little ones did ample justice. A merry day it was to them, for our boy Martin had made them a little sledge, and there was a famous snow drift against the garden fence, which was hard packed and frozen smooth and glare—up and down this frozen heap did James and Kate with their playmates glide and roll. It was a Christmas treat to watch those joyous faces, buoyant with mirth, and brightened by the keen air, through the frosty panes; and often was the graver converse of the parents interrupted by the merry shout and gleesome voices of their little ones; and if a sadder train of thought brought back the memory of former days, and home, country, and friends, from whom we were for ever parted ; such sadness was not without its benefit, linking us in spirit to that home, and all that made it precious to our hearts ; for we knew on that day our vacant places would be eyed with tender regret, and "some kind voice would murmur,

'Ah would they were here.'"

That night unwilling to part too soon, I accompanied my sister and her little ones home. Just as we were issuing forth for our moonlight drive through the woods, our ears were saluted by a merry peal of sleigh bells, and a loud hurrah greeted our homely turn-out, as a party of lively boys and girls, crammed into a smart painted cutter, rushed past at full speed. They were returning from a Christmas merry-making at a neighbour's house, where they too had been enjoying a happy Christmas; and long the still woods echoed with the gay tones of their voices, and the clear jingle of their merry bells, as a bend in the river-road, brought them back on the night breeze to our ears. There then we were breaking the Sabbath stillness of the dark forest with the hum of joyous voices, and the wild bursts of mirth that gushed forth from those glad children, who had as yet known little of the cares and regrets that later years bring with them as the inevitable consequence of a mature age. But soon overpowered by excess of happiness, and lulled by the low monotonous creaking of the runners of the sleigh, and heavy footfall of the oxen, one by one, our happy companions dropped off to sleep, and we were left in silence to enjoy the peculiar beauties of that snow clad scene, by the dreamy light that stole down upon our narrow road through the snow laden branches above our heads. And often in after years, when far removed from those forest scenes, has that Christmas night returned to my memory, and still I love to recall it for it, brings with it the freshness of former days, and the array of infant faces now grown up and fulfilling the state of life into which they have been called by their Heavenly Father.

C. P. T.

Christmas, 1853, Oaklands, Rice Lake.

INDIAN SUMMER.

This mysterious second summer comes for a brief season to quicken the vegetation of the new sown grain, and to perfect the buds that contain the embryo leaves and blossoms of the future year, before the frost of winter shall have bound up the earth with its fetters of ice.

The misty warmth of the Indian Summer steals drowsily upon our senses. We linger lovingly over each soft day that comes to us, folded in a hazy veil, and fear each one will be the last. They seem to us

"Like joys that linger as they fall,
Whose last are dearest."—

We watch with anxious eye the sun go down in the smoky horizon, and wonder if we shall see another Indian Summer day arise on the morrow.

The earth is rendering up her increase on nature's great altar, giving back to us some of the teeming warmth that she had collected during the long hot days of July, August and September.

It is natural to suppose that the mist that softens the atmosphere at this peculiar season arises from vegetable decomposition.

Or may be it has its origin in a remoter cause : the commencement of the polar winter. This subject has puzzled wiser heads than mine; therefore I will dismiss that part of my subject to the natural philosophers of this enlightened, reasoning age.

Among the peculiarities of this season, may be noticed, frosty nights, followed by warm soft days; sometimes a hot stirring breeze comes on about noon, at other times a stillness almost sultry continues through the day. From notes made in my journal during a succession of years, I have remarked that the Indian Summer comes on directly after the rains which prevail during the equinox, and the first two weeks in October. From the tenth or 15th of October to the first week in November, I should fix as the usual period of Indian Summer. Old settlers say that it comes earlier now than in former years. The date used to be as late as the 20th of November, but it is rarely so late now, whatever be the cause.

The Northern lights are frequently seen about the commencement of the Indian Summer, often being visible for many successive nights. The termination of this lovely serene season is very generally accompanied with a tempest, a hurricane, a violent rain, ending in snow and sharp frost.

INDIAN-SUMMER.

Though so lovely to the senses, it is not always a season of health: autumnal fevers and agues, with affections of the chest, are common. Nevertheless, this Indian-Summer is hailed by the Indian people with joy. It is, emphatically speaking, indeed the INDIAN'S SUMMER—his own peculiar season—his harvest in which he gathers in the winter-stores.

At this time the men forsake the villages and summer-lodges, and go off to their far-off hunting-grounds, for venison and furs. Now is their fishing-season ; and it is in the month of October, that the lakes swarm with myriads of wild-fowl.

The term *Indian-Summer*, always sounds to me as so expressive of the wants, habits and circumstances of the race. Their summer is not our summer. Like the people it is peculiar to this continent.— *They* reap while *we* sow. While *they* collect, *we* scatter abroad the seed for the future harvest.

It is by minute observation upon the objects with which he is most familiar, that the Indian obtains his knowledge :—a knowledge which has hitherto been sufficient for the supply of his very limited wants. He knows by the thickness of the down on the breasts of the wild fowl, and the fur of his peltries, whether the coming winter will be a severe one or otherwise. By the number of small animals that congregate in their several haunts, and the stores which they lay up, whether the season will be of longer or shorter duration. By the beavers repairing their dams ; and the muskrats building their houses earlier than usual, that the cold will also set in early.

In all these things the Indian trusts to the instinct of the lower animals, which is a knowledge given from God above—a great gift to help the weakest of his creatures. *

The unlettered Indian, in the simple faith of his heart, believes that the Almighty Creator—whom he adores as the GOOD SPIRIT, speaks to his creatures, tells them of his will, and guides them how to act, and provide for the winter's cold, be it little or be it much.

A great deal of the fruitfulness of the next year's harvest, may depend upon the length or shortness of the Indian-Summer.

It is during this season that the farmer stores his root-crops, and prepares his fallow lands. If, as it sometimes happens, the Indian-summer is short, and early frosts stop the ploughing operations, the Spring crops must suffer.

---

* " God's gift to the weak :" as says Mrs. Southey.

Therefore the thoughtful settler naturally regards the length of the Indian-summer as a great blessing.

Nature has now exhausted her rich store of buds and blossoms.—The rains and winds of October have scattered the last bright leaves upon the earth. The scarlet maple, the crimson oak and cherry, the dark purple of the black-ash, the lighter yellow of the birch and beech, lie withering at our feet—"the fading glories of the dying year."

Is there nothing but sadness and decay, in those fallen leaves? In those grey, leafless branches, through which the wind is sighing a requiem over the faded flowers and foliage? In yon grey elder, those round knobs contain the embryo blossoms, closely packed like green seeds; yet each tiny flower-cup is as perfect as it will be in the month of May:—it is only abiding its time! Yes, truly, there is much of hope and promise, revealed to us at this season. There is a savour of death;—but it is a death unto LIFE!

Look on those broad fields of emerald verdure, brightening into Spring-like beauty, with the rays of the noonday sun. Do they not speak to us of the future harvest—of the fruits of the coming year, which the harvestman is to reap.

He, too, must bide the time: first the blade; then the ear; then the ripened grain; then, again, the seed cast upon the earth—the renewal of his toil and his trust. Thus, then, we perceive that the Fall of the year is the renewal of Hope. In its darkest gloom, there is ever a gleam of sunlight, pointing onward to future joys.—*Revised from the original copy published in the Old Countryman, Nov, 2d, 1853.*

THE SCOTTISH EMIGRANT'S SONG.

    She turns her wheel wi busy hand
        But her thoughts are far away
    'Mid the bonnie braes o' her native land,
        While she sings this simple lay :—

    "I think upon the heathery hills
        I ay hae lov'd sae dearly,
    I think upon the wimpling burn
        That wandered by sae clearly.

    The little gowans tipped wi dew
        That 'mang the grass shone brightly ;
    The harebell waving in the breeze
        That bowed its head sae lightly.

    The lavrock singing in the cloud
        Wi' note sae blythe and cheery,
    That made my heart forget its load
        O' grief and care sae eerie.

    I think upon the moss grown grave
        O' those sae dear to me
    Wha' slumber in the auld kirk yard—
        My bonnie bairnies three.

    An' I would gie a mint o' gowd—
        If gowd were mine to gie—
    To wander through that auld kirk yard
        Thae bairns' wee graves to see."

    She ceased her sang—the briny tears
        Fell frae her glistening ee—
    For her heart throbbed fast as she thought upon
        These graves ayont the sea.

CONCLUSION.

And now, having touched upon almost every subject likely to prove useful to the emigrant's wife or daughter, in her Canadian home, I will take my leave, with the sincere hope that some among my readers may derive profit and assistance from the pages, which, with much toil and pains, I have written for their instruction. Very happy I shall be, if I find that my labours have not been entirely fruitless, and that my little book has been indeed, what it professes to be, a Guide and a Friend to the Female Emigrant.

If I have sometimes stepped aside to address the men, on matters that were connected with their department, it has still been with a view to serve their wives, daughters or sisters ; and such hints I hope may be well taken, and acted upon, for the ultimate benefit and comfort of all. In writing this little book, I have been influenced by no other desire than that of benefitting my countrywomen, and endeavouring to smooth for them the rough path which I have trodden before them, and in which, therefore, I may not be an incompetent guide.

I have urged upon no one the expediency of leaving their native land ; but I have laboured to show them that Canada, especially the Western or Upper portion of the Province, is preferable in many respects, to any other country to which they might feel inclined to turn their steps. Here the capitalist will find safe investment for his surplus wealth : the agriculturist will find a large field open to him, for the exercise of his knowledge, with a ready market for his produce, and the protection of a mild government, under the name of Her whom Britons delight to call their Queen. Here the labour of the poor man is amply rewarded, and he has it in his power in a few years, to become independent, and owe no man anything but that debt of brotherly love, which all Christians are bound to pay to each other.

It is a pleasant thing to contemplate the growing prosperity of a new country. To see thriving farmers, with well-stored barns, and sunny pastures covered with flocks and herds ; with fruitful gardens and orchards, extending over spaces where once lay the trackless and impenetrable forest ; and to reflect that these things have been the result of industry and well-directed energy ;—that by far the greater number of the men who own these blessings, have raised themselves from a state of abject poverty to a respectable position among their fellow-men.

The Irish emigrant can now listen to tales of famine and misery endured by his countrymen, while he looks round with complacency and contentment upon his own healthy, well-fed, well-clothed family, and thinks how different is his lot from that of his less fortunate brethren at home.

He sees his wife and children warmly clad with the wool spun from the fleeces of the flock before his door ; fed by the produce of his farm ; and remembers the day when he landed in the strange country, hungry, naked, forlorn, and friendless ; with drooping head, and crushed heart—scarcely even daring to hope that better things were in store for him and that pale, wasted creature at his side, his partner in misery and despair.

How many such have I seen and known ! How many of those who came to this Province eighteen years ago, under such sad circumstances as I have described, were among the settlers who came forward, with willing mind and liberal hand, to offer their subscriptions towards the relief of the famine-stricken Irish peasantry, in those sad years when a funeral pall seemed to have fallen over their native land. Do not these facts speak well for Canada ?

When I cast my eyes over this improving country, and behold such undoubted proofs of the prosperity of its inhabitants, I cannot but rejoice and feel glad in my very heart, that such things are ; and naturally wish that the poor among my countrymen and women, were as happily situated as those I have described.

Let me add yet a few words ere we part, on a subject that doubtless is very dear to you—I mean your Church. If your lot be cast as a resident in any of the towns or villages, of which now there are

CONCLUSION.

so many ; or in the long-cleared and populous portions of the Province ; you will find churches and ministers of every denomination ; with ready access to Sunday-schools, for the better instruction of your children : in the cleared townships services are held at stated times, in the school-houses, of which there are one or more in each section of every township : but you may be far from a church, and your opportunities may be few and far between, of attending divine worship. Nevertheless, suffer not your God to be forgotten in the lonely wilderness ; for you have need of his fatherly care over you and yours.— His ear is ever open to hear, and his holy arm stretched over you to save. He is at hand in the desert, as well as in the busy city : forsake him not, and bring up your children in his love and in his ways ; so shall his blessing be upon yourselves and your substance.

The first church in which I bent my knee in heartfelt thankfulness to the Almighty, for his saving care over me and my husband, in preserving us from the perils of the great deep, and the perils of the pestilence which had brought me down very low, almost to the very gates of Death—was in a log church of the rudest description ; and subsequently, it was in a barn, where two of my elder children were baptized by the good rector of Peterboro', long since called away from his pastoral labours by his Heavenly Master. But there was no lack of reverence among the little flock in the wilderness, who were gathered together that day ; for they felt that the rudest building can be made holy by the invisible presence of that Great God who has said, " Where two or three are gathered together in my name, there am I in the midst of them."

On that very spot, or within a few yards of it, the walls of a stone church are raised, and it will not be without a missionary of the Church, to administer the holy ordinances : so you see that while we were yet but a little flock, scattered and without frequent means of obtaining religious instruction, there were those who cared for the spiritual destitution of the poor colonists in the Backwoods ; and many liberal donations were sent from the mother-country for the erection of this church : many others in like manner, have been built by funds supplied from England, and this fact will, I hope, encourage and cheer those whose first settlement may be made in remote and less-favoured situations. It is also encouraging to the poor Canadian emigrants to know that kind and pious hearts care for them.

Much has been effected by the government with respect to the establishing of schools in every township and in all the principal towns; and much improvement will yet be made ; for we are what the Yankees would call a progressing people, *and must go forward*, till a satisfactory system of education has been established in the country, to meet this great want.

And now, farewell ; and I trust you will find kind hearts and friends, and much prosperity, in the land of your adoption ; never forgetting that you still belong to that land, which is the glory of all lands, and are subjects to a mild and merciful Sovereign, who is no less beloved in her Province of Canada, than she is by her loyal people of Britain.

APPENDIX.

INFORMATION FOR EMIGRANTS.
1854.

ROUTES, DISTANCES AND RATES OF PASSAGE.

From Quebec to Montreal.
180 miles, by steamers, every day, at five o'clock, through in fourteen hours.

	Steerage.		Cabin.	
	Stg.	Cy.	Stg.	Cy.
By the Royal Mail Packets	3s 0d	3s 9d	12s 15s 0d	
" Tait's Line	2s 0d	2s 6d	10s	12s 6d

From Montreal to Western Canada.
Daily by the Royal Mail Line Steamer, at nine o'clock, A.M., or by Rail Road to Lachine, at 12 o'clock.

Distances. Miles.	Deck fare.		Cabin fare.	
	Stg.	Cy.	Stg.	Cy.
From Montreal to				
Cornwall 78	5s	6s 3d	11s	13s 9d
Prescott 127	6s	7s 6d	14s	17s 6d
Brockville 139	8s	10s 0d	20s	25s 0d
Kingston 189	8s	10s 0d	20s	25s 0d
Cobourg 292	12s	15s 0d	28s	35s 0d
Port Hope 298	12s	15s 0d	28s	35s 0d
Bond Head.....313	14s	17s 6d	34s	42s 6d
Darlington 317	14s	17s 6d	34s	42s 6d
Whitby 337	14s	17s 6d	34s	42s 6d
Toronto........367	16s	20s 0d	26s	45s 0d
Hamilton 410	16s	20s 0d	26s	45s 0d
Detroit 596	24s	30s 0d	56s	$14
Chicago 874	32s	40s 0d	80s	$20

Passengers by foregoing line tranship at Kingston to the Lake Steamers, and at Toronto or Buffalo.

Daily by the American Line Steamer, at 1 o'clock, p.m.

From Montreal to Miles.	Deck fare.		Cabin fare.	
	Stg.	Cy.	Stg.	Cy.
Ogdensburgh ...133	6s	7s 6d	14s	17s 0d
Cape Vincent ..190	8s	10s 0d	20s	25s 0d
Sacket's Harbor 242	12s	15s 0d	24s	30s 0d
Oswego 286	14s	17s 6d	26s	32s 6d
Rochester 349	16s	20s 0d	30s	37s 6d
Lewiston 436	16s	20s 0d	34s	42s 6d
Buffalo........467	20s	25s 0d	38s	47s 6d
Cleveland 661	26s	32s 6d	—	—
Sandusky 721	28s	35s 0d	—	—
Toledo & Monroe 975	28s	35s 0d	—	—

Passengers by this line tranship at Ogdensburg to the Lake Steamers for Oswego and Lewiston.

The Passengers for both Lines embark at the Canal Basin, Montreal.

Steerage Passage from Quebec to Hamilton..23s 9d
" " Buffalo..............28s 9d

From Hamilton to the Western States,
By the Great Western Rail-road.

The new short route to the West.

Trains leave Hamilton daily for Detroit, connecting at that City with the Michigan Central Rail-Road for Chicago.

Distance.	Miles.	Emigrant Train. Stg.	Cy.	First-Class Train. Stg.	Cy.
To Dundas	6	0s 6d	0s 7½d	1s 0d	1s 3d
Flamboro	9	"	"	"	"
Paris	20	2s 0d	2s 6d	3s 8d	4s 6d
Woodstock	43	3s 0d	3s 9d	5s 0d	6s 3d
Ingersoll	47	3s 6d	4s 4d	7s 0d	8s 9d
London	76	4s 9d	6s 0d	9s 0d	11s 3d
Eckford	96	6s 0d	7s 6d	14s 0d	17s 6d
Chatham	140	7s 0d	3s 9d	"	"
Windsor } Detroit, Michigan	186	8s 0d	10s 0d	20s 0d	25s 0d
Chicago, Illinois	465	16s 0d	20s 0d	44s 0d	55s 0d

Steamers leave Chicago daily for Milwaukie and all other Ports on Lake Michigan.

Emigrants on arriving at Chicago, if proceeding further, will, on application to Mr. H. J. Spalding, Agent of the Michigan Central Railroad Company, receive correct advice and direction as to route.

Passengers for the Western parts of the United States of New York, Ohio, Pennsylvania, and Indiana, must take the route via Buffalo.

Ottawa River and Rideau Canal.

From Montreal to Bytown and places on the Rideau Canal, by Steam every evening.

By Robertson, Jones & Co.'s Line.

From Montreal to	Distance. Miles.	Deck Passengers. Stg.	Cy.	Deck Passengers. Stg.	Cy.
Carillon	54	2s	2s 6d		
Grenville	66	3s	3s 9d		
L'Original	73	3s	3s 9d		
Bytown	129	4s	5s 0d		
Kemptville	157				
Merrickville	175				
Smith's Falls	190				
Oliver's Ferry	199	6s	7s 6d		
Isthmus	216				
Jones' Falls	226				
Kingston	258				

(Rideau Canal)

Passengers proceeding to Perth, Lanark, or any of the adjoining Settlements, should land at Oliver's Ferry, seven miles from Perth.

Route to the Eastern Parts of the United States.

Emigrants, proceeding to any of the following States of the American Union, viz.:—Maine, New Hampshire, Massachusetts, Connecticut, Vermont, New York, and Pennsylvania,

By the Champlain and St. Lawrence Railroad Company,—Mr. W. A. Merry, Secy.

Office opposite to the Steamboat Landing, Montreal.

EMIGRANT TRAIN.

From Montreal to	Stg.	Cy.
Burlington	8s 0d	10s 0d
Whitehall	12s 0d	15s 6d
Troy	18s 0d	22s 6d
New York	19s 0d	23s 9d
Boston	26s 0d	32s 6d

Trains of the above Company leave Montreal daily.

From Toronto Steamers leave daily for Port Credit, 15 miles; Oakville, 25 miles; Wellington Square, 37 miles; Hamilton, 43; also Port Dalhousie on the entrance of the Welland Canal, Niagara, Queenston and Lewiston—passage, 3s. 9d.

Steamers leave Kingston daily for the Bay of Quinte and the River Trent, calling at Picton, Adolphustown, Belleville, and other landing-places in the Bay.

To New Brunswick.

The best and most expeditious route is by the St. Lawrence and Atlantic Railroad, from Montreal to Portland,—thence by Steamer, which leaves for St. John's N. B. every Monday and Wednesday evening, at eight o'clock.

Route:	Stg.	Cy.
From Quebec to Montreal, by Steamer,	3s	3s 9d
Montreal to Portland, by Railroad,	24s	30s 0d
Portland to St. John's, by Steamer,	16s	20s 0d
	43s	53s 9d

Throughout these Passages, Children under twelve years of age are charged half-price, and those under three years are free.

Passengers by steamers from Quebec to Hamilton—Luggage free; if by Railroads, 100 lbs. is allowed to each passenger, all over that quantity will be charged.

The Gold Sovereign is at present worth 24s. 4d. cy.; the English Shilling, 1s. 3d.; and the English Crown-piece, 6s. 1d.

Through Tickets can be obtained on application to this Office.

A. C. BUCHANAN, CHIEF AGENT.

EMIGRATION DEPARTMENT,
Quebec, June, 1854.

NOTE.—It should be observed that the above information applies more particularly to the present year. There are some parts of it, however, which will be found useful to intending emigrants and their friends here.

Any further information or new arrangements will appear in future numbers or editions.

EQUIVALENT VALUE OF CURRENCY AND CENTS,

FROM ONE COPPER TO ONE DOLLAR.

(Copied from The Old Countryman Newspaper, Toronto.)

Currency. d.	Cents.	Currency. s. d.	Cents.
½ equal to	5-6	1 0 equal to	20
3-5 "	1	1 0 3-5	21
1 "	1⅔	1 1	21⅔
1 1-5 "	2	1 1 1-5	22
1½	2½	1 1 4-5	23
1 4-5	3	1 2	23½
2	3⅓	1 2 2-5	24
2 2-5	4	1 3	25
2½	4 1-6	1 3 3-5	26
3	5	1 4	26⅔
3½	5 5-6	1 4 1-5	27
3 3-5	6	1 4½	27½
4	6⅔	1 4 4-5	28
4 1-5	7	1 5	28⅓
4½	7½	1 5 2-5	29
4 4-5	8	1 6	30
5	8⅓	1 6 3-5	31
5 2-5	9	1 7	31⅔
5½	9 1-6	1 7 1-5	32
6	10	1 7½	32½
6½	10 5-6	1 7 4-5	33
6 3-5	11	1 8	33⅓
7	11⅔	1 8 2-5	34
7 1-5	12	1 9	35
7½	12½	1 9 3-5	36
7 4-5	13	1 10	36⅔
8	13⅓	1 10 1-5	37
8 2-5	14	1 10½	37½
8½	14 1-6	1 10 4-5	38
9	15	1 11	38⅓
9½	15 5-6	1 11 2-5	39
9 3-5	16	2 0	40
10	16⅔	2 3	45
10 1-5	17	2 6	50
10½	17½	3 0	60
10 4-5	18	3 6	70
11	18⅓	4 0	80
11 2-5	19	4 6	90
11½	19 1-6	5 0	100

APPENDIX. 5

TABLE FOR CALCULATING THE DIFFERENCE BETWEEN STERLING MONEY AND CURRENCY.

One Pound Sterling equal to One Pound Four Shillings and Four Pence Currency.

PENCE.			POUNDS.			POUNDS.			POUNDS.		
Stg.	Currency.		Stg.	Currency.		Stg.	Currency.		Stg.	Currency.	
d.	£ s.	d.	£	£ s.	d.	£	£ s.	d.	£	£ s.	d.
1	0 0	1¼	1	1 4	4	38	46 4	8	75	91 5	0
2	0 0	2½	2	2 8	8	39	47 9	0	76	92 9	4
3	0 0	3¾	3	3 13	0	40	48 13	4	77	93 13	8
4	0 0	5	4	4 17	4	41	49 17	8	78	94 18	0
5	0 0	6¼	5	6 1	8	42	51 2	0	79	96 2	4
6	0 0	7½	6	7 6	0	43	52 6	4	80	97 6	8
7	0 0	9	7	8 10	4	44	53 10	8	81	98 11	0
8	0 0	10	8	9 14	8	45	54 15	0	82	99 15	4
9	0 0	11¼	9	10 19	0	46	55 19	4	83	100 19	8
10	0 1	0½	10	12 3	4	47	57 3	8	84	102 4	0
11	0 1	1¾	11	13 7	8	48	58 8	0	85	103 8	4
12	0 1	3	12	14 12	0	49	59 12	4	86	104 12	8
			13	15 16	4	50	60 16	8	87	105 17	0
			14	17 0	8	51	62 1	0	88	107 1	4
SHILLINGS.			15	18 5	0	52	63 5	4	89	108 5	8
			16	19 9	4	53	64 9	8	90	109 10	0
s.	£ s.	d.	17	20 13	8	54	65 14	0	91	110 14	4
			18	21 18	0	55	66 18	4	92	111 18	8
1	0 1	2⅜	19	23 2	4	56	68 2	8	93	113 3	0
2	0 2	5¼	20	24 6	8	57	69 7	0	94	114 7	4
3	0 3	8¼	21	25 11	0	58	70 11	4	95	115 11	8
4	0 4	10½	22	26 15	4	59	71 15	8	96	116 16	0
5	0 6	1	23	27 19	8	60	73 0	0	97	118 0	4
6	0 7	3¾	24	29 4	0	61	74 4	4	98	119 4	8
7	0 8	6¼	25	30 8	4	62	75 8	8	99	120 9	0
8	0 9	9	26	31 12	8	63	76 13	0	100	121 13	4
9	0 10	11¾	27	32 17	0	64	77 17	4	200	243 6	8
10	0 12	2	28	34 1	4	65	79 1	8	300	365 0	0
11	0 13	4¾	29	35 5	8	66	80 6	0	400	486 13	4
12	0 14	7½	30	36 10	0	67	81 10	4	500	608 6	8
13	0 15	10¼	31	37 14	4	68	82 14	8	600	730 0	0
14	0 17	1	32	38 18	8	69	83 19	0	700	851 13	4
15	0 18	3	33	40 3	0	70	85 3	4	800	973 6	8
16	0 19	5¾	34	41 7	4	71	86 7	8	900	1095 0	0
17	1 0	8½	35	42 11	8	72	87 12	0	1000	1216 13	4
18	1 1	11¼	36	43 16	0	73	88 16	4			
19	1 3	1¼	37	45 0	4	74	90 0	8			
20	1 4	4									

COMPARATIVE PRICES AT FOLLOWING PERIODS IN TORONTO MARKET.

	May, 1845.	May, 1849.	July, 1853.	December, 1854.
	s. d. s. d.	s. d. s. d.	s. d. s. d.	s. d. s. d.
Flour, per barrel.........196 lbs.	15 0 to 20 0	16 3 to 21 3	17 6 to 19 0	35 0 to 37 6
Wheat, (Spring,) per bushel, 60 lbs.	3 9 to 4 0	3 0 to 4 0	4 0 to 4 9	0 0 to 0 0
" (Fall) " "	3 4 to 6 0	3 6 to 4 6½	5 0 to 5 3	7 0 to 7 6
Barley " 48 lbs.	2 4 to 3 0	1 8 to 1 10½	2 6 to 3 0	4 6 to 4 8
Rye, " 56 lbs.	3 0 to 3 6	3 0 to 3 4	2 0 to 3 6	6 9 to 7 0
Oats, " 34 lbs.	1 8 to 1 10½	1 0 to 1 2	1 10½ to 2 0	3 3 to 3 6
Oatmeal, per barrel,......196 lbs.	16 3 to 18 9	17 6 to 20 0	22 6 to 23 9	38 9 to 40 0
Peas, per bushel	1 8 to 2 6	1 6 to 2 0	2 6 to 2 10	4 0 to 5 0
Potatoes, "	1 2 to 1 8	3 6 to 3 9	1 8 to 2 0	1 10½ to 2 6
Beef, per lb.	0 2 to 0 6	0 2 to 0 4	0 3½ to 0 4	0 6 to 0 7
Beef, per 100 lbs	15 0 to 26 0	12 6 to 20 0	20 0 to 22 6	25 0 to 27 6
Pork, per lb.	0 2 to 0 4	0 2½ to 0 2¾	0 4 to 0 4½	
Pork, per 100 lbs.	16 3 to 22 6	16 3 to 20 0	25 0 to 27 6	25 0 to 30 0
Veal, by the quarter	0 2 to 0 3	0 2½ to 0 4	0 3½ to 0 4	0 4½ to 0 5
Bacon,	0 0 to 0 0	0 2½ to 0 4	0 5 to 0 6	55 0 to 62 6
Mutton, per lb. per quarter	0 3 to 0 5	0 2¼ to 0 4	0 4½ to 0 5½	0 6 to 0 7
" " carcass	0 0 to 0 0	0 2 to 0 3	0 3½ to 0 4	0 4 to 0 5
Lamb, per quarter	0 0 to 0 0	2 6 to 5 0	2 0 to 2 6	
Fresh Butter, per lb.	0 6 to 0 7	0 7 to 0 9	0 7½ to 0 8	1 0 to 1 3
" " firkin	0 0 to 0 0	0 6 to 0 7½	0 6½ to 0 7	0 9 to 0 10
Cheese,	0 0 to 0 0	0 3½ to 0 5	0 5 to 0 6	0 10 to 1 0
Lard,	0 0 to 0 0	0 0 to 0 3½	0 5 to 0 6½	0 6 to 0 7
Eggs,	0 3½ to 0 4½	0 5½ to 0 6	0 0 to 0 7½	1 0 to 1 3
Turkeys,	0 0 to 0 0	2 6 to 5 0	3 6 to 4 0	3 0 to 4 0
Fowls, per pair	1 6 to 2 0	2 0 to 2 6	1 9 to 2 6	1 3 to 1 10
Straw, per ton	22 6 to 25 0	25 0 to 30 0	30 0 to 35 0	60 0 to 90 6
Hay, "	40 0 to 55 0	35 0 to 45 0	40 0 to 50 0	120 0 to 110 0
Firewood, per cord	0 0 to 0 0	10 0 to 12 6	15 0 to 17 6	27 6 to 30 0
Sheepskins, fresh slaughtered	0 0 to 0 0	0 0 to 0 0	1 8 to 2 0	2 6 to 3 10
Wool,	0 7 to 0 9	0 10 to 1 0	1 7 to 1 8½	1 0 to 1 3
Coal,	to	to	to	32 6 to 50 0

APPENDIX. 7

PROGRESSIVE VALUE OF FARMING STOCK.

	1833.			1650.			1853.			1855.		
	£.	s.	d.	£.	s.	d.	£.	s.	d.	£.	s.	d.
Horses..................	15	0	0 to	17	10	0 to	25	0	0 to 35	40	0	0 to 50 0 0
Working Oxen per pair...	15	0	0 to 20 10	0	0	0	20	0	0 to 22 10	25	0	0 to 35 0 0
Sheep...................	0	5	0 to 0 17 10	0	5	0	0	17	0 to *17 10	1	5	0 to 2 0 0
Cows....................	3	15	0 to 4 0 0	5	0	0	6	0	0 to 7 10	6	0	0 to 10 0 0
Pigs, of 300 lbs. each, per cwt.	0	12	0 to 0 17 6	0	15	0	1	5	0 to 1 10	1	10	0 to 1 15 0
Lambs...................	0	3	0 to 0 5 0	0	7	6	0	10	0 to 0 12 6	0	15	0 to 0 17 6
Oxen for slaughter, per cwt.	0	15	0 to 1 0 0	1	5	0	1	5	0 to 1 10 0	30	0	0 to 40 0 0
							*Leicesters.					

WAGES IN CANADA.

	s.	d.		s.	d.
Bricklayers..............	8	9	to 8	11	3
Masons..................	8	9	to 9	10	0
Stone-Cutters............	6	3	to 10	8	0
Joiners..................	6	3	to 10	8	0
Carpenters..............	6	3	to 10	7	6
Tinsmiths...............	6	3	to 10	6	10½
Painters.................	6	3	to 10	7	6
Grainers................	7	6	to 10	8	9
Hatters (Compositors)....	6	3	to 10	8	9
Printers (Compositors)...	7	6	to 10	7	6
Do. (Power-Pressmen)..	7	6	to 10	8	4
Tailors (Male)...........	5	0	to 6	6	3
Do. (Female).........	1	3	to 2	2	6
Shoemakers..............	5	0	to 10	5	3
Upholsterers.............	6	3	to 10	7	6
Coopers.................	3	9	to 10	5	0
Farm-Laborers (with board)	2	6	to 10	3	9
Day-Laborers............	3	9	to 5	5	3
Boys and Girls (12 to 14).	1	3	to 1	1	9
Dress-Makers (with board)	1	6	to 10	2	6
Railway-Laborers........	5	0	to	6	3
Needle-Women (with board)	1	3	to 10	2	6
Servant-Maids (per month)	15	0	to 25	0	0

Servant-Boys..................20 0 to 35 0
Servant-Men..................50 0 to 70 0

USEFUL TO FARMERS.

WEIGHTS OF VARIOUS ARTICLES OF PRODUCE, AND THE RATES BY WHICH THEY SHOULD BE BOUGHT AND SOLD.

A bushel of wheat, sixty pounds.
Of Indian corn, fifty-six pounds.
Of corn in the cob, seventy pounds.
Of rye, fifty-six pounds. Of oats, thirty-four pounds.
Of barley, forty-eight pounds.
Of potatoes, sixty pounds.
Of beans, sixty pounds. Of bran, twenty pounds.
Of clover seed, sixty pounds.
Of timothy-seed, forty-eight pounds.
Of flax-seed, forty-six pounds.
Of hemp-seed, forty-four pounds.
Of buckwheat, fifty pounds.
Of blue-grass seed, fourteen pounds.
Of onions, fifty-seven pounds.
Of castor beans, forty pounds.
Of dried peaches, thirty-three pounds.
Of dried apples, twenty-four pounds.
Of salt, fifty-six pounds.

Government Emigration Department.

PARTIES desirous of bringing out their friends from Europe, are hereby notified, that the Chief Agent for Emigration has received the sanction of the Provincial Government to a plan for facilitating the same, which will obviate all risk of loss or misapplication of the money.

Upon payment of any sum of money to the Chief Agent, a Certificate will be issued (see annexed form,) at the rate of Five Dollars to the Pound Sterling.

This Certificate will be available for transmission, and will secure the parties holding the same passage by vessels from any port in the United Kingdom, or from Bremen and Hamburg, bound for Quebec.

Parties in Western Canada will be furnished with the necessary Certificate, on application to A. B. HAWKE, Esq., the Chief Emigration Agent at Toronto, or the undersigned at Quebec. They may also at the same time arrange with this Department for their inland transport to any point on the line of steamboat or railroad travel nearest to their place of final destination. Application, if by letter, to be post-paid.

A. C. BUCHANAN,
Chief Agent.

Emigration Department,
Quebec, May, 1854.

CERTIFICATE.

GOVERNMENT EMIGRATION DEPARTMENT.
Quebec, --------, 1854.

No------

£------Sterling. ------ has this day deposited with me, the sum of ------Pounds ------Shillings Sterling, to promote the emigration from ------ to this country of ------Persons. Equal to ------ Adults.

Now, the said sum of ------Pounds ------Shillings Sterling will be paid, or accounted for by this Department, to such ship as shall convey to the Port of Quebec the said ------ on presentation of this Certificate.

If the said sum of ------Sterling should prove more than sufficient to cover the passage of the above parties, at the rates to be agreed upon, the surplus to be paid in like manner to the said ------ or order.

N.B.—Should this Certificate not be made use of, it must be returned to the depositors to enable them to recover their money here.

The sum of two shillings and sixpence will be charged for each Certificate, issued in Upper Canada, under £10, and five shillings for sums above that amount, and this charge will cover all expenses of transmission and agency.

A. B.—Persons holding this Certificate are referred in case of need, to the Government Emigration Office in the United Kingdom at the following Ports:—

London,	Glasgow,	Dublin,	Limerick,
Liverpool,	Belfast,	Waterford,	Galway,
Plymouth,	Londonderry,	Cork,	Sligo.

APPENDIX.

GENERAL TABLE OF LAND MEASURE.

```
62.7264 Sq. Inches=   1 Sq. Link.
   144     =    2.2936   =    1 Sq. Foot.
  1296     =   20.6611   =    9     =   1 Sq. Yard.
 39204     =     625     =  272.25  =   30.25   =   1 Perch.
627264     =   10000     = 4356     =  484      =  16  =  1 Sq. Chain.
1568160    =   25000     = 1890     = 1210      =  40  =  2.5   =   1 Rood.
6272640    =  100000     = 43560    = 4840      = 160  =  10    =   4 = 1 Acre.
```

Six hundred and forty acres make a square mile.

TABLE OF THE LENGTH AND BREADTH OF AN IMPERIAL ACRE OF LAND.

Width of Row.		LENGTH PER ACRE.				
Feet.	In.	Plants.	Yards.	Rods of 5½ Yards.	Roods of 36 Yards.	Miles—1760 Yards.
0	1	6,272,640	174,240	31,671¼	4,840	99
0	2	1,568,160	87,120	15,840	2,420	49.5
0	3	696,960	58,080	10,560	1,613 12 yds.	33
0	4	392,040	43,560	7,920	1,210	24.75
0	5	250,906	34,848	6,336	968	19.8
0	10	62,726	17,424	3,168	484	9.9
1	0	43,560	14,520	2,640	403 12	8.25
1	3	27,878	11,616	2,112	322 24	6.6
1	6	19,360	9,680	1,760	268 32	5.5
1	9	14,224	8,297	1,508½	230 17	4.71
2	0	10,890	7,260	1,501½	201 24	4.12
2	3	8,604	6,453	1,355	179 9	3.66
2	6	6,970	5,808	1,237½	161 12	3.3
2	9	5,760	5,280	960	146 24	3
3	0	4,840	4,840	880	134 16	2.75
4	0	2,723	3,630	660	100 30	2.06
5	0	1,742	2,904	528	80 23	1.66
6	0	1,210	2,420	440	67 12	1.37
7	0	889	2,074	377	57 22	1.17
8	0	681	1,815	330	50 15	1 03
9	0	538	1,613	293¼	44 29	.916
10	0	436	1,452	264	40 12	.125
11	0	360	1,320	240	36 24	.756
12	0	303	1,210	220	33 22	.647
13	0	258	1,116	203	31	.634
14	0	224	1,037	188½	28 29	.5-9
15	0	194	968	176	26 32	.552
16	0	170	907	165	25 7	.515
17	0	151	854	155½	23 26	.485
18	0	134	806	146¼	22 14	.457
19	0	121	764	139	21 8	.434
20	0	109	726	132	20 6	.412
25	0	70	580	105¼	16 4	.313

EXPLANATION.—In the above Table the first column may represent the width of rough furrows, drills, or ridges. The second column is ruled by the first, and shows the number of plants required for an acre, when they are planted at equal distances from each other in all directions. The remaining columns give the length of an acre at the various widths specified in the first column. The distances travelled in a day by a sower or a ploughman can in this way be readily ascertained, if the acres completed and the widths of ridges or furrows are known.

MEAN TEMPERATURE

The following Table gives the MEAN TEMPERATURE of the various places named.

1854	Jan.	Feb.	March.	April.	May.	June.	July.	Aug.	Sep.	Oct.	Nov.	Dec.
LONDON	36.02	39.75	42.6	47.57	55.26	60.68	63.17	62.78	57.	50.37	43.12	40.09
PARIS	35.44	39.54	43.99	49.78	58.08	62.74	65.66	65.35	60.17	52.25	44.17	38.57
TORONTO	25.0	23.71	30.37	43.38	53.28	60.88	66.28	66.73	58.71	45.69	36.03	27.24
SEBASTOPOL	34.27	36.52	42.37	50.92	61.54	70.09	71.15	70.40	63.41	53.76	44.08	74.03
England	36.34	39.6	42.	47.29	54.31	59.76	62.45	61.63	57.7	51.16	42.78	39.42
Scotland	37.24	37.88	40.76	44.78	50.55	56.11	58.83	57.05	53.52	48.28	42.46	39.84
Philadelphia	30.08	29.4	38.78	49.45	61.18	68.85	73.92	71.51	63.6	51.7	40.32	30.72
St. Petersburg	14.74	14.74	25.5	37.18	48.52	59.95	63.91	61.17	51.31	41.38	30.38	22.57
New Zealand	65.	67.	65.	61.	55.48	53.	52.	53.	54.	59.	61.	67.
Vienna	29.28	33.53	40.8	51.85	62.15	67.47	70.75	69.96	70.07	51.22	40.35	33.04
Madrid	42.44	44.42	48.2	55.28	63.1	71.96	78.26	78.98	68.	56.48	47.84	42.62
Cairo	58.1	56.12	64.58	77.9	78.26	83.66	85.82	85.83	79.10	72.32	62.69	61.34
Lisbon	52.52	53.6	56.3	59.	63.64	69.44	72.14	71.24	69.44	62.6	55.4	51.44

NOTE.—The authoress is indebted to an excellent Count025-Gentleman's Newspaper, published in London, England, called THE FIELD, for the three foregoing and most of the Tables immediately following. The Calendar for the past year is worth a year's Subscription. The Editor of the "Old Countryman", Toronto, has kindly consented to act as Agent for it in the Canadas.

LENGTH OF A MILE IN DIFFERENT COUNTRIES.

English mile	contains	1,760 yards.	Spanish mile	contains	5,028 yards.
Russian mile	"	1,100 "	German mile	"	5,866 "
Irish and Scotch mile	"	2,200 "	Swedish and Danish mi'e }	"	7,233 "
Italian mile	"	1,467 "			
Polish mile	"	4,400 "	Hungarian mile	"	8,830 "

In France they measure by the mean league of 8,660 yards.

T A B L E S ,

Accurately calculated, converting Short Weight into Long Weight, and Long Weight into Short Weight.

Sh. Wt. T.	C.	Q.	*Long Wt.* T.	C.	Q.	lb.	*Long Wt.* T.	C.	Q.	*Short Wt.* T.	C.	Q.	lb.
0	0	1	0	0	0	28	0	0	1	0	0	1	2
0	0	2	0	0	1	26	0	0	2	0	0	2	4
0	0	3	0	0	2	24	0	0	3	0	0	3	6
0	1	0	0	0	3	22	0	1	0	0	1	0	8
0	2	0	0	1	3	14	0	2	0	0	2	0	16
0	3	0	0	2	3	6	0	3	0	0	3	0	24
0	4	0	0	3	2	28	0	4	0	0	4	1	4
0	5	0	0	4	2	20	0	5	0	0	5	1	12
0	6	0	0	5	2	12	0	6	0	0	6	1	20
0	7	0	0	6	2	4	0	7	0	0	7	2	0
0	8	0	0	7	1	26	0	8	0	0	8	2	8
0	9	0	0	8	1	18	0	9	0	0	9	2	16
0	10	0	0	9	1	10	0	10	0	0	10	2	24
0	11	0	0	10	1	2	0	11	0	0	11	3	4
0	12	0	0	11	0	24	0	12	0	0	12	3	12
0	13	0	0	12	0	16	0	13	0	0	13	3	20
0	14	0	0	13	0	8	0	14	0	0	15	0	0
0	15	0	0	14	0	0	0	15	0	0	16	0	8
0	16	0	0	14	3	22	0	16	0	0	17	0	16
0	17	0	0	15	3	14	0	17	0	0	18	0	24
0	18	0	0	16	3	6	0	18	0	0	19	1	4
0	19	0	0	17	2	28	0	19	0	1	0	1	12
1	0	0	0	18	2	20	1	0	0	1	1	1	20

A TABLE

For buying or Selling by the Great Hundred.

D.	L.	S.	D.	D.	L.	S.	D.	D.	L.	S.	D.	D.	L.	S.	D.
	0	0	0	6	2	16	0	12	5	12	0	18	8	8	0
¼	0	2	4	6¼	2	18	4	12¼	5	14	4	18¼	8	10	4
	0	4	8	6½	3	0	8	12½	5	16	8	18½	8	12	8
	0	7	0	6¾	3	3	0	12¾	5	19	0	18¾	8	15	0
1	0	9	4	7	3	5	4	13	6	1	4	19	8	17	4
1¼	0	11	8	7¼	3	7	8	13¼	6	3	8	19¼	8	19	8
1½	0	14	0	7½	3	10	0	13½	6	6	0	19½	9	2	0
1¾	0	16	4	7¾	3	12	4	13¾	6	8	4	19¾	9	4	4
2	0	18	8	8	3	14	8	14	6	10	8	20	9	6	8
2	1	1	0	8	3	17	0	14¼	6	13	0	20¼	9	9	0
2½	1	3	4	8½	3	19	4	14½	6	15	4	20½	9	11	4
2¾	1	5	8	8¾	4	1	8	14¾	6	17	8	20¾	9	13	8
3	1	8	0	9	4	4	0	15	7	0	0	21	9	16	0
3¼	1	10	4	9¼	4	6	4	15¼	7	2	4	21¼	9	18	4
3½	1	12	8	9½	4	8	8	15½	7	4	8	21½	10	0	8
3¾	1	15	0	9¾	4	11	0	15¾	7	7	0	21¾	10	3	0
4	1	17	4	10	4	13	4	16	7	9	4	22	10	5	4
4¼	1	19	8	10¼	4	15	8	16¼	7	11	8	22¼	10	7	8
4½	2	2	0	10½	4	18	0	16½	7	14	0	22½	10	10	0
4¾	2	4	4	10¾	5	0	4	16	7	16	4	22¾	10	12	4
5	2	6	8	11	5	2	8	17	7	18	8	23	10	14	8
5¼	2	9	0	11¼	5	5	0	17¼	8	1	0	23¼	10	17	0
5½	2	11	4	11½	5	7	4	17	8	3	4	23½	10	19	4
5¾	2	13	8	11¾	5	9	8	17¾	8	5	8	23¾	11	1	8

Example.—First, at 5¾d. the lb., what is the great Cwt?—Look in the table for 5¾d. in the first column, and against it, in the second, you will find £2 13s 8d., and so much will 112 lbs. cost. Again, if a Cwt. cost £4 8s. 8d., find £4 8s. 8d., and against it, in the column towards the left hand, there you will find 9½d., and so much it is by the lb. For every ¼ that 1 lb. costs, reckon 2s. 4d.; that is the price of the great Cwt.

INTEREST TABLE.

By which the Interest of £100, at any Rate, and for any Time, may be readily found.

Days.	3 ₩ cent. L.	s.	D.	3½ ₩ cent. L.	s.	D.	4 ₩ cent. L.	s.	D.	4½ ₩ cent. L.	s.	D.	5 ₩ cent. L.	s.	D.
1	0	0	1¾	0	0	2¼	0	0	2½	0	0	3	0	0	3¼
2	0	0	3¾	0	0	4½	0	0	5¼	0	0	6	0	0	6½
3	0	0	5¾	0	0	6¾	0	0	7¾	0	0	8¾	0	0	9¾
4	0	0	7¾	0	0	9	0	0	10¼	0	0	11¾	0	1	1
5	0	0	9¾	0	0	11½	0	1	1¼	0	1	2¾	0	1	4¼
6	0	0	11¾	0	1	1¾	0	1	3¾	0	1	5¾	0	1	7½
7	0	1	1¼	0	1	4	0	1	6¼	0	1	8¾	0	1	11½
8	0	1	3¾	0	1	6¼	0	1	9	0	1	11¼	0	2	2¼
9	0	1	5¾	0	1	8½	0	1	11¾	0	2	3½	0	2	5½
10	0	1	7½	0	1	11	0	2	4½	0	3	5¼	0	2	8¾
20	0	3	4¼	0	3	10	0	4	6½	0	4	11¼	0	5	5¾
30	0	4	10	0	5	9	0	6	9¾	0	7	4½	0	8	3½
40	0	6	6¾	0	7	8	0	8	0	0	9	10¼	0	10	11½
50	0	8	2¼	0	9	7	0	10	10¼	0	12	3¾	0	13	8¼
60	0	9	10¼	0	11	6	0	13	0¾	0	14	9½	0	16	5¼
70	0	11	6	0	13	5	0	15	4	0	17	3¾	0	19	2
80	0	13	1¾	0	15	4	0	17	6¼	0	19	8¾	1	1	11
90	0	14	9½	0	17	3	0	19	8¼	1	2	2¼	1	4	7¾
100	0	16	5¼	0	19	2	1	1	11	1	4	8	1	7	4¾

TABLE TO CALCULATE WAGES AND OTHER PAYMENTS.

Per Year. £	Per Month. £	s.	d.	Per Week. £	s.	d	Per Day. £	s.	d.	Per Year. £	Per Month. £	s.	d.	Per Week. £	s.	d.	Per Day. £	s.	d.
1	0	1	8	0	0	4¾	0	0	0¾	15	1	5	0	0	5	9	0	0	10
2	0	3	4	0	0	9¼	0	0	1¼	16	1	6	8	0	6	1½	0	0	10½
3	0	5	0	0	1	1¾	0	0	2	17	1	8	4	0	6	6¼	0	0	11¼
4	0	6	8	0	1	6½	0	0	2¾	18	1	10	0	0	6	10¾	0	0	11¾
5	0	8	4	0	1	11	0	0	3¼	19	1	11	8	0	7	3½	0	1	0½
6	0	10	0	0	2	3½	0	0	4	20	1	13	4	0	7	8	0	1	1¼
7	0	11	8	0	2	8¼	0	0	4½	30	2	10	0	0	11	6	0	1	7¾
8	0	13	4	0	3	0¾	0	0	5¼	40	3	6	8	0	15	4	0	2	2¼
9	0	15	0	0	3	5½	0	0	6	50	4	3	4	0	19	2	0	2	9
10	0	16	8	0	3	10	0	0	6½	60	5	0	0	1	3	0¼	0	3	3¼
11	0	18	4	0	4	2¾	0	0	7¼	70	5	16	8	1	6	10¼	0	3	10¼
12	1	0	0	0	4	7¼	0	0	8	80		13	4	1	10	8¼	0	4	4½
13	1	1	8	0	4	11¾	0	0	8½	90	7	10	0	1	14	6¼	0	4	11¼
14	1	3	4	0	5	4¼	0	0	9¼	100	8	6	8	1	18	4½	0	5	5¾

DEATHS AND CAUSES OF DEATH IN 1853.

Class of Disease.	Upper C.	Lower C.
Epidemic, Endemic and Contagious...	1782	3088
Nervous System..................	509	409
Respiratory and Circulatory Organs...	1053	1070
Digestive " ...	674	418
Urinary " ...	37	21
Generative " ...	148	150
Locomotive " ...	35	44
Tegumentary " ...	5	3
Diseases of Uncertain Seat	480	211
Violent or Sudden Deaths...........	422	318
Causes of Death, not classed........	717	708
Total of causes specified..........	5838	6500
" not specified.......	1939	5174

USEFUL INFORMATION.

A dicker of hides, 10 skins
Ditto of gloves, 10 dozen pairs.
A last of hides, 20 dickers.
A standard gallon contains 10 ℔ avoirdupois of distilled water.
A weigh of cheese, 236 ℔.
The (long) hundredweight is 112 ℔.
Barrel of beer, 36 gallons.
Hogshead of beer, 54 gallons.
Herrings are measured by the barrel of 26½, or cran of 37¾ gallons.
A stone of fish, 14 ℔: and of wool, 14 ℔. The same for horseman's weight, hay, iron, shot, &c.
A stone of glass, 5 ℔; a seam of ditto, 24 stone
A cade of red herrings, 500; and sprats, 1,000.
A load of timber unhewn, 40 cubic feet.
A bag of hops, nearly 3½ cwt.
A ton contains 42 cubic feet.

Oranges, lemons, corks, and a few other articles, are often sold by the gross; nails, tacks, &c., have six score to the hundred.
A solid yard of well-wrought clay will make 460 bricks. Thirty-two common bricks will cover a square yard. A common brick is 9 inches long, 4½ inches wide, and 2½ inches thick.
8 pounds, 1 stone of meat.
Sheet lead is from 6 ℔ to 10 ℔ to the square foot.
A pipe of an inch bore is commonly 13 ℔ or 14 ℔ per yard long.
An imperial gallon of whale or seal oil should weigh 9 ℔; spermaceti, 8 ℔; which test of quality all consumers are recommended to employ, as many use the old measure, which is one-fifth less.
Plain tiles are 10½ inches long, 6¼ wide, and ⅝ inch thick.

REGULATIONS FOR THE POSTAGE OF BOOKS, MSS. &c, IN ENGLAND.

All books under one pound weight may be sent by post in wrappers open at each end, for sixpence in stamps; all books over one pound weight, and under two, are charged one shilling, and so onward, sixpence for every additional pound, a fraction over being charged as a pound.

MSS. may be transmitted by post without limit as to weight, at the rate of twopence per ounce, the smallest fraction being charged as an ounce.

No money postage will be now received for Books, Letters, or MSS. Stamps alone are to represent payment, and everything unstamped will go as unpaid, payment in money not being recognised.

WEIGHT OF WATER ON LAND.

A cubic foot of water contains 6¾ gallons, each weighing 10 ℔. If 4000 gallons of liquid manure are applied to an acre, the cubic capacity of the application is 23 yards 19 feet, and its weight 17 tons 17 cwts. 16 ℔. This dressing, if not imbibed by the soil or allowed to run off, would cover it with a sheet of water having a depth of nearly 3-16ths of an inch, and would be equivalent to a very heavy thunder-shower.

CONDITION OF CANADA.

For the following information, the Authoress is indebted to the valuable Census Returns of William Hutton, Esq., which are deeply interesting to every one wishing well to Canada, and which would, if known, attract many persons hither, to whom her vast resources and healthy climate are unknown:—

"The Home consumption is probably very nearly five and a-half Bushels for each individual; the seed required in 1853 would be for the increased number of acres under Wheat in 1854.

In the United States the Home consumption is calculated at six bushels per head,—but there appears to be no ground for such a calculation, especially as so much Indian Corn is used for food—and in fact the whole growth of Wheat in 1850, as given on page fifty-seven of the Abstract of the last Census of the United States, divided into the population of the same year, gives only 4$\frac{15}{60}$ bushels for each inhabitant, whilst the Returns of the Canada Census give more than double that amount, viz: 8$\frac{46}{60}$ bushels.

It is true that the quantity of Indian Corn per individual is much larger in the United States than in Canada, but, it is well worth observing, that, deducting the Exports of that year, amounting to about 12$\frac{1}{4}$ millions of bushels, (allowing five bushels to the barrel of Flour,) as appears in page fifty-seven of the Abstract of their last Census,—and allowing 12$\frac{1}{2}$ millions for seed at 1$\frac{1}{2}$ bushel per acre, their individual consumption of Wheat is little more than three bushels per head—whilst that of Canada is 5$\frac{1}{2}$—this may be accounted for by the increased consumption of Rice as well as Indian Corn.

In the United States the growth of Wheat has increased about forty-eight per cent. during the last ten years, whilst in all Canada, during the same period, it has increased upwards of 400 per cent.!! And taking the article of Indian Corn, which is the production that compares most favorably for the United States, the increase on it for the ten years between 1840 and 1850, has been equal to 56 per cent. viz: from 377$\frac{1}{2}$ mil-

APPENDIX. 15

bushels of Wheat are one-twelfth less, being in Ohio 14,487,000 to 16,202,272.

Ohio, in cultivated acres, possesses $1\frac{1}{2}$ of all the United States. In uncultivated acres, possesses $\frac{1}{2\frac{1}{2}}$ of the same.

She possesses one-fourth more cultivated land per inhabitant than Canada, having five acres to four.

All Canada produces one-seventh more bushels of Wheat than Ohio, and $1\frac{1}{2}$ bushel more per individual. Upper Canada, however, produces six bushels more Wheat per individual than Ohio—the latter producing in her staple Indian Corn twenty-nine times more than Canada, which produces 77 times more Peas, and 54 per cent. more Oats than Ohio. The land of Ohio is valued at nearly double that of the average of the Union,—(see the Report of Mr. Kennedy, page 49,)—and has more than three times as many inhabitants to the square mile as the Average of the Union—she having $49\frac{55}{100}$ and the average of the States being $15\frac{75}{100}$.

The produce of wheat per acre in Upper Canada is $16\frac{44}{100}$ and in Lower Canada $7\frac{8}{60}$ bushels per acre. The Census Superintendent in the

lions of bushels to $592\frac{1}{2}$ millions,—(see page 60 of Mr. Kennedy's Report,)—whilst the increase in Canada for the last nine years has been 163 per cent. the Census having been taken in 1842 and not in 1841. During the same period also, the increase in the growth of Oats in the United States has been 17 per cent., whilst in Upper Canada it has been 133 per cent.,—in Lower Canada, 41 per cent.,—and in both united 70 per cent.

In Pease we find the increase in Upper Canada has been 140 per cent, in nine years—that of the United States, or any of them, is not given in the Abstract of the Census; but, with them, it appears to be an article of little importance, the whole crop of all the States and Territories being only a few bushels over the produce of Canada.

In comparing the different columns of the foregoing tables, some not uninteresting inferences and deductions may be drawn.

It will be perceived that though the number of cultivated acres in Ohio is one-fourth greater than those of Canada, being 9,800,000 to 7,300,000, or rather more than ten to seven, yet the

Again, Ohio produced 7½ bushels for each inhabitant, whilst the whole of the United States produced only 4⅓—the former having one-eighth of her cultivated land under wheat, whilst the whole Union has not one-twentieth of the whole cultivated land under that crop.

With perhaps equal advantages we find an enormous discrepancy in some of our own wheat-growing districts. In the year 1850, the township of Esquesing, in the County of Halton, produced 26 bushels of wheat to the acre, and that of Adolphustown, in the County of Lennox, only 6 bushels to the acre, and this with soil and climate perhaps equally good. This is at once accounted for by the ravages of that fearful plague to the farmer—the Weevil. The worst wheat crops in Canada West, in the year 1851, were in those counties where the Weevil was prevalent. It committed the most serious depredations, in very many cases having rendered whole fields of most promising wheat not worth the thrashing. This fly, which deposits its larvæ in the blossom of the wheat in order to feed upon the milk of the grain as it ripens, was, unfortunately in that year most abundant in the Counties of Frontenac,

States has followed in the footsteps of the English Superintendent in not giving an account of the number of acres under any particular description of crop, and thus we can form no just opinion of acreable produce. This is much to be regretted as the more we particularize comparisons, not only of county with county, or State with State, but townships with townships, fields with fields, and acres with acres, the more easy shall we find it to draw useful deductions to account for success here, or failure there, and to ascertain whether it be climate or soil, or management, or skill, or the absence of them, or defect in them, that gives one locality an advantage over another.

To give an example of this, it is only necessary to see the vast difference which exists in the amount and value of different productions in different parts of the same country.

In the article of wheat, we find that the United States produced in 1850, only 100,479,000 bushels, whilst the one State of Ohio—one out of 32 and 4 large Territories—produced more than ⅐th of the whole Union.

cows. How to account for so great a difference, the prices being taken at the same rate in both countries, is a very difficult matter. The having a more congenial climate than Canada East, shorter winter, and the supply of green food continuing for a larger period, may account for a great deal, but certainly not for such a serious discrepancy. The natural inference is that the breed of cows in Canada must be very inferior to those of Ohio.

It may, however, fairly be observed that Ohio exceeds the average of the whole United States, in the amount of butter per cow, 27 per cent., and in the amount of cheese, 133 per cent.; Upper Canada exceeds the average of the whole Union by about 9 per cent. in butter, but is very deficient in Cheese. The difference in the value of the yield of one cow in Upper Canada and Ohio, calculating the price of butter at 7½d. per lb., and the cheese at 5d., in both places, would be 16s. 10½d. in favour of Ohio, and the extra milk and whey would make 20s., supposing the returns to be correct, which there is no good reason for doubting. As a proof, however, if proof were necessary, that the climate of Ohio is much less

Lennox, Addington, Hastings, and Prince Edward, and is travelling gradually West at the rate of about nine miles every summer, and remains from 5 to 7 years in a locality. The only prevention yet discovered has been to sow early seed on early land, and very early in the autumn, so that the wheat may blossom before its enemy takes wing, the period for which depends much upon the earliness of the season. So destructive was the fly in 1851, that the fine agricultural county of Lennox produced only 6 bushels per acre, Hastings about 10, and Prince Edward, Addington and Frontenac, about 11. It had not in that year reached the County of Northumberland, but was very destructive in that county the following year, 1852.

Canada possessed, in 1851, 46,939 more milch cows than Ohio, and yet Ohio produces ⅔ more butter, and nearly eight times as much cheese as Canada.

This is a most important feature in the difference between the two countries—amounting annually to the large sum of £276,122 for butter, and £376,703 for cheese, in favour of Ohio, although Canada possesses nearly 47,000 more

The number of sheep in Canada, in round numbers, is 1,600,000, in Ohio 4,000,000, although the number of acres *occupied* is very nearly the same, and the number of acres *cultivated* only about one-third greater than in our Provinces. In the value of wool alone the annual difference in favour of the former is - - - £606,564
And in sheep at 7s. 6d. each it is -   879,405

                                      £1,485,969

the latter item, being capital, which, deducting the expense of keep, &c., pays at least 33 per cent. per annum, net profit, and allowing for increase in numbers every year, might fairly be calculated at fifty per cent.

It must, however, be observed, that notwithstanding the striking superiority of Ohio in this particular, the rate of increase in the number of sheep, as compared with that in the United States would appear, from page 67 of Mr. Kennedy's Report, to be greatly in favour of Canada, for in ten years the increase in the States has been only 10 per cent., and in the weight of the fleece only 32 per cent., whereas in Canada the increase in wool has, in nine years, been 64 per cent., and

severe than that of Canada, it may be stated that although she has ⅓ more horses, viz: 78,020—about 63,000 more young cattle, and 2¼ millions more sheep, she produces less hay by 204,293 tons, and very much less straw and other fodder, even allowing that she has 29 times more corn stalks.

The increase in the production of the articles of butter and cheese in Canada, has notwithstanding been enormous, and we find that within the three years, 1849, 1850 and 1851, the amount of butter produced has, in the Upper Province, increased 372 per cent., and that of cheese during the same period, 233 per cent., which leads to the inference, that our milch cows are rapidly improving in quality. The Census Returns of the Lower Province, previous to the year 1851, are very deficient as to the amount of these articles.

The next most important feature in the difference between Ohio and Canada, is the number of their sheep, and the consequent value of their wool. Here, too, the amazing difference is difficult to be accounted for, but the fact should open the eyes of the Canadian farmers to their interest.

that of sheep, 35 per cent., showing an improvement in the weight of the fleece of not far off 30 per cent.

The average weight in Canada is found to be:

In Upper Canada - - - - $2\frac{14}{16}$ lbs.
In Lower Canada - - - - $2\frac{4}{16}$ "
In all Canada - - - - $2\frac{10}{16}$ "

whilst in the United States it is, as per page 67 of the Abstract, $2\frac{7}{16}$ or $2\frac{43}{100}$ lbs., shewing an excess in favour of Canada in the average of nearly 3 oz. per fleece. The proportion too in both countries i. e. the whole United States and Canada, is about the same, being about 9 sheep to every 10 inhabitants. Upper Canada has about ten sheep to every 100 acres occupied; Lower Canada has 8, and the United States has $7\frac{17}{100}$.

With regard to horses, there are in both Canadas, according to the Census Returns 385,377, or very nearly one to every five inhabitants, and they have increased during the last nine years 48 per cent. In some counties the increase has been very much greater than this, for we find in Oxford an increase of 350 per cent. and in some townships in that county even 400 per cent.; this would induce a belief that there was some great error in the Returns of 1842, and there seems to be no good reason why the number of horses should not have kept pace with the population; the wealth of the latter having, also, during that time so materially increased. If in 9 or 10 years, the population has increased cent. per cent.; it is almost unaccountable that the number of horses should not have increased in a similar ratio.

It is stated by the Census Superintendent, that in the United States, where Railways have been extensively constructed, the number of horses has been very much decreased, and according to the Abstract accompanying his last Report, the number in New York has decreased by 26,566; in Pennsylvania by 13,000; in New England by 77,000, or more than 25 per cent., "while in all the States" (he remarks) "Railroad conveyance has almost superseded the use of horses for travelling purposes along main routes." He adds, "we would more readily attribute the apparent diminution to the omission to enumerate the horses in cities and towns than to any superseding of horse power."

There can be no doubt that this must be the

with that of the population, and so also in Canada West the new townships shew a far greater increase than the older ones.

From this kind of comparison it will be seen that there are various branches of Agriculture well deserving of the increased attention of the Canadian farmer.

Ohio far exceeds Canada in Indian corn, butter and cheese, grass seed, wool, tobacco, and beef and pork.

Canada far exceeds Ohio in wheat, peas, rye, barley, oats, buckwheat, hay, hemp and flax, hops, maple sugar and potatoes; and also considering that Ohio has one-third more cultivated land, in total value of live stock. This bears a proportion of only $12\frac{1}{2}$ to 11, whilst the cultivated land in Ohio to that of Canada is as 10 to $7\frac{1}{2}$.

In all the above enumerated articles, viz: live stock, grain, other farm produce, articles manufactured from flax, hemp and wool, beef and pork, Ohio exceeds Canada by £8,199,310, being very little over $\frac{1}{3}$ more than the produce of Canada, and if the produce of the *Forest* be calculated, of which Canada exported in 1851, value for up-

---

reason for any apparent decrease, for the experience of other countries shews a very different effect, as produced by Railway travelling.

In Great Britain, the number of horses employed at the Great Railway Termini, and the numerous intermediate stations, very far exceeds the number formerly employed in the Stage and Posting Departments. The facilities afforded by Railway communication, and the saving of time, combined with so much greater comfort, has led to an enormous increase of travellers, and the tens who formerly travelled between the chief cities and towns of a country, either on business or for pleasure, are now multiplied to hundreds. The main routes may be comparatively deserted, but it is difficult to believe that the construction of Railways, which must be fed at every point with their freights, living as well as dead, can have any other effect than an increase in the employment of horses.

The horses and mules of the whole Union, constitute a proportion of 1 to 5 of the inhabitants. New York has only 1 to 7; Pennsylvania 1 to $6\frac{6}{10}$; and Ohio has 1 to $4\frac{3}{10}$. In the new States of the West, the increase in horses has kept pace the United States and Canada, and they are both numerous and important, the following brief remarks embrace those perhaps most worthy of notice:

1st. Canada should attend to the improvement of the breed of milch cows; the value of butter and cheese produced in Ohio from 47,000 fewer cows, and calculated at the same price in both places, being about 70 per cent. more than in Canada.

2nd. Canada should make more cheese. Ohio produces 760 per cent. more than Canada, and 28 per cent. more butter. Canada depends too much on foreign countries for her supply of cheese, and the demand for American cheese in Canada causes its production in such large quantities in Ohio. At present cheese is much the more profitable of the dairy produce. The value of cheese in Ohio, at 5d. per lb., is £433,740, against £57,037, the value of cheese in Canada at the same price—making a difference in favour of Ohio of £376,703.

3rd. Canada should grow more clover seed and grass seed for which her climate is quite as well adapted as Ohio. Of these two articles, the lat-

---

wards of one million and a half of pounds, the relative wealth per acre would be in favour of Canada.

The ratio of increase of population in Ohio for 10 years, from 1840 to 1850, is $33\frac{33}{100}$ per cent.—that of Upper Canada, in the same period, has been $104\frac{58}{100}$ per cent.—that of Lower Canada for 7 years, from 1844 to 1851, has been 20 per cent.

When it is considered that there are 31 States, 1 District and 4 Territories; and that Ohio has 8 per cent. of the whole population of the Union,—$8\frac{3}{4}$ per cent. of the grain of the whole Union except Rice,—and about $10\frac{1}{2}$ per cent. of all other agricultural produce not manufactured, and 7 per cent. of butter, cheese, beef, pork and domestic manufactures of the whole Union, and that Canada equals Ohio in *acreable* produce, is there not good reason for expecting that Canada, with her more extended scope, and her more rapidly increasing population, will, in a very few years, make a much nearer approximation to the produce of the whole Union than Ohio does now.

As a *summary* of the inferences which may be drawn from this comparison between Ohio and ter grows 130 per cent. more than Canada, making a difference of £80,000 against Canada, always bearing in mind that the cultivated land of Ohio is 33 per cent. more than that of Canada. The farmer should not be under the necessity of purchasing clover seed—the very purchase makes him sparing, and a field of wheat or barley should not be sown without seeding it down with 10 or 12 lbs. of red clover per acre. It is a fact equally consistent with practical experience and theoretical science that, other things being equal, the acreable produce of wheat, barley and oats will be in proportion to the amount of clover grown and ploughed under, or consumed by stock on the farm. In regard to the other suggested improvements there may be some arguments against them on the score of climate, but in this no such can apply, for the climate of Canada is quite as good for the production of clover and grass seeds as that of Ohio. Frosts do not injure the seed and it may therefore be allowed to remain in the field late in the fall. A more extended growth of these articles would ensure an increased extent and richness of pasture, and would add to the quantities of butter and cheese.

4th. Canada should keep more Sheep—the value of sheep and wool being both 140 per cent. higher in Ohio than in Canada, though the quality of sheep and weight of fleece is rather better in the latter, and the cultivated land of Ohio only 33½ per cent. more than in Canada.
In value of sheep, Ohio exceeds Canada - £879,405
" Wool, - 606,564
£1,585,969

5th. Canada should grow more Indian Corn. Ohio produces 2800 per cent. more than Canada, although the difference in the climate in the Upper Province does not warrant anything like so great a difference. The average acreable value is not quite so great as that of Wheat—the average crop of Wheat, sixteen bushels at 4s. is £3 4s., and 24 bushels of Indian Corn at 2s. 6d. is £3; but it should be remembered that wheat occupies the land two years and Indian Corn one, and requires more outlay for seed and labour than Indian Corn; and an acre of corn-stalks is more valuable than an acre of straw, and the condition of the land after corn is much better than after wheat.

Taking all these matters into consideration,

APPENDIX. 23

one acre of Indian Corn is as profitable as two acres of wheat where the climate is suitable for the growth of both.

6th. Canada should have fewer acres under wheat as well as more under Corn. There is too large a proportion of the land in Upper Canada under Wheat, nearly one-fifth of the whole cultivated land, say $\frac{4}{19}$.

In Ohio there is said to be only one-eighth of the cultivated land under wheat, but that is much to be doubted, as taking it at that, it gives only 12 bushels average per acre. It is very probable there is not more than $\frac{1}{16}$ under wheat; this would leave the averge 15 bushels per acre—the acres under different crops are not given in the U. S. Census. The wheat crop of Canada is nearly $\frac{1}{5}$, say $\frac{4}{23}$ of that of the whole United States and Territories. It is very doubtful whether she can maintain this proportion for many years without diminishing her acreable produce, unless the new clearances be very extensive.

7th. Canada might grow more tobacco. Ohio produces 850 per cent. more than Canada—and a large portion of Upper Canada is well calculated for its growth. In this article alone Ohio has £230,000 worth more than Canada.

Already the population of Canada is more than $1\frac{1}{3}$ of the Union—the area in square miles, exclusive of the territories, is one-sixth, and of course in acres the same—in occupied acres about $\frac{1}{17}$—in growth of wheat very nearly one-sixth of the whole Union—in barley more than one-fourth; in oats one-seventh, in buck wheat one-eighth; in all grain, including Indian corn, about $\frac{1}{19}$—exclusive of Indian corn, about one-sixth; of rice Canada has none, neither has Ohio; the whole Union produces 215,312,710 lbs., which at three pence per pound would be £2,691,408 in favour of the Union.

Even at present Canada compares most favorably in proportion to her population with the States, and when the railroads now in course of formation shall have united the whole British possessions in North America, the increased facilities and aroused and invigorated energies, and improving climate and more rapidly increasing population, and interminable water communication, and extensive fisheries, will, in a few years, enable the British North American possessions to make no unfavourable comparison with the Union, flourish as she may.

The whole area of the United States and territories is 3,230,572 square miles which multiplied by 640 gives the number of acres 2,057,566,080, certainly a prodigious territory, but the British possessions in North America far exceed this.

The exact amount according to Allison is 4,109,630 square geographical miles, and the water in British America is 1,840,000 square miles—the whole terrestrial globe embrace about 37,000,000 square miles, so that British America contains nearly a ninth part of the whole terrestrial surface of the Globe—the number of acres is 2,630,163,200. Allison remarks that a very large portion is perhaps doomed to everlasting sterility, owing to the severity of the climate—such is no doubt the case, but it should be recollected that as the country becomes cleared up, the climate improves, and that there are at present twenty or thirty millions of acres, to the successful cultivation of which the climate presents no insuperable barrier.

Two or three centuries ago, the Rhine used to be frozen, and the animals, the natives of the Northern regions, were abundant on its banks—how different is the case now. It will be so in British North America, with this difference, that the improving climate will keep pace with the vastly accelerated movements, and more rapidly increasing numbers of the New World settlers.

The means that are taken by Government to promote immigration, and improve the Agriculture of the country, will stimulate progression to an indefinite degree. The formation of a Bureau of Agriculture is an important feature in the history of Canada, and the most important results may be expected from its labours. In industry and perseverance the Canadian farmer stands perhaps unrivalled, and it rests with those who have the power to assist him by the diffusion of that kind of knowledge which, unaided, he has no means of acquiring. The time has happily passed when a perseverance in old habits and prejudices was thought to be a virtue—let the results of science and the experience of our own and other countries, be placed within the reach of our industrial population, and a blessing will result to the individual and the country, with a certainty and speed unattainable without this aid, &c. &c.

REMARKS ON THE CENSUS OF GREAT BRITAIN, &c.

The population of Great Britain stood thus on the 31st March, 1851:—

England,	16,921,888
Wales	1,005,721
Scotland	2,888,742
Islands in British Seas	143,126
Persons at Sea or abroad	162,490
	21,121,967

In Great Britain the families are considerably smaller than in Canada, owing no doubt, to the youthfulness of our colony, and the constant accession of young people to our shores, leaving the elder branches at home. In Great Britain each family consists of $4\frac{73}{100}$ and each house contains $5\frac{7}{00}$. In Canada the families and houses average $6\frac{1}{4}$ to each. In Great Britain, 12 per cent. or 1 in 8 or 9 of these families keep servants. In Canada, probably not more than 1 in 20—but this part of the Census not being completed it cannot be ascertained at present, nor hereafter with any accuracy, as the enumerators have classed the servants in many cases under the head of labourers. In Great Britain there are 2 acres to each person, and 11 acres to each inhabited house. In Canada there are nearly $9\frac{1}{4}$ acres to each person and 58 acres to each house.

In Great Britain the mean distance between each house is 252 yards, and between each persons 108 yards.

In London the mean distance between each house is 38 yards, and between each person 14 yards.

In towns in Great Britain there are $5\frac{2}{100}$ persons to an acre, and in the country $5\frac{3}{100}$ acres to a person.

The density of population in the counties is 120 to a square mile, in towns 3,337 to a square mile.

London extends over 78,029 acres, and has $30\frac{1}{4}$ persons and about 7 houses to the acre; whilst the population of the counties and towns increased 71 per cent. in 50 years, that of the large towns increased 189 per cent. In watering place, the increase was the largest, viz: $2\frac{561}{1000}$ per cent. per annum. The next largest was in manufacturing towns, $2\frac{380}{1000}$; next in Seaports, $2\frac{191}{1000}$; in London, $1\frac{820}{1000}$; and in country towns, $1\frac{609}{1000}$ per cent per annum.

Great Britain has 815 towns of various magnitudes; 580 in England and Wales; 215 in Scotland, and 10 in the Channel Islands. The population of the 815 towns is 10,556,288; that of the country, 10,403,189. Small towns with markets are included in the country. In fact the town and country population differ so little that they may be considered equal. The average population to each town in Scotland is 6,654, to each town in England and Wales, 15,501. The Scottish towns therefore contain less than half the population of the English. (Page 46, census of Great Britain, 1851.) The English towns are on an average at a distance of $10\frac{8}{10}$ miles from the centre of one to the centre of the other. The Scotch towns are $12\frac{7}{10}$ miles apart.

Very few persons being aware of the number of Islands lying around Great Britain, it may be mentioned that there were 175 Islands found inhabited on the morning of the 31st March, 1851, though 500 islands and rocks had been numbered. Those of Anglesey, Jersey, Man and Wight, have over 50,000 each; Guernsey has very nearly 30,000, and the whole 175 have a population of 423,000. The area of the Islands in the British Seas is 394 square miles. England has in the average 332 persons to a square mile; Wales 136; Scotland only 92, and the Islands 363, whilst Upper Canada has 29; Lower Canada 4, and in all Canada $7\frac{59}{100}$; Ohio $49\frac{55}{100}$, and all the United States $15\frac{75}{100}$; so that the land even now occupied in Upper Canada would hold more than eleven times its present population, say 11,000,000 inhabitants, to be as densely peopled as England.

TABLES SHOWING THE POPULATION OF UPPER AND LOWER CANADA, AND THE UNITED STATES, THE RATIO OF DEATHS TO THE NUMBER LIVING, AND THE AVERAGE PRODUCE OF WHEAT IN UPPER AND LOWER CANADA.

UPPER CANADA.

Counties.	Total Population.	Ratio to the Number living.	Average produce of Wheat per acre. Bushels.
Addington	15165	1 to 98	
Brant	25426	" 115	19
Bruce	2837	" 157	20
Carleton	23637	" 211	
Dundas	13811	" 215	
Durham	30732	" 128	16
Elgin	25418	" 134	17
Essex	16817	" 151	
Frontenac	13150	" 157	
Grey	12845	" 151	
Glengary	17596	" 139	
Grenville	20707	" 146	
Haldimand	18788	" 113	17
Halton	18322	" 125	18
Hastings	31977	" 142	
Huron	10198	" 158	
Kent	17469	" 84	18
Lambton	10815	" 138	
Lanark	27317	" 139	
Leeds	30280	" 170	
Lennox	7955	" 103	
Lincoln	20868	" 97	
Middlesex	32863	" 111	
Northumberland	31220	" 118	
Norfolk	21281	" 117	
Ontario	30576	" 100	17
Oxford	32638	" 87	18
Peel	24816	" 194	18
Perth	15545	" 207	
Peterborough	15237	" 111	16
Prescott	10487	" 190	
Prince Edward	18857	" 156	
Renfrew	9415	" 136	
Russell	2870	" 220	
Simcoe	27105	" 167	16
Stormont	14643	" 240	
Victoria	11656	" 140	
Waterloo	26537	" 119	16
Wellington	26796	" 184	
Welland	20141	" 120	
Wentworth	28507	" 102	
York	48944	" 130	18
Toronto City	30775	" 65	
Hamilton	14112	" 70	
Kingston	11697	" 68	
Bytown	7760	" 86	
London	7035	" 70	

The average of produce of Peas in these counties is about 18 bushels an acre, and of Indian-corn 25. The produce of Wheat in the County of Peterboro is the nearest the average of all Upper Canada, which is 16 bushels 14 lbs. per acre.

The Longevity of Canada West when compared with that of other Countries, speaks volumes for its general healthfulness, and it is most interesting to compare the rates of death to the number of living in Canada and the United States, the number of deaths in the latter exceeding that of Upper Canada in proportion to the population by about 36 per ct. and of Lower Canada by 25 per ct. The ratio given by Mr. Kennedy in his report on the United States Census is inserted with that of the two provinces for the sake of comparison, the average ratio in the United States having *one* to *seventy-four*—in Upper Canada *one* to *one hundred and two*; and in Lower Canada *one* to *ninety-four* of the number living. The greatest mortality in the United States is in Louisiana, 1 in 43; and the greatest in Canada is in Leinster, 1 in 60; exclusive of the Cities, where deaths are always more numerous in proportion to population.

LOWER CANADA.

Counties.	Total-Population.	Ratio to the Number living.	Average produce of Wheat per acre. Bushels.
Beauharnois,	40213	1 to 138	12
Bellechasse,	17982	" 75	
Berthier,	34608	" 88	
Bonaventure,	10844	" 190	14
Chambly,	20576	" 74	
Champlain,	13896	" 77	13
Dorchester,	43105	" 48	9
Drummond,	16562	" 112	12
Gaspe,	10904	" 111	7
Huntingdon,	40645	" 106	
Kamouraska,	20396	" 98	
Leinster,	29690	" 60	11
L'Islet,	19641	" 63	6
Lotbiniere,	16657	" 90	
Megantic,	13835	" 72	15
Missisquoi,	13484	" 129	12
Montmorency,	9598	" 59	10
Montreal,	19066	" 120	8
Nicolet,	19657	" 84	12
Ottawa,	22903	" 112	12
Portneuf,	19366	" 70	10
Quebec,	19474	" 56	14
Richelieu,	25086	" 82	
Rouville,	27031	" 98	
Rimouski,	26892	" 118	
Saguenay,	20783	" 80	7
St. Maurice,	27502	" 124	10
St. Hyacinthe,	30623	" 102	
Sherbrooke,	20011	" 132	11
Shefford,	16482	" 103	
Stanstead,	13898	" 157	12
Terrebonne,	26701	" 64	10
Two Mountains,	30470	" 116	12
Vaudreuil,	21429	" 121	11
Vercheres,	14393	" 145	10
Yamaska,	14748	" 74	10
City of Montreal,	57715	" 33	
City of Quebec,	42052	" 39	

The average produce of Peas is about 13 bushels an acre, and of Indian Corn about 23.
Megantic is the best county for Wheat, viz..................15 bushels.
Quebec   "   Peas, viz......................22   "
Missisquoi "   Oats, viz......................35   "

Dorchester produces the largest quantity of Hay. Then Stanstead and Huntingdon.

In the four Eastern Townships, the Land was estimated in acres and the Grain in bushels. In all the others the arpents have been converted into acres, and the minots into bushels.

APPENDIX.

	Brls.	Bush.
Total Export of Wheat in 1851,		933,756
Total Export of Flour in 1851,	668,623 or	3,343,115
Total Home consumption, allowing 5 bushels for each inhabitant, in a population of 1,842,265,		9,211,325
Total Seed at 1¼ Bushel per acre:		
Upper Canada,	780,385	
Lower Canada,	335,926	
	1,116,311	
At 1½ Bushel per acre		1,674,466
Total number of Bushels of Wheat on these calculations,		15,162,662
Total returned by Census:	Bush.	
Upper Province,	12,802,272	
Lower Province, about	3,400,000	
		16,202,272
Total growth of Wheat in all Canada, calculating the Flour at 5 Bushels per Barrel,—the consumption at 5 Bushels per head—and the Seed at 1¼ Bushel per acre,		15,162,662
Leaving to be accounted for in some other way 1,039,610 bushels.		1,039,610

UNITED STATES.

	Population.	Ratio to the Number living.
Maine,	583188	1 to 77.29
New Hampshire	317964	" 74.49
Vermont,	314120	" 100.29
Massachusetts,	994499	" 51.23
Rhode Island,	147544	" 65.83
Connecticut,	370791	" 64.13
New York,	3097394	" 69.85
New Jersey,	489555	" 75.70
Pennsylvania,	2311786	" 81.63
Delaware,	91535	" 75.71
Maryland,	583035	" 60.77
Virginia,	1421661	" 74.61
North Carolina,	868903	" 85.13
South Carolina,	668507	" 53.59
Georgia,	905999	" 91.33
Alabama,	771671	" 84.94
Mississippi,	606555	" 69.63
Louisiana,	517739	" 42.85
Texas,	212592	" 69.79
Florida,	87401	" 93.67
Kentucky,	982405	" 64.60
Tenessee,	1002625	" 85.26
Missouri,	682043	" 55.85
Arkansas,	209639	" 70.18
Ohio,	1980408	" 68.41
Indiana,	988416	" 77.65
Illinois,	851470	" 73.28
Michigan,	397654	" 87.97
Iowa,	192214	" 94.03
Wisconsin,	305191	" 105.82
Minnesota,	6077	" 202.56
Oregon,	13293	" 232.82
New Mexico,	61547	" 53.19
Utah,	11380	" 47.61
District of Columbia,	51687	" 61.03

TABLE OF EXPENSES, INCOME OR WAGES.

Giving at one view what any sum from One Pound to One Thousand per Annum, is per Calendar Month, Week, or Day.

Pr. A.		Pr. Month			Pr. Week.			Pr. Day.			Pr. Yr.		Pr. Mth.			Pr. Week.			Per Day.			Pr. Year.		Pr. Mnth.			Per. Week.			Per Day.		
£	s.	£	s.	d.	£	s.	d.	£	s.	d.	£	s.	£	s.	d.	£	s.	d.	£	s.	d.	£	s.	£	s.	d.	£	s.	d.	£	s.	d.
1	0is	0	1	8	0	0	4½	0	0	0¾	8	8is	0	14	0	0	3	2¾	0	0	5½	18	18is	1	11	6	0	7	3	0	1	0½
1	10	0	2	6	0	0	7	0	0	1	8	10	0	14	2	0	3	3¼	0	0	5½	19	0	1	11	8	0	7	3½	0	1	0½
2	0	0	3	4	0	0	9¼	0	0	1¼	9	0	0	15	0	0	3	5½	0	0	6	20	0	1	13	4	0	7	8	0	1	1¼
2	2	0	3	6	0	0	9¾	0	0	1½	9	9	0	15	9	0	3	7½	0	0	6¼	30	0	2	10	0	0	11	6	0	1	7¾
2	10	0	4	2	0	0	11½	0	0	1¾	10	0	0	16	8	0	3	10	0	0	6½	40	0	3	6	8	0	15	4½	0	2	2¼
3	0	0	5	0	0	1	1¾	0	0	2	10	10	0	17	6	0	4	0½	0	0	7	50	0	4	3	4	0	19	3	0	2	9
3	3	0	5	3	0	1	2½	0	0	2	11	0	0	18	4	0	4	3	0	0	7¼	60	0	5	0	0	1	3	0¾	0	3	3½
3	10	0	5	10	0	1	4¼	0	0	2¼	11	11	0	19	3	0	4	5¼	0	0	7½	70	0	5	16	8	1	6	11	0	3	10
4	0	0	6	8	0	1	6½	0	0	2¾	12	0	1	0	0	0	4	7½	0	0	8	80	0	6	13	4	1	10	9	0	4	4½
4	4	0	7	0	0	1	7½	0	0	2¾	12	12	1	1	0	0	4	10	0	0	8¼	90	0	7	10	0	1	14	7¼	0	4	11
4	10	0	7	6	0	1	8¾	0	0	3	13	0	1	1	8	0	5	0	0	0	8½	100	0	8	6	8	1	18	5	0	5	5¾
5	0	0	8	4	0	1	11	0	0	3¼	13	13	1	2	9	0	5	3	0	0	9	200	0	16	13	4	3	16	11	0	10	11½
5	5	0	8	9	0	2	0¼	0	0	3½	14	0	1	3	4	0	5	4½	0	0	9¼	300	0	25	0	0	5	15	4½	0	16	5¼
5	10	0	9	2	0	2	1½	0	0	3¾	14	14	1	4	6	0	5	8	0	0	9¾	400	0	33	6	8	7	13	10	1	1	11
6	0	0	10	0	0	2	3¾	0	0	4	15	0	1	5	0	0	5	9	0	0	10	500	0	41	13	5	9	12	3½	1	7	4¾
6	6	0	10	6	0	2	5	0	0	4¼	15	15	1	6	3	0	6	0½	0	0	10¼	600	0	50	0	0	11	10	9	1	12	10½
6	10	0	10	10	0	2	6	0	0	4¼	16	0	1	6	8	0	6	2	0	0	10½	700	0	58	6	8	13	9	2¾	1	18	4¼
7	0	0	11	8	0	2	8¼	0	0	4½	16	16	1	8	0	0	6	5½	0	0	11	800	0	66	13	4	15	7	8¼	2	3	10
7	7	0	12	3	0	2	10	0	0	4¾	17	0	1	8	4	0	6	6½	0	0	11½	900	0	75	0	0	17	6	1¾	2	9	3¾
7	10	0	12	6	0	1	10½	0	0	5	17	17	1	9	6	0	6	10	0	0	11¾	1000	0	83	6	8	19	4	7¼	2	14	9½
8	0	0	13	4	0	3	1	0	0	5¼	18	0	1	10	0	0	6	11	0	0	11¾											

Tariff of Duties.

PAYABLE ON IMPORTS INTO CANADA, UNDER THE ACT 12 VICTORIA, CAP 1, AND THE ACTS AMENDING SAME OF APRIL, 1853, AND DECEMBER, 1854.

To take effect on the 5th of April, 1855.

Animals, specially imported for the improvement of Stock, Free; Anatomical Preparations, do; Ashes, Pot, Pearl and Soda, do.
Acids, nitric and oxalic, two and a half per cent; Strong fluid, do; Alum, do.
Biscuit, twelve and a half per cent.
Books, printed, free.
Books, reprints of British copyright works, twelve and a half per cent; Books, Blanks, do.
Books and Drawings of an immoral or indecent character, prohibited.
Boots and Shoes, twelve and a half per cent.
Brandy, three shillings per gallon.
Brooms, twelve and a half per cent; Brushes do.
Bulbs, Roots and Trees, free.
Burr Stones, wrought, twelve and a half per cent.
Busts and Casts of Marble, Bronze, Alabaster, or Plaster of Paris, free.
Bleaching powders, two and a half per cent; Blue, ultra marine and paste, do; Borax, do; Brick, fire, do; Brimstone, do.
Cabinets of Coins, Medals, or Gems, and other collections of antiquity, free.
Candles, twelve and a half per cent.
Cassia, Cinnamon, Cloves, three-pence half-penny per pound.
Castings, twelve and a half per cent.
Iron Chains of all sorts, two and a half per cent, Cider, twelve and a half per sent; Clocks, do.
Coffee, green, one half-penny per pound.
Coffee, other than green, three pence per pound.
Coin and Bullion, free.
Coin, base or counterfeit, prohibited.
Cordials, four shillings per gallon.
Cotton Wool, free.
Cotton Manufactures, twelve and a half per cent.
Cochineal, two and a half per cent; Copperas, do.
Cotton Batting, twelve and a half per cent.
Cotton Warp and Wick, two and a half per cent
Drugs, twelve and a half per cent; Earthenware do.
Engravings, Etchings and Drawings, free.
Feathers, twelve and a half per cent.
Fruits, dried, one penny per pound.
Furs, twelve and a half per cent; Furniture do;
Fisheries, the following articles for the use of, Seines, Fishing Nets and Hooks, Twines, and Lines, Boat Sails and Hawsers, Fishermen's Boots, Tarred Rope and Rigging, do.
Gin, two and sixpence per gallon.
Ginger, three pence per pound.
Glass, and Manufactures of, twelve and a half per cent; Glue, do; Hair, and Manufactures of, do;

Harness, do; Hardware, do; Hats, do; Honey, do; Indian Corn, free.

Indian Rubber, and Manufactures, twelve and a half per cent; Ink, do.

Iron, when imported to be used in the manufacture of Locomotive Engines, two and a half per cent; Bar and Rod, do; Sheet, do; Hoop, not over two inches broad, do; Hoop or Tire for driving wheels, bent and welded, do; Connecting Rods, in pieces, do; Frames and Pedestals, rough from the forge, do; Brass or Copper Tubes do; Boiler Plates, do; Railroad Bars, do; Scrap, do, Rolled Plate from a quarter to half an inch thick, do; Round and Square, four inch and upwards, do; Iron Cranks, wrought, six cwt. and upwards; do.

Iron Manufactures, twelve and a half per cent; Jewelry, do; Lamps, do; Lead Manufactures, do; Leather, and Manufactures of, do; Lemon Syrup, do; Linen, and Manufactures of, do.

Liquors, four shillings per gallon.

Maccaroni, one penny per pound.

Mace, sevenpence half penny per pound.

Machinery, all kinds, twelve and a half per cent; Mahogany, do.

Manures, all kinds, free; Maps do.

Marble, twelve and a half per ct; Medicines, do.

Models of Machinery, and other inventions and improvements in the Arts, free.

Molasses, two pence per gallon.

Musical Instruments, twelve and a half per cent; Nails, do.

Nutmegs, seven pence half penny per pound. Nitre, two and a half per cent.

Oil, twelve and a half per cent; Oysters, do; Packages containing free goods, or goods rated under twelve and a half per cent, do; Packages, other, charged the same as the *ad valorem* rate on their contents, Paints, do.

Paintings, free.

Paper and Paper Manufactures, twelve and a half per cent; Perfumery, do.

Philosophical Instruments & Apparatus, free.

Pickles and Sauces, twelve and a half per cent.

Pimento, Pepper and Alspice, one penny per lb

Pipes, smoking, twelve and a half per cent;

Pork, mess, do.

Preserved Fruits, 12*l* 10 per cent.

Phosphorous, two and a half per cent; Potash, prussiate of, do.

Quills, twelve and a half per cent.

Quinces, thirty per cent.

Raisins, one penny per pound.

Rice, twelve and a half per cent.

Rope, old, two and a half per cent.

Rum, at proof by Sykes' Hydrometer, one shilling and eight pence per gallon.

Sail Cloth, two and a half per cent.

Salaratus, twelve and a half per cent.

Salt, free; Seeds, do.

Segars, two shillings per pound.

Snuff, four pence per pound.

Soap, twelve and a half per cent.

Specimens of Natural History, Mineralogy and

Telegraph Wire, two and a half per cent
Varnish, twelve and a half per cent
Vermicelli, one penny per pound
Vinegar, three pence per gallon
Vitriol, two and a half per cent
Watches, twelve and a half per cent; Wax, do;
Whalebone, do
Wheat, free.
Whiskey at proof, five pence per gallon
Wine of all kinds in Wood or other vessels not being Bottles, not exceeding in value £15 the pipe of 126 gallons, one shilling per gallon, and if exceeding £15 the Pipe is one shilling and sixpence per gallon
Wine of all kinds in Bottles per dozen Quarts, seven shillings and six pence
Wine of all kinds in Bottles per dozen Pints, three shillings and nine pence
Woollen Yarn, twelve and a half per cent;
Wool Manufactures, do
All Goods, Wares and Merchandise not enumerated, twelve and a half per cent.

FREE GOODS.

The following articles, in addition to those marked "free" in the columns above, are now made free—subject to the exception, that if the Governor of this Province shall at any time declare the suspension of the Treaty between Her Majesty and the United States of America, signed on the 5th day of June, 1854, then, while such

Botany, free.
Spices, unenumerated, three pence per pound.
Spikes, twelve and a half per cent
Spirits, except Rum and Whiskey at proof, two shillings and sixpence per gallon.
Spirits or Cordials, sweetened so that the strength cannot be found by the Hydrometer, four shillings per gallon.
Spirits of Turpentine, twelve and a half per cnt.
Steel, two and a half per cent.
Steel Manufactures, twelve and a half per cent.
Sugar, Refined, in Loaves, Crushed, or Candy or other Sugars rendered equal thereto by any process, twelve shillings per cwt
White and Brown, Clayed or Yellow Bastard Sugars, or other Sugars rendered by any process equal in quality thereto, eight shillings and sixence per cwt
Sugar, Raw, and other kinds not being equal to White or Brown, Clayed or Yellow Bastard Sugars, six shillings and six pence per cwt
Syrups, twelve and a half per cent.
Do Sugar, two pence per gallon and, do.
Sal Ammoniac, two and a half per cent; Seed; Mustard, do; Shellac, do; Slate, do; Straps for Walking Beams, do; Sulphur, roll, do.
Sulphur, flour, twelve and a half per cent.
Tea, two pence per pound.
Tin, two and a half per cent
Tobacco, Manufactured, or Unmanufactured, other than Segars or Snuff, two pence per pound.
Toys, twelve and a half per cent

suspension shall continue, the several articles mentioned in the schedule to the Act last aforesaid, being the growth and produce of the said United States, shall be subject to the duties to which they are now subject; and no such article shall then be admitted free of duty, unless it was so admitted immediately before the passing of the said Act.

Animals of all kinds, meats of all kinds (except mess pork), butter, cheese, flour, barley, buckwheat, bear and bigg, oats, rye, beans and peas, meal of the above grain, and wheat not bolted, bran in shorts, and hops.

Anchors, chain cables, veneers, hay, pig iron, green fruits, bark berries, nuts, vegetables, woods and drugs used solely in dyeing, and indigo, bristles, bur-stones unwrought, coal and coke, grease and scraps, hemp, flax, and tow undressed, hides, junk and oakum, lard, lead (pig or sheet), marble in blocks unpolished, oil, cocoanut, pine and palm only, ores of all kinds of metals, pipeclay, resin and rosin, saw logs, ships' watercasks in use, teazles, broom corn, wood used in making carpenters' or joiners' tools, tallow, tar and pitch, type metal in block or pigs, wool, caoutchouc, cordage of all kinds, sail cloth, copper in bars, rods or in sheets, yellow metal in bars or in sheets, bright or black varnish, marine cement, trenails, bunting, felt sheeting, printing presses, printing types, printers' ink, printing implements of all kinds, bookbinders' tools and presses and implements of all kinds, old nets and ropes, cotton and flax waste, rags, fire-clay, and Russian hemp yarn.

ORDERS IN COUNCIL.

The following articles are admitted at the rates set after them, by orders in Council, viz.:—

Ships' sails, prepared rigging, tin, zinc, hoop iron, candle wick, and spelter, at 2½ per cent.—Order of 4th June, 1853.

Brass in pigs or sheets, magnetic telegraph insulators, relay magnets, registers and batteries, at 2½ per cent.—Order of 4th Nov., 1853.

Locomotive, passenger, baggage, and freight cars, running upon any line of railroad crossing the frontier between Canada and the United States, free.—Order of 13th Jan., 1854.

Iron wheels and axles, imported expressly for railroad purposes, 2½ per cent.—Order of 13th Nov., 1854.

Printing paper, draining tiles, and oil cake, 2½ per cent.—Order of 6th Dec., 1854.

EXEMPTIONS.

Arms, Clothing, Cattle, Provisions and stores of every description, which any Commissary or Commissaries, Contractor or Contractors shall import or bring, or which may be imported or brought by the principal or other Officer or Officers of Her Majesty's Ordnance into the Province for the use of her Majesty's Army or Navy, or for the use of the Indian Nations in this Province; provided the duty otherwise payable thereon

And the following articles, when imported directly from the United Kingdom, the British North American Provinces, the Island of Prince Edward and Newfoundland, and being the growth produce, or manufacture of the said United Kingdom, or of such Province respectively, viz:—

Animals, beef, pork, biscuit, bread, butter, cocoa paste, corn or grain of all kinds, flour, fish, fresh or salted, dried or pickled, fish oil, furs or skins, the produce of fish or creatures living in the sea, gypsum, horns, mess poultry, plants, shrubs and trees, potatoes and vegetables of all kinds. Seeds of all kinds, pelts, skins, furs or tails undressed. Wood, viz: boards, planks, staves, timber and firewood.

And the following articles when imported direct from the Provinces of Nova Scotia, New Brunswick and Prince Edward's island, and being the growth, produce, or manufacture of said Provinces respectively, viz:

Grain and Breadstuffs of all kinds, vegetables, fruits, seeds; hay and straw, hops, animals, salted and fresh meats, butter, cheese, chocolate, and other preparations of cocoa, lard, tallow, hides, horns, wool, undressed skins, and furs of all kinds, ores of all kinds, iron in pigs and blooms, copper, lead in pigs, grindstones and stones of all kinds, earth, coals, lime, ochres, gypsum ground or unground, rock-salt, wood, bark, timber and lumber of all kinds, firewood, ashes, fish, fish oil, viz: train oil, spermaceti oil, head matter and blubber, fins and skins, the produce of fish or creatures living in the sea.

would be defrayed or borne by the Treasurer of the United Kingdom of this Province.

Horses and carriages of travellers, and horses cattle and carriages and other vehicles when employed in carrying merchandise, together with the necessary harness and tackle, so long as the same shall be *bona fide* in use for that purpose, except the horses, cattle, carriages, vehicles and harness, of persons hawking goods, wares and merchandise through the Province, for the purpose of retailing the same, and the horses, cattle, carriages, and harness of any circus or equestrian troops for exhibition; the horses, cattle, carriages and harness of any Menagerie to be free.

Donations of clothing especially imported for the use of or to be distributed gratuitously by any charitable society in this Province.

Seeds of all kinds, farming utensils and implements of husbandry, when specially imported in good faith by any society incorporated or established for the encouragement of agriculture.

Salt for the use of the fisheries, military clothing and wine for the use of regimental messes.

The following Articles in the occupation or employment of persons coming into the Province for the purpose of actual settling therein, viz:—

Wearing Apparel in actual use, and other personal effects not merchandise; horses and cattle; implements and tools of trade of handy-craftsmen. The personal household effects, not merchandize, of inhabitants of this province, being subjects of Her Majesty and dying abroad.

CROWN LANDS DEPARTMENT.

NOTICES to the effect of that which follows are issued from time to time from the *Crown Lands Department* which has hitherto sold Lands at prices varying from Seven Shillings and Six-pence to Twelve Shillings and Sixpence per acre, upon these conditions:—

The price to be   Shillings per acre, payable in Ten equal Annual Instalments, with interest; the first instalment to be paid upon receiving authority to enter upon the land. Actual occupation to be immediate and continuous; the land to be cleared at the rate of two acres annually for each hundred acres, during the first five years; a dwelling house, at least sixteen feet by eighteen, to be erected; the Timber to be reserved until the land has been paid for in full and patented, and to be subject to any general timber duty thereafter; a License of Occupation, not assignable without permission, the Sale and License of Occupation to become null and void in case of neglect or violation of any of the conditions; the Settler to be entitled to obtain a Patent upon complying with all the conditions; not more than two hundred acres to be sold to any one person on these terms.

GOVERNMENT EMIGRATION DEPARTMENT
TORONTO, 1855.

IN consequence of the frequent misapplication of Money sent from Canada, for the purpose of bringing out *Emigrants*, an arrangement has been made by this Department, sanctioned by the Government, which will render such misapplication impossible.

This Department will receive in deposit, any sum of Money, parties in Upper Canada may be disposed to remit, for which they will receive a certificate, which will insure the passage of the person or persons named therein.

The advantages of this plan are as follows :

The parties remitting the certificate will be assured that their money cannot be applied to any other purpose than that intended.

The parties named in the certificate will have their choice of Port of departure, as also selection of Ship, and can arrange for the rate of passage, as the certificate will be received in payment of their passage in any Port of the United Kingdom, by the Owner or Master of any ship bound to Quebec.

If the sum named in the certificate is more than the passage amounts to, the Master or Owner of the Ship can advance the difference in cash, if so disposed; if not, the surplus will be repaid to the person or persons named in the Certificate, on his or their arrival at Quebec.

For further particulars apply to A. C. BUCHANAN, Esq., Chief Emigrant Agent, Quebec, or to A. B. HAWKE, Chief Emigrant Agent for Upper Canada, Toronto.

Toronto, March 5, 1855.

APPENDIX. 37

TABLE SHOWING THE COMPARATIVE METEOROLOGY AT TORONTO, U. C., AND HIGH-FIELD HOUSE, NOTTINGHAM, ENGLAND, FOR THE YEAR 1854.

Month.	Mean Temperature.		Highest Temperature.		Lowest Temperature.		Mean Daily Highest.		Mean Daily Lowest.		Monthly Range of Temperature.		Mean Daily Range.	
	Toronto, U.C.	Nottingham, England.	Toronto.	Nottingham.	Toronto.	Nottingham.	Toronto.	Nottingham.	Toronto.	Nottingham.	Toronto.	Nottingham.	Toronto.	Nottingham.
January.	23.6	37.0	46.4	55.2	−5.4	−4.0	29.3	42.7	13.5	30.3	51.8	59.2	15.8	12.4
February.	21.1	39.2	42.8	56.0	−10.8	24.8	29.6	46.7	9.1	31.4	53.6	31.2	20.5	15.3
March.	30.7	43.7	55.1	64.3	7.4	23.4	36.3	53.9	22.9	34.6	47.7	40.9	13.4	19.3
April.	41.0	46.4	65.1	74.8	20.2	26.4	47.8	59.2	30.7	35.1	44.9	48.4	17.1	24.1
May.	52.2	50.0	71.4	73.0	25.2	31.4	61.8	62.8	37.9	37.7	46.2	41.6	23.9	25.1
June.	64.1	55.2	92.5	79.8	35.2	41.0	74.5	65.2	49.8	46.8	57.3	38.8	24.7	18.4
July.	72.5	59.4	98.0	86.0	42.5	39.0	84.8	69.4	58.5	50.9	55.5	47.0	26.3	18.5
August.	68.0	59.4	99.2	81.5	45.6	40.8	80.7	70.2	55.3	49.9	53.6	40.7	25.5	20.3
September.	61.0	56.9	93.6	82.1	35.8	33.5	72.6	69.9	49.1	45.1	57.8	48.6	23.5	24.8
October.	49.5	47.6	75.4	66.4	26.4	24.6	59.0	57.2	41.3	38.5	49.0	41.8	17.6	18.7
November.	36.8	39.7	55.4	57.2	13.8	18.7	42.1	46.3	28.1	32.8	41.6	38.5	13.9	13.5
December.	21.9	40.7	44.8	56.6	−7.0	24.0	29.5	46.4	14.4	34.2	51.8	32.6	15.1	12.2
Year.	45.2	47.9	99.2	86.0	−10.8	−4.0					110.0	90.0	19.8	18.6

N. B.—For a note to this table see next page.

COMPARATIVE METEOROLOGY. *(See page 37 for Table.)*

The depth of rain that fell during the year at Nottingham was 17.3 inches, which however, is nearly 12 inches less than the usual amount; that at Toronto was 23.5 inches being 8 inches less than the average: the fall at Nottingham was distributed over 174 days, and at Toronto over 114. The depth of snow that fell at Toronto was 49.5 inches, distributed over 52 days, thus leaving at Toronto 199 perfectly fair days, on which neither rain nor snow fell. The whole period, however, occupied by fall of rain or snow is remarkably small, not amounting quite to 26 days. The climate of Upper Canada, as compared with that of Great Britain, presents a much greater range of temperature in the course of the year, the winters being much colder and the summers much hotter, and combines a remarkable regularity from year to year with excessive variability on particular days. These extremes are however more than compensated for by the general fineness of the weather, the dryness of the atmosphere, and the almost total absence of mist or fog and continuous rain.

TABLE SHOWING THE COMPARATIVE TEMPERATURES FOR THE YEAR AND DIFFERENT SEASONS, AND ALSO THE EXTREMES OF TEMPERATURE AND CLIMATIC DIFFERENCES FOR VARIOUS PLACES IN GREAT BRITAIN AND UPPER CANADA.

	Latitude N.	Mean of year.	Winter.	Spring.	Summer.	Autumn.	Hottest Month.	Coldest Month.	Difference between hottest and coldest months.	Difference between Summer and Winter.
Isle of Wight,	50.45	50.4	39.0	48.7	63.0	51.0	65.0	37.0	28.0	24.0
Greenwich,	51.23	49.0	37.7	48.4	60.3	49.4	62.7	35.4	27.2	22.6
Boston,	52.48	49.1	37.7	48.2	62.0	48.5	63.0	36.0	27.0	24.2
Dublin,	53.21	50.1	40.7	48.5	61.1	50.1	61.5	39.3	22.2	20.4
Isle of Man,	54.12	49.8	41.7	47.4	59.0	51.3	60.3	40.5	19.8	17.3
Carlisle,	54.54	47.0	37.2	45.5	57.4	47.8	58.5	36.2	22.3	20.1
Edinburgh,	55.58	47.1	38.4	45.0	57.2	47.9	58.7	37.4	21.3	18.7
Aberdeen,	57.9	49.2	39.0	48.2	59.5	50.0	60.5	37.8	22.6	20.5
Toronto, C.W.	43.39	44.3	24.9	40.9	65.0	46.7	66.6	23.3	43.3	40.1
Niagara, C.W.	43.15	51.7	30.5	47.2	72.2	57.0	74.6	25.2	49.4	41.7

The Authoress has to express her acknowledgements for the two foregoing tables to Professor Cherriman, M. A., St. John's College, Cambridge, now of the Observatory, Toronto.

GENERAL ABSTRACT OF AGRICULTURAL PRODUCE &c., COLLECTED FROM THE CENSUS REPORT 1851-2.

Occupiers of Lands in Acres.	Upper Canada.	Lower Canada.
Total.	99,906	95,003
10 acres and under.	9,746	14,477
10 " to 20	2,671	2,702
20 " to 50	19,143	17,522
50 " to 100	47,427	37,893
100 " to 200	17,515	18,629
Above 200 acres	3,404	4,590
Lands in Acres.		
Held	9,825,915	8,113,408
Under Cultivation	3,702,783	3,605,167
Under Crops	2,282,928	2,072,341
Under Pasture	1,361,346	1,502,697
Gardens	58,509	30,129
Wood and Wild Land	6,123,132	4,508,241

AGRICULTURAL PRODUCE.

	Upper Canada.		Lower Canada.	
	Acres.	Bushels.	Acres.	Bushels.
Wheat,	798,275	*12,682,550	410,043	3,073,943
Barley,	30,129	625,452	42,844	494,766
Rye,	49,066	318,429	43,438	325,422
Peas,	186,643	3,127,681	162,030	1,415,806
Oats,	413,508	11,391,867	591,521	8,977,380
Buck Wheat,	44,264	579,935	52,814	532,412
Indian Corn,	72,047	1,688,805	22,507	401,284
Potatoes,	77,966	4,982,186	73,227	4,424,016
Turnips,	17,048	3,110,318	3,720	334,250

*The average produce of wheat in the Upper Province is 16 bushels an acre.

AGRICULTURAL PRODUCTS, &C.

	U. Canada	L. Canada.
Clover, Timothy or other Grass Seeds, bushels.	39,029	19,073
Carrots, bshls.	174,686	81,685
Mangel Wurtzel, bshls.	54,206	110,126
Beans, bshls.	18,309	22,860
Hops, lbs.	113,527	145,735
Hay, tons,	693,727	755,579
Flax or Hemp, lbs.	59,680	1,189,018
Tobacco, lbs.	777,426	443,059
Wool, lbs.	2,619,434	1,428,783
Maple Sugar, lbs.	3,669,874	6,067,542
Cider, galns.	742,840	43,092
Butter, lbs.	16,064,532	9,610,036
Cheese, lbs.	2,292,600	764,304
Beef, brls.	113,445	43,031
Pork,	317,010	161,257
Cured Fish, brls.	11,886	80,338
Fulled cloth, yds.	531,560	746,532
Linen, yds.	14,712	929,259
Flannel, yds.	1,157,221	836,445
Cattle.		
Bulls, Oxen or Steers,	192,140	112,128
Milch Cows,	297,070	295,552
Calves or Heifers,	255,249	183,972
Horses,	201,670	184,620
Sheep,	1,050,168	647,465
Pigs,	671,496	257,794

BOOK POST.
(From The Old Countryman March 12, 1855.)

We are authorised to state, on the 1st March the privileges of the Inland Book Post will be extended to the Colonial Book Post; and thus, except as regards the charge, the difference in the regulations of the two Book Posts (which has been a frequent source of error) will cease. Under the new regulation it will be allowable to send any number of separate publications in the same cover, to write marginal notes in the books, (except letters) and to forward any other manuscript that is open to inspection.

In order to provide for cases in which, from inadvertence, a book-packet may be insufficiently pre-paid, it has been ordered that after the first of March every such book-packet having affixed thereupon postage stamps equal to a single book rate, (generally 6d.) shall be charged, not as heretofore, with the letter rate, but only with the deficient book postage—*plus* an additional single book rate.

NOTE.—The above regulations have just been announced, and must be taken in lieu of those which appear in page 13.

March.

BARRIE,
COUNTY TOWN OF SIMCOE, C.W.

SOUTH FRONT OF THE NORMAL AND MODEL SCHOOLS

ELEVATION OF A SUBURBAN VILLA.

TRINITY COLLEGE, TORONTO, C.W.

REV. PETER JACOBS, INDIAN MISSIONARY.

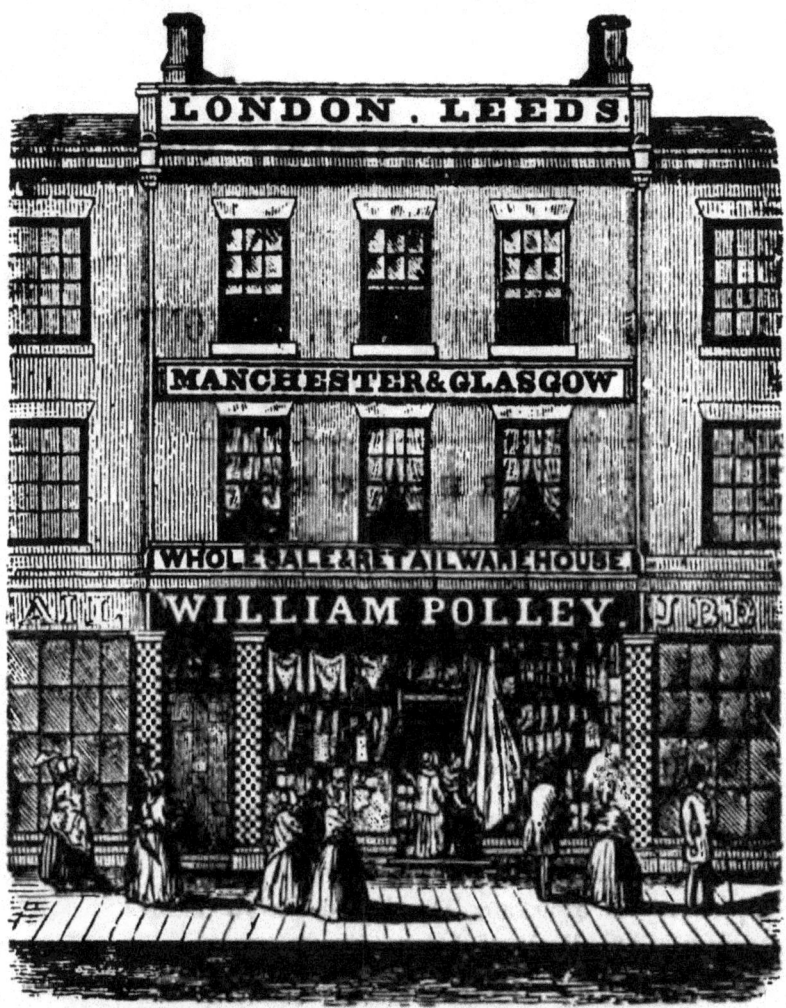

WILLIAM POLLEY

BEGS leave to call attention to his Superb Stock of **STAPLE AND FANCY DRY-GOODS,** replete with every article in the line, suitable for every Season. Intending purchasers will find it to their advantage to examine the Stock and prices of this far-famed establishment, which for style, variety and excellent value, is not surpassed by any House in the trade, Toronto or elsewhere.

N.B. Every article warranted—in no case goods misrepresented, the lowest Cash-price named, and no abatement! One-price System. Determined not to be undersold.

Chequered Warehouse,
66, KING-STREET EAST,
Third door *West of Church-Street.*
WILLIAM POLLEY.

Toronto, Jan'y 1855.

THE NEW PROVIDENT BUILDING & INVESTMENT SOCIETY,

54, KING STREET EAST, TORONTO,

(Next door to the Colonist Office.)

DIRECTORS.

B. W. Smith, Esq., Sheriff, Co. Simcoe—*President*.
R. A. Parker, Esq.,—*Vice-President*.
George Wright, Esq.,
Peter Hutty, Esq.,
T. J. Preston, Esq.,
I. Stoughton Dennis, Esq.,
R. G. Barrett, Esq.,

Managing Director and Treasurer,—W. H. Smith.
Solicitors,—Messrs. Duggan and Barrett.
Inspectors,—I. Stoughton Dennis and Joseph Dixon.
Bankers,—The Bank of Upper Canada.

MONEY RECEIVED FOR INVESTMENT in sums of £5 and upwards. On sums deposited from *three* to *six* months, FIVE per cent interest allowed, and on sums deposited for *six* months and *upwards*, at the rate of SIX per cent per annum.

Interest payable half-yearly or quarterly, at the option of the Invester.

January 12th, 1855.

TOWN OF COLLINGWOOD.

This newly-created TOWN is situated on LAKE HURON, about thirty miles north-west of BARRIE, the County-town of SIMCOE, and is the TERMINUS of the

ONTARIO, SIMCOE, & HURON RAIL-ROAD.

It is in the direct line of communication from TORONTO to GREEN-BAY, the SAULT DE ST. MARIE, and the newly-opened territory of MINNESOTA, which promises to become a District of great importance. The TOWN is laid out in

QUARTER ACRE LOTS:

and is now rapidly increasing in population.

A year ago it had not more than *six inhabitants*—it has now more than SIX HUNDRED! and every month adds to its number. The LOCALITY is delightfully picturesque and beautiful—the AIR most salubrious—the SOIL excellent. Being accessible by *railway* from TORONTO in little more than three hours, COLLINGWOOD affords an opening for SETTLERS and general enterprise rarely to be met with.

LAND AND TOWN LOTS

May be obtained on application to Mr. JAMES H. SMITH, at COLLINGWOOD, or to Mr. SHERRIFF SMITH BARRIE.

GEORGE B. WYLLIE,
18 KING STREET, EAST,
TORONTO,

Linen and Woollen Draper, Silk Mercer, Haberdasher,

Damask

AND CARPET WAREHOUSEMAN, &c. &c.

Wholesale and Retail.

RAILROAD HOTEL, ORILLIA, ALEXANDER DUNLOP, Near Steamboat Landing.

Good accommodation for Travellers or Sportsmen visiting Lakes Simcoe, Couchiching, and their Islands.

1855.

MILLINERY AND DRY GOODS. | WHOLESALE AND RETAIL.

THE TORONTO HOUSE, No. 60
J. CHARLESWORTH.

J. CHARLESWORTH would respectfully call the attention of the Citizens of Toronto, and the Public generally to his large and well assorted stock of

MILLINERY STAPLE & FANCY DRY GOODS,

J. C.'s Dry Goods department will be found to consist of all that is Seasonable and suitable for family furnishing. In his Millinery department will be found all that is requisite for Fashion and economy combined with usefulness, entirely too numerous to mention.

An Inspection is respectfully solicited before buying elsewhere.

NO SECOND PRICE.

J. CHARLESWORTH,
The Toronto House, No. 60, King Street East,
opposite the Wesleyan Book Store,
Toronto.

FRANK H. BADGLEY,

**Advocate, Barrister, Attorney, &c.,
LOWER CANADA.**

OFFICE—*Easton's Buildings, Little St. James' Street, Montreal.*

MR. BADGLEY'S extensive connection in Montreal affords him every facility for the transaction of all Agency Business, either strictly legal or of a more general character.

Toronto Savings Bank.

(Established under the authority of the Legislature)
and under the patronage of his Lordship the
Rt. Rev. A. F. M. DeCharbonnell.

Honorary Directors.

Hon. J. Elmsley, Dr. Hayes, Dr. King, Dr. Trenor. Messrs. M. Scollard, Chas Donlevy, Albert Furniss, Frans. O'Dea, M. P. Hayes, Jas Hallinan, John McGee, T. J. O'Neil, J. O Donohoe, P. J. O'Neil, D. Kohoe, Jas Stock, P. Foy, W. J. Macdonell, John Shea, M. Manamara, S. G. Lynn, J. Wallis, Charles Robertson, Angus Macdonell, J P. DeLaHaye.

Trustees and Directors.

Elected to serve during the present year.)
W. J. MACDONELL,—President,
P. J. O'NEILL,—Vice-President,
Messrs. S. G. LYNN, P. FOY, & Dr. HAYES,
BANKERS—BANK OF UPPER CANADA.
SOLICITOR—JAS. HALLINAN, Esq.

This Institution is now opened for the transaction of business on every day (Sundays and Holidays excepted,) from 10 o'clock, a. m. to 3 p.m., when sums from One Shilling upwards will be received on deposit, and Interest allowed according to its Rules and Regulations, which may be seen at any time by applying at the Bank.

The Toronto Savings Bank has been founded solely with a view towards encouraging habits of economy amongst the operative classes, by offering them a place for the secure deposit of their savings, and the most liberal terms of interest for the money they pay in—to accomplish these ends, and to ensure public confidence in the Institution, the Rules provide—

1. That there shall always be a numerous directory.
2. That ample securities be given by the Officers, and that both Officers and Trustees be sworn to the faithful discharge of their duties.
3. That the utmost publicity shall be given to the manner in which its affairs shall be conducted, by submitting a statement at every Session of Parliament to each branch of the Legislature, and publishing the same in the city newspapers.
4. All the profits made by investments are to be paid to depositors, and the interest can never be less than four per cent.
5. Interest is paid from the last day of each month in which the deposit is made, and continues until the day that the money be withdrawn, which may be done at any time.
6. The services of the Trustees and Directors are entirely gratuitous, and it is not permitted that they shall derive any advantage whatever from the funds—even as accommodation.

Office on Colborne Street, corner of the Old Post Office Lane.

D. K. FEEHAN, Manager.

ONTARIO SNUFF, AND TOBACCO FACTORY.

Depot, 48 King Street, Toronto.
J. LYONS & Co.

WILLIAM WHARIN

BEGS respectfully to intimate to the public, that he is now in receipt of a large assortment of
Gold and Silver Watches,
Gold Vest and Fob Chains,
Ladies' Gold Chains,
Gold Keys and Seals,
Silver and Gold Brooches,
Gold and Pebble Bracelets,
Ruby and Opal Crosses,
Wood and Bronze Case Clocks.

And a choice selection of such other articles as constitute a well assorted JEWELLERY STOCK. He undertakes to offer *Ladies Watches* at unusually low prices, and would direct the attention of Gentlemen to his Hunting "*Railroad Levers.*"

WILLIAM WHARIN,
Watchmaker and Jeweller, Church Street,
(*First door South of King Street,*) Toronto.

FINISHING SCHOOL FOR YOUNG LADIES.

MRS. FORSTER, having hitherto received a limited number of Pupils for tuition in special subjects, has been reqested to extend the advantages of her system of instruction by enlarging her classes.

Mrs. Forster having determined to accede to this request, has secured the assistance of the best Masters, and is prepared to give instruction in the following branches of Edusation:

English, French, Italian, German,

Music, Piano & Harp, Drawing,

Singing, &c.

In the Senior or Finishing Class, to which pupils are admitted by examination, the course of instruction is specially adapted for completing the education of Young Ladies; including a thorough review of the subjects ordinarily taught, Critical readings of the French and English Poets, Ancient and Modern Historians and the Study of Philosophy and Astronomy.

References are kindly permitted to Judge Draper, Dr. Bovell, Mr. Gzowski, and Dr. Ryerson, all of whom have daughters under Mrs. Forster's instruction.

For particulars apply to the Rev. T. S. Kennedy, Church Society's Office, King Street; or to Mrs. Forster, Pinehurst.

Toronto, January, 1855.

NICHOLAS HOPKINS,
No. 72, King Street,
CORNER OF CHURCH STREET, TORONTO.

THE Subscriber has now in Stock, and daily opening out a large and very complete assortment of

Staple and Fancy Dry Goods,

IN WHICH WILL BE FOUND

All the Novelties of the Seasons;

In Dress Goods,	Milliners' Goods
Trimmings	Ribbons, Flowers,
New Silk,	Shawls and Cloaks,

Cloakings, Flannels, Blankets, Shirtings, Linens, &c., &c.,

☞ Small Profits and quick returns.

Jan., 1855.

ANDREW H. ARMOUR & CO., Bookbinders, Stationers, Binders, & Print-Seller King Street, Toronto.

D. O. FRENCH,
DENTIST,
BAY STREET, CORNER OF MELINDA ST.,
TORONTO.

HEARN & POTTER,

(FROM DOLLONDS',)

JEWELLERS, MATHEMATICAL INSTRUMENT MAKERS & OPTICIANS,

54, *KING STREET, TORONTO.*

THEODOLITES, Levels, Drawing Instruments, Barometers, Telescopes, Microscopes, Opera Glasses, Hydrometers, Sachrometers, Lenses, &c. &c.

SPECTACLES

To suit all Sights. Royal Admiralty Charts of the St. Lawrence and the Lakes. All descriptions of Surveying Instruments, repaired and adjusted; Glasses Fitted to Spectacles, Telescopes, &c. &c.

London made Gold and Silver Lever Watches, and Electro Plate and Jewellery of all descriptions.

Watches and Jewellery Repaired and Warranted.

ALL ORDERS BY POST PUNCTUALLY ATTENDED TO.

JOSEPH GREEN, MANUFACTURER AND IMPORTER of all kinds of Tin, Copper, and Japanned Ware.

114, King Street East, (next door to Roach's Hotel,) Toronto.

Hats and Furs,

OF EVERY VARIETY.

North West Buffalo, Fox, Wolf, *and other Robes, Cheap.*

T. McCROSSON & Co., Toronto.

JAMES GRAND,

ARCHITECT AND SURVEYOR,

Offices removed to his residence, 63 Adelaide Street, West, (opposite Mr. Ritchey's Buildings,) Toronto.

Watches, Clocks and Jewellery.

THE Subscriber begs to acquaint his numerous Friends and the Public, that he has Removed to the Newly Erected Premises, East Market Square, second door from Mr. Platt's Hotel, where he is now receiving direct from the Manufacturers—a superior assortment of English Patent Lever Gold and Silver Watches; Church, Office, Marine and Fancy Mantlepiece Clocks; Silver Spoons, Wedding Rings, Electro Plate, &c., &c.

Watches and Clocks repaired in the most skilful manner, and shortest notice.

☞ All goods sold or repaired, warranted.

JOHN MOORE.
Toronto.

PROTECTION.

A SPLENDID ASSORTMENT OF PISTOLS,—Comprising Colt's and other Revolvers,—Double and Single Barrelled Pistols, with the celebrated Prussian Arms, now so much in demand, at the Gun and Rifle Manufactory of

SAMUEL T. GREEN,

48, *Yonge Street, Toronto.*

☞ Ammunition and Sporting Implements always on hand. 1

Dr. Cadwell,

NOTICE.

ANY PERSON DESIROUS OF A COPY of Dr. Cadwell's TREATISE ON THE EYE AND EAR, just published, and containing a large report of very interesting Cases, will receive the same FREE OF CHARGE, by forwarding their address, post-paid, to the Subscriber.
F. A. CADWELL, M.D.
Toronto.

JAMES COCKBURN,
BARRISTER, &c.,

KING STREET,

COBOURG.

MR. KIVAS TULLY, ARCHITECT and CIVIL ENGINEER, King Street West, TORONTO.

THE undersigned begs to notify the public that in addition to his "BROKERAGE" business, he offers his services as

INSURANCE BROKER,

and is prepared to execute orders for either Fire or Marine Insurance promptly, having made arrangements with the leading Insurance Offices for that purpose.

P.S.—All orders left at his Office, York Chambers, will meet with immediate attention. If sent by post, must be pre-paid.

STEPHEN HEWARD.

Toronto.

JAMES E. ELLIS,

IMPORTER OF

WATCHES, PLATE,

AND

FINE JEWELLERY,

30, KING STREET, TORONTO.

A large and well Assorted Stock always on hand.

Boston Lamp Store.

A BEAUTIFUL and well selected assortment of **Paper Mache Wares,** with many other articles too numerous to mention, for Sale.

J. BRIGGS.

OUR Stock of **Lamps** and **Fancy Goods** are better than ever. Always on hand Oils, Burning Fluid, and Camphine.

J. BRIGGS.

KEEP IT BEFORE THE MILLERS.

BOSTON BELTING COMPANY'S **Vulcanized Rubber Belting,** Hose and Packing, Best Oak Tanned Stretched Leather Belting.

J. BRIGGS,

Toronto.

ROBINSON & ROBINSON,

SOLICITORS, &c.

JAMES LUKIN ROBINSON,
CHRISTOPHER ROBINSON,

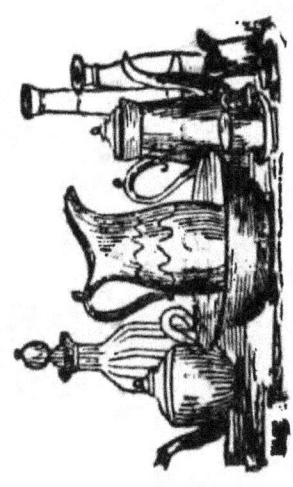

S. G. LYNN,

IMPORTER of *Crockery, China* and *Glassware,* No. 39, Front Street, Toronto.

Mr. William Eyre,
DESIGNER & ENGRAVER ON WOOD,
CORNER OF QUEEN & PETER STREETS, TORONTO.

C. READING,
(LATE J. WILSON & Co.,)

Dealer in Family Groceries, Provisions, &c. &c.

ENGLISH-CURED HAMS AND BACON.
Genuine Wines and Liquors,

CHEWETT'S BUILDINGS,

98, *King Street, West.*

Toronto.

EDUCATION.

MRS. COSENS receives a Limited Number of Young LADIES for BOARD and EDUCATION. The best Masters are engaged for Music, Singing, French, German, &c.

Terms can be known on application to Mrs COSENS, Yonge Street, Toronto.

References are kindly permitted to
The Honorable and Right Rev. the Lord Bishop of Toronto.
The Hon. the Chief Justice.
The Hon. Mr. Justice Draper.
The Rev. H. J. Grasett.
Vice Chancellor Esten.

STRACHAN & BROTHER,

Barristers and Attorneys-at-Law, Notaries Public, &c

WEST STREET,

GODERICH,

Canada West.

JOHN STRACHAN,
ALEXANDER WOOD STRACHAN,

LANDS FOR SALE.

5000 ACRES in the Township of Dover
1,200 Acres in the Township of Collingwood.

1,500 Acres in the Township of Mara.		
4,350	"	Medonte.
3,850	"	Oro.
3,528	"	Nottawasaga.
1,757	"	Osprey.
400	"	Mulmur.
200	"	Flos.

Also, in Brock, Erin, Eramosa, Essa, Fenelon, Garafraxa, Georgina, Gwillimsbury, Orillia, Ops, Scott, Tay, Tecumseth, Tossorontio, &c.

The above Lands are worthy the attention of speculators or settlers.

Apply personally, or by letter, to Mr. H. BOVELL HOPE, Land Agent, &c., Corner of Church on Front Street, Toronto.

Marine and Life Assurance.

THE subscriber is Agent for the following highly respectable companies:

Ætna Insurance Company, of Hartford, Conn.—one of the oldest established Agencies in Canada.

Home Insurance Company of New York.

Risks at fair rates, and losses adjusted fairly and honorably.

E. F. WHITTEMORE.

Toronto.

HOUSE OF ALL NATIONS!

40, *King Street, East opposite Toronto Street,*

near the New Post Office.

CLOAKS, MANTLES, FURS, BONNETS, PLAIDS, COBOURGS, CASHMERES, DELAINES, FRENCH MERINO, RIBBONS, HOSIERY, GLOVES, &c., &c., &c.

☞ An early inspection is respectfully solicited.

HOUSE OF ALL NATIONS,

SAMUEL HEAKES,

Toronto.

G. C. HORWOOD,

North American Hotel,

TORONTO.

1855.

Canada Western Assurance Company,
CHARTERED BY ACT OF PARLIAMENT,
CAPITAL £100,000; In Shares of £10 Each.

HOME OFFICE—TORONTO.

President, - - - J. C. GILMOR, Esq.
Vice-President, - THOMAS HAWORTH, Esq.

DIRECTORS.

GEORGE MICHIE,	RICE LEWIS,
WILLIAM HENDERSON,	WALTER MACFARLANE,
M. P. HAYES,	T. P. ROBARTS,

E. F. WHITTEMORE, Esq.

Secretary and Treasurer, - ROBERT STANTON, Esq.
Solicitor, - - ANGUS MORRISON, Esq.
Bank, - - - - BANK OF UPPER CANADA.

APPLICATIONS FOR FIRE RISKS
Received at the Home Office, Toronto, and at the several Agencies in the Province.

The Largest French Paper in Canada.

PRICE, $2 PER ANNUM.

Le Moniteur Canadien, Journal du Peuple.

THE *Moniteur* is Published, as formerly, with regard of the interests of every class of Society. Local and Foreign Politics, Literature, Science, Commerce, Agriculture, &c., &c., are brought before our readers in order to satisfy every taste. As to Foreign Intelligence we offer extracts from the best European and United States publications.

C. G. N. MONTIGNY,
Proprietor and Editor.

Owing to its large circulation in Canada, the United States and Europe, it is a most desirable medium for Advertising.

Letters should be addressed (*p. epaid*) to
C. G. N. de MONTIGNY
55, St. Paul Street, Montreal.

WESLEYAN BOOK-ROOM
AND
General Printing Establishment,

No. 9, WELLINGTON BUILDINGS,

TORONTO.

Where may be obtained a great variety of Religious, Literary and Scientific Works.

PRINTING & BINDING

IN ALL THEIR BRANCHES.

Saloon and Eating House.

LATE PURDY'S.

CORNER OF CHURCH AND FRONT STREETS.

Late McPherson's Store.

MARTIN ACKERMAN has opened an Eating House at the above stand. He trusts that by careful attention to his customers, moderate charges, and a supply of the best Refreshments, Wines, &c., he will obtain a share of the favors of the public and his friends.

Distinct entrance for parties of ladies and gentlemen on Church-street. ☞ Meals at all hours.

Toronto.

MRS. HIGGINS,

NO. 76, KING STREET WEST,

Toronto Circulating Library and Fancy Goods and Stationery Store.

Toronto.

CHARLES FLETCHER, Bookseller & Stationer, 54, Yonge Street, Toronto.

JAMES SHANLY, JUN'R,
BARRISTER,

MASTER EXTRAORDINARY IN CHANCERY,

NOTARY PUBLIC, &C.

LONDON, C. W.

Reprint Publishing

For People Who Go For Originals.

This book is a facsimile reprint of the original edition. The term refers to the facsimile with an original in size and design exactly matching simulation as photographic or scanned reproduction.

Facsimile editions offer us the chance to join in the library of historical, cultural and scientific history of mankind, and to rediscover.

The books of the facsimile edition may have marks, notations and other marginalia and pages with errors contained in the original volume. These traces of the past refers to the historical journey that has covered the book.

ISBN 978-3-95940-046-6

Facsimile reprint of the original edition
Copyright © 2015 Reprint Publishing
All rights reserved.

www.reprintpublishing.com

www.ingramcontent.com/pod-product-compliance
Lightning Source LLC
Chambersburg PA
CBHW070722160426
43192CB00009B/1279